Making & Marketing a Successful
Art & Craft Business

FIONA PULLEN

Search Press

This revised and expanded edition published in 2019

First published as *Craft a Creative Business* in 2015

Search Press Limited,
Wellwood, North Farm Road,
Tunbridge Wells, Kent TN2 3DR

Photographs used with permission. All photographs by Fiona Pullen except
for page 22, by Louise Dyer; page 23 top, by Holly Booth Photography;
page 23 bottom, by Welbeck Tiles Ltd; pages 56 and 57, by Annie Barker;
page 83, by Torie Jayne; page 84, by Roddy Paine Photographic Studios; page
89 and 93, by Lyndsey James; page 91, by Kangan Arora; page 94 bottom, by
Charlotte's Web; page 95, by Laura Strutt; page 96, by Plush Addict; page 120, by
Paper Panda; pages 124–25, by Tatty Devine; page 130, by Sew Me Something;
page 141, by Claire-Louise Hardie; page 147, by Rachel Pinheiro; page 148, by
Garie Hind; page 194, by Shae Baxter; page 235, by Julie Bonnar; page 236 by
Alice Hadley; and page 253, by Poppy Treffry.

ISBN: 978-1-78221-529-5

The Publishers and author can accept no responsibility for any consequences
arising from the information, advice or instructions given in this publication.

Printed in China by 1010 Printing International Ltd

CONTENTS

Making & Marketing a Successful
Art & Craft Business

Dedication

Thank you to everyone who has contributed to this book for sharing your knowledge with my readers. I would also like to thank all the readers of the first edition of this book. I have loved your messages and watching your businesses grow. I am very grateful for all your social media shares, blog posts and reviews too.

With special thanks to my amazing husband and son, Alex and James, and my supportive business partner Julie Briggs.

FOREWORD

BY ABBY GLASSENBERG AND KRISTIN LINK

When you have a job with a title, regular paycheck and perks, it is easy to speak confidently and proudly about what you do for a living. Everyone knows you are working hard to support yourself or support your family. But when you are self-employed in the craft industry and your business evolved from your passion, expressing that same level of confidence and legitimacy can be difficult. You may find that it takes extra effort to convince family and friends that what you do is your career, not your hobby. Sometimes, you may even have trouble convincing yourself.

You might be a maker, a book author, or a shop owner, but to be a successful entrepreneur you also have to be an accountant, a social media expert, a web developer, a writer, and a photographer. Being a small business owner means wearing many hats and learning many skills. Most of us hit the ground running and learn those skills as we go, which is both exciting and challenging (to say the least).

There are many advantages of working for yourself — setting your own hours, steering your own ship, and working in your pyjamas, to name just a few. But running your own business can also be lonely, exhausting and frustrating. It is important to seek out a community of fellow creative business owners who can support you and help you along the way. Search for a local get-together or join the online trade organization we founded, Craft Industry Alliance, to connect with fellow makers around the world.

Abby Glassenberg *and* **Kristin Link** *are the co-founders of* **Craft Industry Alliance: craftindustryalliance.org**

CRAFT
INDUSTRY
alliance

Making & Marketing a Successful Art & Craft Business is the book you need to launch your business and grow it into an endeavour that will sustain you in the long term. This book is for anyone who does creative work including knitters, crocheters, papercrafters, woodworkers, quilters, and more.

Whether you want to sell your wares online or at craft shows and galleries, you will find all the information you need to create a strong business foundation. Apply what you have learned here and soon you will be fulfilling the dream of making a living doing what you love.

INTRODUCTION

The National Office of Statistics (UK) reported in 2016 that the rate of self-employment had risen to fifteen per cent. 4.75 million of us are now running our own businesses and still more are getting ready to start up. For many people the idea of turning their much loved hobby into a business seems like to perfect way to start earning an income.

The UK's creative industries in particular are proving to be increasingly popular, growing by nearly nine per cent in 2014 and accounting for 9.6 million pounds of income per hour! What better time to start up your own creative enterprise?

Your business and this book

Although many creative people can easily identify what products to make or what services to offer, they often find the technical sides of running a business harder to manage. It can be difficult to find the time to make your products while learning about accounts, legislation, social media, search engine optimization, marketing and all the other aspects of the business. I intend this book to be a guiding hand to help you through those sides of the business as quickly and easily as possible, allowing you more time to enjoy the creative parts.

I have spent the past few years avidly learning as much as possible while starting up and running my own business, The Sewing Directory. I have gone from being new to this industry in 2010 to running one of the UK's top sewing websites, which attracts almost 1.5 million hits a year and has a social media following of over 80,000. I have been sharing the information that I have learned through business guides on my website, in magazines, in training sessions and at seminars. I decided it was time to lay out all I had learned so people can access it all in one place, and that leads us to this book.

Activity: Preparing yourself

Fetch a notebook and pen. Keep them to hand as you read this book and work through the activities.

By the end of the book, you will have a complete set of notes that will help you to apply what you learn to your business, and to get you started with a useful record of what you have achieved.

You can, of course, read this book from cover to cover, but it is designed to be dipped into so that you can go straight to the aspect you want to learn about at any given time. Each chapter has a different coloured background so you can see at a glance if you are in the right part of the book.

If you have ever read any of my business guides you will know that I like to provide detailed information, tips on how to apply the information to your own business, and useful links for you to learn more, should you wish to do so. I have continued this format with this book: you will find activities like the one on the opposite page, with exercises to get you putting the information into practice; information boxes (see below left) that provide illustrative examples, important notes, and insights from other professional craft businesses; and there are also tips (see below right) with notes and advice drawn from my own experiences.

Furthermore you will find spaces where you can fill in your own notes in the book. There are new websites and useful articles popping up daily, so I have included space for you to add your own links or notes at the end of each section.

I hope you find this book useful and wish you every success with your creative enterprise.

WHAT HAS CHANGED?

Since the first edition of this book, the popularity of video in social media has exploded. The social media section of this book has been almost completely re-written, with more focus on using video to promote your business.

Legislative and tax changes have been updated, as has information relating to online market places and search engine optimization which constantly evolves. I have also checked all the links at the end of each section, removing any that are no longer working and adding in new ones for your reference.

Another change is that all downloads which are mentioned in the book are now available from the **Search Press** website: searchpress.com. Just search for 'Making & Marketing a Successful Art & Craft Business' and you will find them on the same page as my book.

MY EXPERIENCE

My background is not in the creative industries; I took a degree in law then worked in the legal team of a firm of loss adjusters. While on maternity leave in 2009, I wanted something which would better fit around my son.

Having built the website for my mum's dressmaking business, I could not find anywhere to promote it online, and so formed the idea of The Sewing Directory as a service for small businesses who wanted an affordable way to promote themselves online.

I avidly studied everything I could find about running my own business and still do to this day. The world of business constantly changes, so it pays to keep on top of these changes to use them in a way that benefits your business.

WHERE DO

I START ?

SELF-EMPLOYMENT AND YOU

The first thing you need to consider before getting into the nitty-gritty of setting up your own business is whether self-employment is for you. There are many benefits to self-employment, but there can be a lot of downsides too. I am not going to sugarcoat it and make self-employment sound like the easy option, but equally I can tell you that having set up my own business, I cannot imagine working for anyone else ever again!

I love running my own business and most of the entrepreneurs I have spoken to say the same. This section of the book will help you to make sure you are prepared for what self-employment involves.

Making the leap

The move from employment to self- employment can be uncertain; even scary. You want to be as well-prepared as possible to ease the transition.

Some people, myself included, start up their business while still working another job, in order to mitigate the financial risks. This gives you the benefit of still having an income during the early stages of a business, when income is typically low. However, do bear in mind that this can be exhausting and may mean you cannot put as much time and energy into your business as you would like.

A NOTE ON WEBSITES AND LINKS

For clarity, any prefixes to web addresses (URLs), such as 'http' or 'www' have been removed. Most browsers will automatically account for this, so you can type the addresses in just as they appear.

I have included a list of useful links to websites referenced repeatedly, or intended for further reading, at the end of each section. Where space and readability allows, I have included a link within the text.

THE REALITIES OF SELF-EMPLOYMENT

Being self-employed means that you can ensure that you spend most of your day doing things you love. You are in control. If it is a sunny day and you want an afternoon at the beach, you do not have to ask anyone's approval. If you are just having one of those days where you do not feel like doing anything, then you can take some time off.

You do not have to wear a set work wardrobe dictated by anyone else. If you are working from home, then you also have no commute with which to contend either. Another great advantage is that your earning potential is unlimited. Unlike most jobs where you have a fixed monthly wage, you have the potential to work more and earn more; and ideally, as your business grows, so will your income.

The downside of having an unfixed wage is that you could earn less than expected, so you need to have a contingency fund ready to cover any quieter periods. You will also probably find that you work many more hours than you ever did in regular employment. Several years into running my business I found I was working sixty-hour weeks. It can also be hard to take holidays or sick days because you normally will not get paid for them, and you know you have to make up the work when you get back.

If you are not afraid of hard work, are passionate about your idea, and love the thought of being your own boss, then read on.

MAKING IT WORK FOR ME

Using my business as an example, I can fit my hours around my young son and his school holidays; and because I run an online business I can work from almost anywhere: I was able to relocate from Wales to England without it affecting my work or income. (I can also sit on the sofa watching television while I work!)

Is self-employment for you?

To set up and run your own business, there are certain character traits which will help to ensure that it becomes a success. You need to be:

Self-motivating You will be your own boss, so there is no one else to tell you what to do and when to do it. You have to be able to stick to the deadlines you have promised your customers or the other businesses with which you are working. You will need to make sure that you spend the day being productive rather than procrastinating. We all have days like that sometimes, but you alone will be responsible for making sure it is not most of your days!

Organized Any business has a lot to co-ordinate. From buying in supplies to setting up a website; and from doing the administration to managing your accounts, there are many tasks to be done. When self-employed, you need to be able to structure your working week to make sure you keep on top of all of these routine aspects of running a business, as well as spending time doing the things you love or find more stimulating.

Willing There are likely to be many things in which you have no experience that you nevertheless have to confront when you are self-employed. Some things like accounts, sales, marketing or administration can be delegated to other members of staff if you have them, or you can hire freelancers to help you with specific tasks. Note that paying someone else to do them will reduce your profit, of course. A willingness to approach and complete tasks with which you are unfamiliar or inexperienced is particularly important if it you are working alone, as you cannot delegate the daunting tasks to other people.

Positive Quite often people are investing not just in your product, but in you as a person. If you are positive and friendly, people are more likely to want to work with you or buy from you. Furthermore, there will be days where things do not go your way. You have to be able to pick yourself up and carry on, rather than become demotivated and give up.

Adaptable If you can respond quickly and are willing to adapt your business plan to suit demand, you can keep on top of current trends, customer demands and other changes in your industry. This responsiveness is a crucial advantage that small businesses naturally have over more bureaucratic larger businesses. Their corporate structure means that it takes time for changes to be implemented, whereas a responsive business can do it straight away and reap the rewards.

Honest Trust has to be earned over time and, if you are true to your word, your reputation for being trustworthy will spread. Equally a bad reputation spreads quickly in this highly-connected age, and it can be very hard to win back lost good will.

Driven It is your energy and drive that will help determine the success of your business. Particularly when you are starting out, you need to be prepared to work seven days a week, to work past midnight to fulfil an urgent order, or forgo a day out to catch up on work. Your drive and willingness to make these short-term sacrifices will help in making your business a success in the long term.

Passionate Most of all, you should love what you do. Then you will not mind the late nights, paperwork, and lack of free time. Passion will come across to your customers and make them more interested in being involved with you. It is quite easy to tell when someone is not passionate about what they are doing and it can be a big turn-off to potential customers.

Some of these traits can be learnt. There are books and courses that can teach you how to improve your organization, how to cultivate a positive attitude or to learn how to stay motivated. Other traits, like honesty, passion and willingness to put in the work necessary to make your business succeed need to be there from the start. Take a good, honest look at yourself and your personality traits to see if you have what it takes to run your own business.

Before you begin

Before you invest money into your business idea, take the time to research your market and make sure there is a demand for the product or service you plan to offer. It could be an amazing concept but if the market is already saturated, or you are trying to pitch it to the wrong people, you will struggle to succeed.

Correctly identifying your market from the outset will save you a lot of time, money and heartache in the long run. Many people are so excited by their business concept, and so keen to get it up and running that they are tempted to skip the research and planning stage. Avoiding this temptation can make the difference between eventual success or failure for your business.

Identifying your target market

Are you aiming your product or service at people with children? People with large incomes? People who are buying for special occasions? People decorating their home?

Try to narrow your target market down as much as possible. It is no good saying that every woman between the ages of twenty and sixty would buy your product, because the truth is they will not. You need to pinpoint, as precisely as possible, what need you are satisfying for your customers. Why would they want or need to buy your product? It is much more cost effective if you are pitching to a narrow, well-targeted audience than trying to appeal to everyone. It is also a lot more likely to help you grow a successful business.

Once you have thought about your ideal customer and how they spend their time, you need to establish if there is a demand for your product. This can be done in a variety of ways, which are summarized on the opposite page.

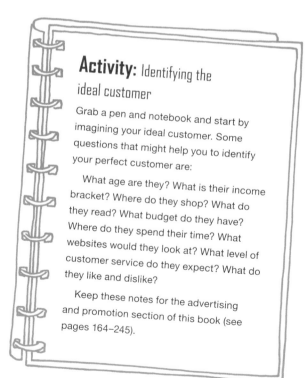

Activity: Identifying the ideal customer

Grab a pen and notebook and start by imagining your ideal customer. Some questions that might help you to identify your perfect customer are:

What age are they? What is their income bracket? Where do they shop? What do they read? What budget do they have? Where do they spend their time? What websites would they look at? What level of customer service do they expect? What do they like and dislike?

Keep these notes for the advertising and promotion section of this book (see pages 164–245).

Ask your customers You could poll some of your target customers by doing a market research questionnaire, either in person or online. Ideally, go to the places where you identified your target customers like to spend their time – both offline and online – and ask them to take part in your survey. You will likely get a higher response rate if there is some kind of incentive to complete the survey, such as being entered into a prize draw.

Do not just ask friends and family; they are more likely to say what you want to hear. Well-intentioned though this may be, honesty is what you need.

Competitor research Research which businesses already exist that offer a similar kind of product or service to what you are planning to offer. Do they seem to be busy? Do they seem to have a lot of customers or are they struggling?

If the latter, is there space for your business in the market too or is the demand not as great as you anticipated? Identify whether they are struggling because they are doing something wrong that you could avoid. Look at where they advertise and how they attract customers. Consider their strengths and weaknesses. What could you learn from them and what could you do better or differently?

Speak to the experts Try speaking to experts in the area you want to go into. Contact relevant magazines and any businesses within your niche, and gauge whether they think your idea is viable. While this approach risks someone else copying your idea, you can get invaluable feedback, so you have to decide if it is worth the risk. Speaking to the experts can be a gamble, but the people already in the industry will have the best idea about what works and what does not. You can get a lot of useful input from speaking with them.

Trials Rather than going through the cost of buying or renting premises, or producing large quantities of products to stock a website or online shop, you could speak to a local shop or an online retailer and see whether they would stock a few of your products on a trial basis.

Such trials can help you to see if there is a demand for your product and if you have priced it correctly. The shop owner may also be able to give you feedback about how it sold compared with other related products.

If you are planning to start teaching your craft, approach an established workshop provider and enquire about becoming a guest tutor. This will allow you to trial your lesson plans without too much cost or hassle.

Focus groups A focus group can be a great way to get honest feedback about your business idea as well as suggestions on how to improve it. You may need to offer some kind of enticement to get people to take part and you will need a place to hold it. Again, try to avoid using your friends and family as your focus group as you are less likely to get honest, unbiased feedback.

Research potential markets

The research you do while investigating whether there is demand for your product will help form the rest of the plan for your business. Finding out where your customers spend their time, what they read, what sites they visit, and their other habits and preferences will help you to decide where you should advertise your business.

Finding out what budget your customers have, and what their income level is, will help you when it comes to pricing your product; while analysing your competitors will help you decide on your business' USP (see pages 22–25).

Market research surveys

One of the easiest methods of research is to conduct a market research survey; but how do you decide what to include, and how do you encourage people to get involved?

Before the days of the internet, entrepreneurs would stop people in the street, asking them to take part in a survey. Nowadays we can do it all from the comfort of home, by harnessing the power of social media using free questionnaire tools like Survey Monkey or Google Forms. Whilst it may seem easiest to do it all online, you need to consider the best way to reach your target audience. If you are planning to run a local business, it may be more useful to get out on the streets and talk to local residents about your idea. These people are your potential audience – and customers – so you need to be connecting with them, rather than people you have contacted online who live hundreds of miles away.

Whether you are running your surveys online or offline, there are a few basic things to consider when planning your questionnaire.

Length Most people are unlikely to complete a survey that will take them more than two or three minutes, so keep your survey short and tightly focused to get a higher participation rate.

The objective Have very clear objectives in mind while you are planning the survey. What do you want to find out?

Clarity Aim to be as specific as possible with your questions, in order to ensure you get the information you want in the shortest survey possible.

Language Leading people into a response you want to hear will not help you. You want their honest opinion, not to spoonfeed them answers. Keep the language as neutral as possible.

EXAMPLE SURVEY QUESTION

How much would you be prepared to pay for a unique and hand-painted wooden sign for your child's bedroom?

A) Less than £10.00

B) Between £10.00 and £15.00

C) Between £15.00 and £20.00

D) More than £20.00

Using closed questions Closed questions are those where the participant has to choose an answer from set responses, as in the example survey question on the opposite page. Closed questions will make it much easier to collate your results into usable data.

Using open questions Bearing the above in mind, it may be worth including one open question at the end of the survey. An open question allows people to give as much detail as they like, and not have to choose from set answers. This will let them expand on anything they wanted to say in response to the earlier questions. You will often see a 'further information' or 'is there anything you would like to add?' option at the end of a survey.

Location Consider where you will ask people to answer your survey. If you try to stop a mother with children in the street she is likely to refuse you, but if you asked her while she was sitting down at a park or play place, watching her children play, she may be more able to give you a couple of minutes of her time. Equally, commuters rushing to work in the morning are less likely to have time to stop than people sitting in a coffee shop or on a train.

Use of the internet You will reach more people if you post a link to your survey on your actively updated social media pages and ask your friends to share it than if you post it on your old neglected blog. If you approach a few complementary businesses and ask them to share it with their followers, that can also lead to a greater response.

Rewards People often respond well to a little enticement. Many surveys use the lure of a prize to get people to participate. Consider offering a cash prize, high street vouchers or a few of your products to tempt participants to reply. Do not forget that you need the participants to give you a way of contacting them if they have won!

Respect for privacy Adding a line to reassure people that you will not be using the data to market to them or passing it on to other companies is always a good idea and will encourage a greater response rate.

Anonymity Some people do not want to leave their details. Making contact details a non-compulsory part of your survey will probably result in more people taking part. It may also encourage people to be more honest because they know you cannot track their response back to them.

TIMINGS AND LIFESTYLE

If you are sending your survey by e-mail, consider the lifestyle of your target participants to get the best response. Sending a survey to an office worker's personal e-mail will get a better response if sent during the evening or weekend, when they have leisure time to read and fill it in. Similarly, if the recipient is likely to be out partying on a Saturday night, that is not the best time to send it to them!

Making use of the survey results

Once you have conducted your survey, do not forget to analyse the data generated by your survey. Pay attention to what people are saying – if most people responded they would only pay an amount for your product that is less than it would cost you to make, then you really need to re-think your business concept. If the majority say they read magazine X, then do not advertise in magazine Y simply because you can get a cheaper deal.

It may be tempting to ignore any negative feedback but this can often be the most valuable feedback of all. Although you do not have to take every single comment on board – you cannot please everyone, after all – you should be aiming to satisfy the majority of your potential customers. We often get too attached to our ideas, which makes it hard for us to see them objectively, so make the most of having objective viewpoints of your concept.

If you have asked the right questions during your market research, you will have a wealth of information that will tell you what people want from your business, where and how to market it, and what price people are prepared to pay for it. Make sure you analyse the data you have gathered to help you make key decisions about your business. It is also worth storing it for future reference.

Finally, remember that there is nothing to stop you conducting more market research at a later date. In fact, this will allow you to continue to refine your business, and make sure you are continuing to offer what your customers want.

Activity: Giving your customers what they want

Having imagined your ideal customer (see the activity on page 16) now it is time to apply the results of your market research to what your customers will expect from you. From the information you have gathered answer the questions below:

- What does that customer want from your product or service? What look? What function? What results when using it?

- What is the best way to reach that customer with your marketing?

- What is the customer likely to pay and what do they expect in return?

- What problem are you resolving for the customer with your product, or how will it enhance their life?

- What criteria does your customer use when choosing your product or service? Price? Style? Customer service? Ease of purchase? A combination?

MARKET RESEARCH TIPS FROM BEFAB'S ZOE & SOLLI

BeFab (befabbecreative.co.uk) is a printer of creative fabrics. The owners, Zoe and Solli, spent over six months planning and researching their business concept, including running several market research surveys.

- Use the resources around you that can help with research and reviewing business plans. An example is Business Gateway (bgateway.com), which offers professional resources and support, such as workshops and advice, to businesses.

- Regional libraries have staff that can assist research too; whether to back up your own findings or discover new information.

- Companies House holds the registration details of all limited companies in the UK. They will have details of your competitors, when they started, some financial information and their business classification.

- When researching your competitors, make sure you identify things that they do which you can or want to do better, in order to better serve your customers.

- Use online tools – survey tools, mailing tools and social media – to promote and collect information, as well as build your customer base in advance.

- Framing your survey questions is really important. Make questions short – people often want to help but are busy, so make things easy for them – but also give the space to give additional information if they want to.

- Trusted friends may not have the knowledge of the business idea but if they have the skills to review documents for grammar and spelling, give pointers in helping you research the chosen subject, or to otherwise assist, get them involved.

- Accept that no matter how much research you do you will not know everything. You have to take a leap of faith; but you will likely be surprised at how much you know.

Your USP

USP stands for 'unique selling point'. When planning your business you need to think about why people will choose to buy from you and not someone else. What makes you different from the other businesses already out there?

Your new business will be up against established businesses who already have a customer base, and if you are simply offering the exact same thing as other businesses, you need to give customers a reason to buy from you rather than one of your competitors. Having something unique about your business will help to make it stand out from the others, and help to convince people to try your business out.

An obvious way to ensure your business has a USP is to sell a product or service that does not yet exist. However, businesses can become very successful by taking something that has been done before, and doing it in a different way. You may have an innovative website in mind that will give the buyer a superior buying experience; or you could plan to sell in a totally different way. You may be combining products that are not usually sold together or you may intend to deliver customer service to a level that is way above your competitors.

If you can establish a niche for your business to occupy, it will be a lot easier for you to both market and sell your product, plus you will have less competition. The examples on these pages highlight a few companies that have excellent USPs that have helped them to become successful.

LOUISE DYER PAPERLACE

USP: Personalization

This company makes personalized papercut family trees including names, dates and quotes. Plus Louise adds silhouettes of the people featured in the tree, or family pets under the tree creating a truly personalized gift.

facebook.com/lousPaperlace

Image credit: Louise Dyer.

JUDITH BROWN JEWELLERY

USP: Unusual supplies

Judith combines vintage haberdashery supplies and lace-making techniques into her jewellery making, producing beautiful unique designs. For instance, she makes necklaces from old hook and eyes and push studs, and earrings from zip pulls or lace.

judithbrownjewellery.co.uk

Image credit: Holly Booth Photography.

WELBECK TILES

USP: Unusual products

Welbeck Tiles produces 'patchwork tiles' – ceramic tiles with prints of beautiful patchwork fabrics on them which when put together look like a patchwork quilt on your wall.

Welbeck Tiles' USP is their prints – they have ditzy floral designs which look just like real fabric.

welbeck.com

Image credit: Welbeck Tiles Ltd.

Market research is a great way to help you find a USP. Ask people what they want, what do they not currently get elsewhere or what they do not like about existing businesses that offer the same products as you. Find out how you can fill a gap in the market and what you can do or offer to stand out. Even once you are up and running you can continue this research by asking customers why they chose you rather than a competitor. They may help to identify a USP that had not occurred to you.

This kind of research does not have to be done through the use of a survey. If you have identified where your target market hangs out, go and join in – whether through online forums, blogs, or at industry events, local cafés or hobby groups. Make friends, join conversations and find out what they really want. If people have come to know you before you start marketing your business to them you are likely to get a much better response. Plus, if they have helped you plan the business, they start to develop an emotional connection to your products too.

Once you have identified a potential USP, double check to make sure none of your competitors are doing the same thing. If you promise to be the only company offering a product or service and your customers find that other businesses do the same, you will have lost their trust.

UNIQUE MARKETING

Your USP does not have to be restricted to your product or service. It could be a clever way of marketing or showcasing your work or products. A great example of marketing your products in a unique way is the 'Fat Quarter Gang'. Like many businesses, Art Gallery Fabrics wanted to get bloggers to demonstrate what could be made with their products. They put a fun – and unique – twist on it by establishing a street gang style for the blog. Bloggers with tongue-in-cheek street names like Stash Slasher, Queen Quilta and MC Hemmer posed for photographs wielding their sewing scissors and rotary cutters.

This unique marketing idea ensured people were talking about their fabrics and sharing links to the projects written by the contributors. It also helped to establish their brand as being fun, modern and different.

agfblog.com/fat-quarter-gang

Activity: Creating your company's USP

Grab your notebook and start writing down what makes your business different from the others.

- Is it your products?
- Is it the way you deliver your product or service?
- Will it be your website?
- Will it be the way you market your concept?

Finally, make sure you tell everyone about it! People will not know how you differ from other similar businesses unless you tell them. If you use Fairtrade or organic materials, make sure this is prominently displayed on the front of your site/shop and highlighted in your product descriptions and your marketing materials. If you promise next-day delivery, remind people of this frequently. If you give a percentage of your profits to charity then make sure this is clearly communicated. The more people know about your USP, the more chance you have to convince them that they should buy from you and not someone else.

CRAIG DE SOUZA'S TIPS ON STARTING A CREATIVE BUSINESS

Craig works for the Association For Creative Industries UK (afci.uk), a not-for-profit trade body whose goal is to increase growth in the craft industry and support businesses within the sector.

- *Passion* It goes without saying that if you do not have passion for the industry then it is a non-starter. Loving what you do will make running your business more rewarding.

- *Point of difference* The craft industry is renowned as being one that goes through 'boom periods' where the market becomes flooded with people who have jumped on a bandwagon. Make sure you are not a 'me too' company and have some innovation in product, or a real USP if you are providing a service. Look at what your potential competitors are doing, identify your differentiation and stay true to it.

- *Cash is king* As with any business, you need to prepare a detailed business plan, which includes not only profit and loss and a balance sheet, but also a cash flow forecast to ensure you have adequate funding to get you through at least the first year. This is normally the reason most new start-ups fail so plan ahead to make sure you always have cash in the bank.

- **Support of friends and family** It may seem exciting, but as with any business you will go through some tough times so having the love and support of those around you will go a long way in helping your business survive and thrive.

- **Keep it real** Do not have your head in the clouds – walk before you can run, do not over-stretch yourself and recognize your limitations. Otherwise, there is the worry you could either implode or run out of financing, in which case it does not matter how great your ideas are.

Study your competitors

Looking closely at the opposition is an essential part of any business plan. Not only do you want to know what other businesses are out there but you want to know what they do well and what they do not. Why do people keep coming back to them, and what do their customers not like about them?

Identify the areas where your competitors excel, and try to think how your business could deliver those things to at least an equivalent standard, if not a better one. Try to pinpoint exactly what it is that makes those parts of their business good. For example, is their website great because it is bright and colourful, because the photography on it is clear, or because it is easy to navigate? This will help to give you a list of the things you want to achieve with your business.

Aim not to simply copy other businesses, but instead be inspired by their strengths and work out how you can apply the lesson to your own business. If you can see that a good website helps to sell a product similar to yours, then you know you need to work hard on your web design. It does not mean you should try to copy their website design.

Imagine that you are considering setting up a fabric shop in your local town. There is already a local fabric shop near you that is always busy and stocks a good selection of dressmaking fabrics. However, the owner has a reputation for being incredibly rude to his customers. Local people say that if there were other places where they could get the same fabrics nearby they would not go to the shop. This information would let you know that what people are seeking is a good range of dressmaking fabrics with nice, polite customer service. With this information, you would know that being friendly and welcoming is as important as having a good selection of dressmaking fabrics in making people come to you instead of the other shop.

That is the kind of information you may not pick up in a survey, or even through looking online, as people are often reluctant to badmouth local businesses publicly. However, spending time at places where you can hear honest word of mouth reviews – local sewing groups and classes, in the case of the example given here – will pay dividends as you will meet your potential customers and hear what they have to say about your competitors.

Looking at the things your competitors do not do well will help you spot gaps that need filling. Perhaps there are things that you can offer that they do not. Do they stock complementary products? If not, perhaps you could. Perhaps you have identified that your customers like to be able to get everything they want in one place and in one transaction: look into whether your competitors can achieve this or not. If your competitors cannot deliver an important service, or supply a vital item, work out why and aim to become the business that can. If your competition is slow at posting orders, find a way to send things out more quickly. This will give a higher level of customer satisfaction. By analysing the mistakes of your competitor's businesses, you can learn without having to make the same mistakes yourself.

CHECK OUT THE COMPETITION ONLINE

Take a look through your competition's social media accounts and see what people are saying about/to them. This will give you an idea of what people like or do not like about their business.

Try searching for online reviews too. Many forums have places where people can recommend businesses or warn people about businesses to avoid; it is worth taking a read through the relevant comments in those as well.

CHECK THE ACCOUNTS

You can now view the accounts for UK-registered companies for free on: beta.companieshouse.gov.uk

Activity: Reviewing the competition

Draw up a three-column table as shown below. In the first column, name at least five of your main competitors. In the second column make a note of what they do well; perhaps 'nice website', 'good prices', 'good online reviews', 'it is easy to find things in their shop' or similar. In the third column make a note of the things they do not do well: 'Items not priced properly in the shop', 'misleading advertising' or 'overpriced', for example.

Competitor name	Strengths	Weaknesses

FORWARD PLANNING PAYS OFF

When I set up The Sewing Directory it was a unique concept and I knew I had to make a big impression before anyone else copied the idea – indeed, several competitors have appeared in the years since my company made its debut.

I prepared an extensive marketing plan which involved me exhibiting at several large shows where key people and businesses in the industry would find out about my site. I also ensured that I had a big presence in magazines, key websites, blogs and on social media. So many became aware of my site that when competitors tried to copy my idea, people would notify me.

Quality really counts. If your products are of a superior quality, people will want to buy your products and not an inferior copy.

A good service will attract positive reviews and a strong reputation which will keep people coming back to you.

Customer satisfaction is very important as well. If your customers are happy with the product or service you are offering, they will not be looking around for someone else doing the same thing. They will feel loyal to you even if approached by other businesses.

Getting started

Once you have decided that running your own business is for you and have identified that there is a market for your product or service, it is time to plan the finer details. What you are going to charge, calculating what profit you can expect and setting your business goals. For the purposes of the pricing exercises in this section, I will use a jeweller making necklaces as an example.

Creating a business plan

Even if you do not want to work to a set business plan, it pays to keep all your notes together in one place. Keep a dedicated business notebook or folder so you can refer back to it in the future. You can download business plans online which have space for you to note the details of your market research and the results, your USPs and your analysis of competitors. Several banks have business plans available for free on the business sections of their websites.

Bplans has over five hundred business plan templates available on its site, many of them free, along with advice on completing a business plan. Some computer software, such as Microsoft Office 2003 or later, includes business plan templates in the free templates that come with the software. I set my own business up through The Prince's Trust using the free business plan template available on their website under the Enterprise Programme section. Links to all of these services are on page 45.

Pricing

Pricing is a very difficult subject when you are first setting up your business. Once you start selling your products at a certain price it can be hard to change it in the future, so it is really important to aim to get the pricing right from the outset. However, until you actually start selling it can be hard to know if you will be able to sell your products at the price you want to achieve. Unfortunately it is all too common in the handmade market to see people selling at cost or even at a loss. Often people only think about the materials cost and not the time or overheads when calculating their price. There are several different formulas for calculating price which we will cover in this section.

> ## RETAIL AND WHOLESALE SELLING
>
> Most of you reading this book will be looking to sell retail, which means you sell your product directly to the consumer. Some businesses sell wholesale, which means they sell their products to a third party, normally a shop, who then sell the products to the end consumer. If you are selling wholesale a second lot of profit needs to be factored into your costings. Not only do you need to make a profit but the shop will also expect to make a profit too. For simplicity, the pricing examples that follow assume that the item is being sold retail.

Cost pricing

There are three factors which are critical to pricing calculations. We will cover each of these in turn to make sure you are arriving at figures which are as accurate as possible when calculating your price.

- **Costs** What you spend to make your product or provide the service you offer.

- **Time** How long it takes you to make your product or provide your service.

- **Profit** How much profit you want to make on top of costs and time expense.

Costs

Your costs are all the expenses involved in making your product. If you offer a service you will normally still have costs too – website hosting, business cards and stationery, electricity, travel costs and so forth. When selling a product your costs could include:

- **Materials** If you are paying postage costs for your materials or tools to be sent to you, do not forget to factor those in too.

- **Tools**

- **Rent**

- **Services** These include electricity, gas, telephone rental and other similar bills.

- **Travel**

- **Products used in giveaways**

- **Website** This includes one-off fees like setup and domain purchase, as well as ongoing maintenance and hosting.

- **Stationery** This includes printer cartridges, business cards, compliment slips and other similar items.

- **Packaging/labels**

- **Selling fees**

- **Waste** This includes supplies used and items produced that are not suitable for sale.

- **Labour** If you are employing anyone else in your business.

Some of the costs listed will be easily calculated per item; like the example to the right, for a glass bead necklace. The other costs listed will need to be split over all your products and taken into account. These are your overheads. The easiest way to do this is to calculate your overhead cost per month (the total amount you pay in rent, services, travel etc.) and then split the result across the average number of products you expect to sell per month.

Assuming the overhead cost of the necklace example is thirty pence, we have a total production cost of £8.80 for our bead necklace.

Note that I have not included postage of the item to your customer, because most people add the postage on separately to the item price when selling online or by mail order. Postage varies depending on how many items are being purchased and what delivery option people choose. However, if you offer free postage, then you will need to factor this into your costs.

Do remember that prices of your supplies or overheads change over time. Periodically check and adjust your figures.

COSTING GLASS BEAD NECKLACES

Assume the following prices for your materials.

- Beading wire: £3.00 per 3m (3¼yd)

- Czech glass beads: £3.50 per 50g (1¾oz)

- Magnetic clasp: £2.00 each

If each necklace you are making requires 1m (1yd) of wire and 75g (2½oz) of beads, your material costs can be calculated as follows:

- £1.00 for the wire

- £5.25 for the beads

- £2.00 for the clasp

This gives you a total materials cost for each necklace of £8.25. If your packaging/labelling costs 25p then you add that on top to get a cost of £8.50.

Activity: Recording your costs

Write down all the costs involved in making your products and cost them out per product. Each time you add a new product to your range do this calculation again and write it here or in your notebook so you have all the costs together in one place.

Product	Cost	Time	Profit	Minimum sale or wholesale price

Time

The £8.80 figure for the glass bead necklace example on the previous page excludes the time element of production, an important consideration. To cost out your time you need to know two things: how long it takes you to make each product or to provide the service you sell, and how much you expect to be paid per hour.

Products The simplest way to calculate the time involved to make a product is to time yourself. We all have days when we are more productive than others, so do this two or three times on different days and then take the average time. Make sure you also factor in the time it takes you to set up, pack away, and the time it takes you to package your product.

Services If you provide a service, the majority of your price will come from the time you take, so make sure you count every minute. You may think the odd few minutes here and there will not matter, but over the year it could make a huge difference to your income. Furthermore do not forget to factor in travel time and preparation time. For example, if you teach craft workshops you may spend half an hour setting up and the same tidying away after. If you forget to count that time in your price calculations you are working unpaid for an hour each time you run a workshop.

When it comes to working out your hourly wage rate, you need to balance up the price for which you can realistically sell your products or charge for your services against what you want to earn per hour.

We would all love to pay ourselves a very generous wage, but the chances are that most of us would never sell our products if we factored a huge hourly rate into our price. That said, do not sell yourself short. You are doing a skilled job and should be paid accordingly. As you gain more experience or qualifications, remember to put your hourly rate up – you have earned it!

MINIMUM WAGE

If you are a resident in the UK, visit gov.uk/national-minimum-wage-rates to see what the current minimum wage is and work up from there as a starting point. US state governments and EU countries have similar webpages for checking minimum wages.

Profit

As with the hourly wage calculation, there is no set figure to which to work. Deciding upon your profit is again a balance between what you want to achieve and what you can realistically charge. A lot of crafters appear to add around fifteen to thirty per cent profit, but this will varying depending on your market.

If you are planning to sell wholesale, retailers will usually expect to buy at half the retail price (this figure can vary depending on the terms you can negotiate; but as fifty per cent mark up is fairly standard, it is assumed for the examples here). To account for this, you need to be able to cover your production costs and make a profit on around half the retail price. A lot of products simply will not have the margin in them to account for the profit margin needed to sell wholesale. You need to calculate your costs plus profit and then compare to the price of other similar products being sold to see if you will be able to sell wholesale. If doubling your end price prices you out of the market, then selling wholesale will not be viable for you.

You can use the calculated starting price (£15.00 in the example) as your retail price – the amount you charge customers if you are selling your product directly. However, if you intend to sell wholesale, then your retail price should be double the starting price you calculated. This is to ensure that you are not undercutting the retailers who stock your products – as mentioned above, they will expect to buy your products at half the price they sell them; so if you want to keep your profit, you must take this into account when selling to wholesalers. In the glass bead necklace example, if you are selling the necklaces wholesale you would sell it to the retailer for £15.00, and the retailer would then charge the customer £30.00. This gives a basic formula to help you calculate a price for your products:

- Production costs + time + profit = retail price; if you are only selling the product directly to the customer.

If you are selling wholesale the formula becomes:

- (Production costs + time + profit) x 2 = retail price. Half of this is the price you want to sell the product at wholesale.

PRICING THE GLASS BEAD NECKLACES

Returning to the necklace example, if one necklace takes you twenty minutes to make, and you want to earn £12.00 an hour, that gives a time cost of £4.00. The other production costs were £8.80 (see 'Costing glass bead necklaces' on page 29).

This gives you a total production cost of £12.80, to which we add a profit margin of around twenty-five per cent of the production cost – an appropriate amount in the market in which it will be sold – would be £2.20.

This gives a basic total of £15.00, which is your starting price.

CHANGING PRICES

If your raw materials vary in price, or are subject to frequent price increases you may want to add an extra ten per cent or so to your profit to account for the fluctuations in price, rather than having to keep increasing your prices or cutting your profit.

Competition pricing

This pricing method involves looking at a group of your competitors and then taking an average of their prices to calculate your own. This method of working out your pricing is quick and simple, and you know customers will buy at this price. In addition, looking at what your competition charge may reveal a 'going rate' for your product or service.

The downside of this method is it takes no account of the costs and time involved in making your product and could lead to your not making a profit. Other people may be able to produce the item more cheaply than you and make a profit on it when you cannot. There are also many 'hobby sellers' who craft because they love it and simply want to earn enough to buy more materials to make something else.

The combination method

I suggest combining the two methods and calculating your prices based upon your costs, then looking at the competition and see how your price compares to theirs. If yours is a lot cheaper then perhaps you could increase your profit.

Remember that cheaper is not always better. Customers will wonder why your product costs less than your competitors and may assume that it is made with cheaper materials, or by someone less skilled. If other people are able to sell the same product at a higher price there is no reason why you should not be able to.

If your price is too high for the market

If your product is going to be a lot more expensive than all your competitors you have a few options:

Pitch to a more expensive market Promote your product as being high end and aim it at those with a larger budget. Popular examples of this are Cath Kidston, Jan Constantine and Poppy Treffry, who are able to sell their homeware at high prices. Like you, even these big, well-established names had to start from nothing and build up their brand. This point also relates to the market research discussed earlier and pinpointing your ideal customer.

Change your product to add value People are prepared to pay a little extra for something unique. If your product is different from all the others, you can get away with charging a little extra. Alternatively could you use more luxurious supplies to justify a higher price. Use wool felt instead of polyester felt, for example, or precious stone beads instead of glass beads. Adding personalization is another way to justify raising your prices.

Buy in bulk You can usually negotiate a much better price on supplies when buying in bulk, which may in turn allow you to lower your prices. You could speak with other businesses and see if you could group together to place a large order to save money.

> ### REMEMBER ONLINE FEES
>
> If you are selling through a site like Etsy, Folksy, Misi or similar, make sure you include any fees involved in selling your product, such as payment processing fees and listing fees, in your price. You should also account for the time you spend in listing your products online.

Source cheaper supplies It is tempting to stick with the supplier(s) you know but you need to make money or your business will not survive. Shop around to find a better deal. I highly recommend attending industry trade shows to find new suppliers. There you will find hundreds of wholesalers, with many products on display and show discounts. For a list of fabric and haberdashery wholesalers, take a look at thesewingdirectory.co.uk/fabric-wholesalers.

Invest or innovate to speed up production Could you invest in a tool or piece of machinery to speed up your work? A different technique or process that could make things quicker, like batching, could help, too. For example, cut out ten bags at once, sew the bags in a batch and then photograph and list them at the same time, rather than making one from start to end before going onto the next one.

Experimenting with your prices

Your pricing is not set in stone, and you do not have to follow a formula to the letter. Such suggestions are good starting points but a lot of handmade products are unique and require a unique price.

Once people get used to paying a set price for something they are generally unhappy if prices increase. As a result, it is better to start at a higher price and lower your prices than to raise your prices. If in doubt when starting out, go higher. If you do need to increase the price it is often better received if you are able to give a justification. People are more understanding if they know you had to increase your price because the price of cotton has increased, or the rent of your shop has risen.

You can trial special offers such as free postage, or money-off sales to see how this affects your income. Running a short-term offer like this gives you a chance to gauge the response and measure the financial effect before you commit to it permanently.

Remember that your prices will need to be regularly reviewed. As your experience and skills grow you can charge more; as your brand grows and becomes more established you can also increase your price. If your materials become more expensive or you move to more expensive premises you may need to increase your costs.

> ### EXPERIMENTING WITH MY START-UP
>
> When starting up my company, The Sewing Directory, I began with high prices. After a few months I ran a summer sale at a forty per cent discount to see if it would make a difference to my sign-up rate.
>
> The sale price proved such a hit that I made it my permanent price and ended up with hundreds of businesses signing up. If I had gone the opposite way and put my prices up I could easily have lost several customers instead.

Setting your goals

A really important part of running a business is to plan ahead, to set goals and then check your progress towards those goals. All too often people write up a business plan before they launch then never return to it once the business is up and running. It is easy to get bogged down in the day-to-day work and never look at the longer term. It may be that you love the creative side of things but not the business side so you tend to ignore it. The reality is that unless you focus on the business side you will not be able to continue doing the creative side. If you do not have clear business objectives in mind, or a good idea of how your business is performing, how do you know if you are going where you want to go?

Activity: Defining your goals

I want you to think about what success means to you. Does it mean being able to work from home, or working around your children's timetable? Does it mean being able to do something you love all day? Does it mean making as much as you used to in your old job? Does it mean earning some extra money for holidays and treats? Is it funding your hobby? Is it having your work admired? Making it into a big gallery or exhibition? Is success to you measured in money? In time? In a frame of mind? A set of circumstances? Is it a combination of factors?

For me success is being able to work from home, doing something I enjoy, while working around my son and earning more than a part-time wage. Now it is your turn. Once you have thought this through, write out and complete the following sentence:

Success to me is ...

Read through your definition of success and pick out the key elements. Jot them down in your notepad. Leave space to add more at a later date.

For example the key elements of success for me are:

- Being able to work from home.
- Enjoying my work.
- Being able to fit my job around my son.
- Earning more than a part-time wage.

The points you have written in your notebook are your goals. They are what you want from your business. Now that you know what your goals for your business are, you need to start thinking about how you are going to achieve them.

When planning how to achieve your goals it is a good idea to make sure each goal is as specific as possible, so that you know precisely what you are aiming for. Take each goal and break it down. For example, one of the key elements of success I identified was earning more than what I consider a part-time wage. I quantified this goal by working out my monthly salary if I returned to work part-time in my previous office job. With this figure in mind, I can quantify that goal and work out precisely how much I am aiming to earn.

Some goals are harder to define than others. How do you set a target for enjoyment, for example? You need to think about what that means to you. To me, enjoying my work is looking forward to doing it as opposed to dreading it, and being willing to work extra because I enjoy what I am doing.

I am happy to say I have achieved that goal. However, I did not achieve it from the outset. When launching my business I had to do a lot of sales, and I hate sales! I am not a natural sales person and I feel very uncomfortable trying to sell myself and my products to people, especially cold calling. So I worked very hard to get to a point where I no longer have to actively sell to people. As a result, my brand and reputation grew, and people began to approach me instead of me having to approach them.

Once you have defined your goals you will know exactly what you want from your business. You will have something to measure against to see whether you have achieved your goals at the end of each year, or month, depending how often you want to review. Now concentrate on how you are going to get there. I think the best way to tackle this is to get the negatives out of the way first.

Activity: Breaking down your goals

Take the list of goals from the previous activity and break down each one as far as you can. Define what you have to achieve to reach that goal, and be as precise as possible.

Put a figure on the income you would need to earn: the number of sales you want to achieve each week, the exact number of magazines you want to be featured in, or the percentage of customers you want to return.

OUTSOURCING

If there is a particular task that is preventing you achieving your goals, consider outsourcing it. If you spend months dreading doing the accounts, hire an accountant.
Sometimes it is worth spending money on these things for your own peace of mind and to allow you to concentrate on the things you love.

Identify what is getting in the way of achieving your goals. Is there too little space to work from home? Can you not sell many products because you do not have the necessary supplies? Are your prices so low that you are not making much profit? Are customers not completing their purchase because your website is difficult to use? Is your website not getting much traffic? Are people struggling to find you because you do not promote yourself well enough? We all have hurdles we need to overcome. Rather than ignoring them – tempting as that may be – tackle them head on!

As with your goals you need to identify and define any obstacles to your success, and then think about what you can do to overcome them. Make them part of your business plan. Do not panic and think you need to overcome them all at once. Write them down, then gradually work through each one, trying to think of some ideas for overcoming them. You could pick one per month to concentrate on, or set some time aside to address them all at once.

If you cannot think of solutions to them, ask around. See if anyone else has had the same problem and find out how they overcame it. Consult online forums, or read magazines for interviews with entrepreneurs or crafters to see how they tackle things. Look at business advice sites, forums, books or magazines for tips on pricing, time management, contracts, dealing with suppliers, promoting yourself and so on. There are plenty of helpful resources available; some of my favourites are listed on page 45.

Activity: Removing obstacles

Use your notebook to write down the things that are stopping you from achieving your goals, then note down ways that you can try to overcome them. As with your goals, try to go into as much detail as possible, as this will help when you are looking back over this in months to come.

You may also find long-term solutions start to come to you as you work out short-term solutions. You may not be able to tackle the whole problem at once but you could well resolve part of it immediately. For example:

Problem

- Lack of space. My work papers are piled up all over the house because I do not have a dedicated work area. I am working from a laptop on the sofa and getting backache. My business cards are strewn all over the house because the boxes are within the reach of my child, who thinks they are fun to play with.

Short-term solutions

- Invest in a small table that goes over the sofa or just in front of the sofa for the laptop. Alternatively, clear the kitchen table to use for working on.

- Move furniture around until I can make space for a filing cabinet. File all papers into the filing cabinet. If I cannot make that space, get some filing boxes and store them under the bed so all documents are together in one place.

- Move the business cards into a high cupboard or shelf away from the child's reach.

Long-term solution

- Save up enough money to convert the garage into an office or look at hiring an office space locally.

Breaking goals and obstacles down into smaller parts makes them a lot more achievable and helps to keep you motivated – you no longer have seemingly insurmountable problems, you have a to-do list of achievable tasks. Now if you find yourself with an hour to spare pick one of the solutions you have written above and make it happen. Before you know it those pesky problems getting in the way of your goals will be gone.

Once you have looked at ways of dealing with potential obstacles to success, begin planning how you are going to reach your goals. Consider each of your goals in turn and establish what steps you need to take to achieve each one.

If your goals are financial, figure out how much you need to sell to reach your goal, and then how you plan to do that. If you want to turn over one thousand pounds a month and your products cost twenty pounds each, write down that you need to sell fifty products a month.

BE REALISTIC

Keep your goals realistic. Do not set yourself up for failure by setting impossibly high targets.

That is the easy bit done; now on to the how. Do you sell at craft fairs? If so, what do you normally sell there? Do you sell through platforms like Folksy and Etsy (see pages 170–171)? If so, make notes of your average sales per month on those platforms. If you sell through your own website make a note of that too. If you add those up and you normally sell forty units per month, start thinking about how you can increase that to fifty. Some ideas that may help you achieve your goals are below and on the following pages.

GOAL: MORE SALES

- Attend extra craft fairs or shows.
- Find a new online platform to sell through.
- Start selling wholesale.
- Send out press releases to relevant magazines and websites.
- Run a sale/give out a discount code.
- Improve your SEO (search engine optimization) to bring more traffic to your site.
- Find more or better stockists.
- Place some adverts.

GOAL: MORE TIME OFF

- Start using a program like Hootsuite or Tweetdeck to schedule your social media updates.
- Work later on a couple of evenings to have an extra day a week off.
- Review your processes to see if there is anything you can stop doing or do more efficiently.
- Raise your prices so you earn more for fewer hours of work.
- Assess whether you can afford to hire help.
- If you have staff, delegate more tasks to them.

GOAL: BUILD BRAND AWARENESS

- If you can afford it, increase your advertising or try advertising in new places to reach different people.
- Write for blogs, sites and magazines. It means people will be seeing your brand name/logo in several different places.
- Create a viral blogging campaign. Blog coverage is very good exposure for a brand.
- Interact with people more frequently on social media, and post content that is likely to be shared.
- Make sure your branding is consistent across all platforms.
- Attend shows, local craft fairs, and networking events to get your name out there.
- Put yourself forward for awards and competitions. If you win, the resultant publicity will help promote your brand.

GOAL: REDUCE COSTS AND INCREASE PROFIT

- Make things in batches to increase productivity. This also works for doing things like social media updates or writing blog posts. It is quicker to preschedule, write or plan several at a time.
- Research suppliers and make sure you are getting your materials at the best price. Attend trade shows to compare several suppliers at once, and see if you can benefit from show discounts.
- Buy in bulk if you can afford to, as you often get bigger discounts that way. If you cannot afford to, see if there are any local crafters who would share a big order with you.
- Review your pricing – are you charging as much as you could be?
- Review your product lines. If certain items are not selling well, reduce their price, clear the stock and fill their place with better-selling products.

GOAL: INCREASE TRAFFIC TO YOUR WEBSITE

- Do a search engine optimization (SEO) review and make sure your site is well-optimized.
- Guest post on blogs and websites to drive traffic to your site, or write for magazines that will include a link to your site on the page.
- Try advertising online – on blogs, websites, Facebook, Google ads or similar.
- Keep adding fresh interesting content to your site to attract visitors and help your SEO.
- Build your social media following and post occasional links back to your site.

Reviewing your goals

There is no point setting goals for your business and then forgetting about them. You need to regularly revisit your goals and review how your business is performing towards those goals. You need to see if you are on target to meet your goals and, if not, what you can do to help reach them. You also need to see whether your goals need revising. Our priorities change over time, so your goals may need updating. What was important to you last year may not be important to you this year. If your business is doing a lot better than predicted, why not set higher goals?

One common thing with entrepreneurs of all types is over-working which results in getting run down, exhausted, or even ill. (I have certainly been there and done that!) If this happens then you may decide that your focus is no longer increasing your profits but perhaps taking more time off.

How frequently you review your goals is up to you, you may want to set aside some time each month to do it or if you think that you are not likely to stick to that make it once a quarter. It is also worth doing a big annual review to look back over the whole year.

Activity: Planning your goals

Go back to your notepad to make notes on how you plan to reach your goals. If you write them in the form of a checklist you can easily cross them off as you go.

Remember your goals are not set in stone. As your business or personal circumstances change, amend your goals accordingly. You may also need to adapt them to fit customer demand.

Write down events such as the launch of a new website, a big sale, a new product range launch, closing the shop while you went on holiday, or exhibiting at a big show – anything that happened during the year which may have affected your statistics, and what dates those things occurred. This will allow you to account for peaks and troughs in the figures in a few years' time when you look back.

You may want to add some extra statistics to your annual review form depending upon the nature of your business, and what your focus is. It can also help to break down the sales of individual items over the year so you can see what is selling well and what is not. This will help you plan your stock for the next year.

It is worth keeping an eye on your conversion rate (the percentage of visitors to your shop or website that end up buying something) so that you can see if any changes you make, such as to the layout of your shop or website, have any impact on the number of conversions.

If you complete the business review form each year you will be able to see the growth of your company from year to year. You can also identify any areas that are not improving, or growing at a slower rate than others, so you can focus on improving them. Once you have more than one year's worth of figures, compare the current year with previous years.

MY REVIEWING HABITS

Personally, I review my figures every month to check that I am on track for my financial target, and keep an eye on my site statistics daily so that if I spot a drop one day I can add something the following day to boost interest.

I also do a big review at the end of the calendar year. This may seem odd because my business year runs from April–April (the UK financial year). However, I find I have more time to review at the end of December as my business has a natural lull between Christmas and New Year. This has the added benefit of giving me three months to address any shortfall I identify so that I still hit my goals by April, the end of my accounting year.

Activity: Reviewing your business

Complete the business review form opposite so that you have a starting point for future reviews. This will give you a snapshot of your business as it stands on this date. If you trade through premises or on a craft stall then pick a week to count your average number of customers and visitors to your shop/stall. Try to use the same week each year so you can accurately measure any growth. Write down which week you have used so you know for the next year. The easiest way to log these figures is to keep a notebook by your till and track the number of customers/browsers.

Photocopy the form before you begin if you want to use it more than once, or download copies from the Search Press website if you do not want to write in your book.

BUSINESS REVIEW FORM

Financial

- Annual turnover
- Annual outgoings
- Annual profit
- Average monthly profit
- Number of sales in the last year
- Average monthly number of sales

Online statistics

- Hits in the last year
- Number of Facebook/Twitter/other social media site followers
- Number of blog followers
- Number of online sales in the last year
- Conversion rate (percentage of website/shop visitors that end up buying something) in the last year

If you sell both online and offline, complete the following:

- Annual turnover from online sales
- Annual profit from online sales
- Average monthly profit from online sales

Offline statistics

- Total people that visited your stall/shop in a week
- Total number that purchased from you that week
- Total number of browsers in that week (visiting/looking but not buying)
- Conversion rate in that week
- Income that week from offline sales
- Income in the whole year from offline sales
- Average monthly income from offline sales

Taking it further

If you have worked through the exercises, you will have ended this section with a written list of business goals, a to-do list of things which will help you achieve your goals, and the up-to-date statistics of your business. The important thing is to make business planning and reviewing part of your routine. Schedule in regular reviews at intervals which best suit you. Aim for mini reviews every month or two and a big annual or biannual review.

Learn to use the tools that will help you with your reviews. Keep your accounts up to date so you can review your financial standing regularly (see pages 58–61 for more on accounts). Learn to use analytical tools like Google Analytics to keep an eye on your web stats (see pages 186–197 and 198–207 for more information on search engine optimization and analytics respectively).

Follow-on activities

Because goal setting and reviewing are so important to your business I have added a few extra activities below to help you continue to monitor your business on an ongoing basis.

Activity: Creating your ideal day

When you are doing something day in and day out you sometimes need to take a step back to assess. Your goals can often change over time as your business evolves or your personal circumstances changes. That is why it is worth taking a day out and starting from scratch with your goals rather than just using the same list as before.

Schedule in a day every six or twelve months where you are away from your business, with a clear mind and no interruptions. Grab your notepad and a pen, visualize your ideal working day and answer the questions below.

- Where are you on that ideal day?
- How does your day start?
- What tasks do you do during that day and what results do you achieve?
- What frame of mind are you in?
- What hours do you work?
- How does your day end?

With that ideal day in mind, and thinking about what success means to you (see page 34), draw up a list of goals that work directly towards achieving that ideal working day. How can you change your business to get you doing more of what you want and less of what you do not want to do? Have your goals changed since the last time you did them? If you identify new goals, remember to break them down into the smaller tasks you need to do to help you achieve them (see page 35).

Sometimes your business can be dragged in directions you have never really planned. Opportunities present themselves and we take them without checking whether they fit with our goals. Regular reviews will help you think such opportunities through so that you can decide whether these things are worth pursuing or if they are just distracting you from your main goals.

Activity: Twenty-four goals in twelve months

Referring to your to-do list (see page 36), and your list of goals (see pages 34), use the table below to allocate one thing from each list to each month of the year. Do not make this one of the big goals or problems, but one of the smaller steps you will need to take to help achieve your goal or overcome your problem. You can download this form from the Search Press website if you do not want to write in the book.

For example, I might add 're-vamp my blog' to the first box for January, and 'sort all my filing into a filing cabinet' into the second box. I might add 'create a press pack' for my February task and 'find a good mailing list program' from my problem list, and so forth.

Month	Task from your to-do list	Item from your list of goals
January		
February		
March		
April		
May		
June		
July		
August		
September		
October		
November		
December		

Start from whichever calendar month it is at the moment and aim to complete the two tasks for this month in the next few weeks. You do not have to do them both at once – start with one now and the other later in the month. When you have completed the task, cross it off or colour the box in so that you know it is done. Think of the sense of achievement you will have when you look at that table in a year's time and see how much you have managed to do.

Do not panic if you cannot do the tasks for one month. Leave them in the table and go back to it later in the year. You will find that some tasks are a lot quicker than others, so one month you may manage three or four tasks and other months only one. The main thing to aim for is to have all twenty-four tasks done at the end of twelve months.

Activity: Make an in-depth business plan

A business plan will help you focus on your goals, and also to plan the long-term future of your business, budget your outgoings, forecast your incomings, research your market and much more. If you never wrote a business plan when you started your business, now is a good time for you to do it. If you did create a business plan, now is the time to update it.

There are several different sites offering business plan templates as well as advice on how to complete them. Several banks have free templates on their sites (some are listed in the useful links opposite). Find your bank's website, go to its business page and look for links to its business plan templates, start-up guides and other useful information.

Writing a thorough business plan is a time-consuming job, but it will give you a much better idea of what you want to achieve when you have finished.

Activity: Studying trends

Using a spreadsheet program (such as Microsoft Excel or Google spreadsheets) or some graph paper, make a graph showing your profit each month for the last year (or two or three years, if you have the records). If you run an online business, do the same thing for your monthly hits as well.

These graphs will likely show you that you earn more, or get more site traffic, in some months than others. If you do this activity with a few years' worth of data, you will be able to see if the same months each year are good or bad for sales and site traffic.

Note down why you think particular months are better or worse than the others. Do you get a sudden rush of traffic and sales in the pre-Christmas period because people are buying presents? Is the summer quieter because people tend to be away on holiday? Do you have a big peak in January and February because you sell lots of products suitable for St. Valentine's Day?

Concentrating on the months where you have a dip in your income or site traffic, brainstorm how you can improve those figures in those months.

Is it worth running a sale? Doing extra advertising? Launching a new product that ties in with a seasonal event that month? Putting some fresh content on your site? Changing your social media strategy?

Bear in mind that some things cannot be overcome. Rather than wasting your time and energy fighting, consider how to usefully use the time. Over December, many people spend less time browsing websites or interacting on blogs or social media: they are busy preparing for Christmas, spending time with their family or simply having time off work. After a couple years of trying to think of ideas to boost my site traffic over that period, I decided to accept it and take some time off myself then too.

Studying these trends can help you plan your business strategy. There is no point putting lots of great content on your site at a time of year when hardly anyone is looking at it. Equally, if you find that certain shows or events on particular months are always quiet and do not make you money, avoid those next year.

USEFUL LINKS

Here are some useful online links to help you with the topics we have discussed in this section.

Free activity templates

searchpress.com

Start-up advice

bgateway.com

businesswales.gov.wales/zones/
    starting-up

enterprisenation.com

europa.eu

gov.uk/browse/business

moo.com/uk/startup-business-
    toolkit

shell-livewire.org

Business plan templates

barclays.co.uk

bplans.co.uk

business.gov.au

lloydsbank.com

santander.co.uk

sba.gov

Advice on planning your business and setting goals

craftindustryalliance.org

entrepreneur.com

enterprisenation.com

thedesigntrust.co.uk

Pricing

ahandcraftedbusiness.com

createandthrive.com

etsy.com/blog

handmadeology.com

ohmyhandmade.com

thedesigntrust.co.uk

ukhandmade.co.uk

Market research

google.com/analytics/surveys

marketingdonut.co.uk/market-
    research

smarta.com

surveymonkey.com

YOUR LINKS AND NOTES

You can use this space to keep a list of links to websites and services you find helpful.

LEGAL

MATTERS

YOUR BUSINESS AND THE LAW

It is sometimes tempting to 'switch off' when looking at the legal and financial aspects of running a business. However, if you want to make a success of your business it is important to do it correctly. You do not want to end up being fined, closed down or even imprisoned because you did not do what you should have done. This chapter gives a simple introduction to the things you should be thinking about and where you can get more information.

We begin with a brief summary of the laws which can apply to creative businesses. Depending upon the exact nature of your business, not all of those listed will apply to you, but do take a read through and think about which ones relate to you. There is an extensive links section at the end of this chapter, so do use these to get more information on all the legislation mentioned here. If you are unsure about any of these requirements, either use the contact numbers on the websites in the links list to get more information or seek professional legal advice.

DISCLAIMER

I am not a legal or financial expert. This chapter is intended simply to give you an idea of where to start when considering the legal requirements of setting up your business. You should always double check the current rules and laws by either using your government website, trading standards, the tax office or seeking professional legal advice.

Learning the law

Familiarizing yourself with local legislation and regulation is essential for any start-up business owner. These laws may cover anything from what you sell to how you sell it, and extends to the people you employ.

Employment laws

Once your business grows to the point where you start employing other people there are more laws that will become applicable to you, including minimum wage laws, pension laws, tax laws and working time regulations. The government website or tax office website for your country of residence is the best place to start obtaining this information.

Health and safety

Depending on where you work and whether you employ people, there may be health and safety regulations that apply to you. These can dictate how you train staff, how you manage risks and how you deal with first aid and accidents. The useful links section at the end of the chapter contains details of where to get more information on this subject.

EMPLOYMENT TIPS FROM KAY HEALD

These tips on employment regulations are from Kay Heald, who runs the human resources consultancy, Heald HR (kayhealdhr.co.uk).

Much business advice suggests that start-ups outsource services and engage freelancers instead of employing staff in order to keep costs down. However, while outsourcing services is usually beneficial, there can be drawbacks to engaging freelancers for regular patterns of work over long periods. An alternative option might be to initially employ part-time staff on short-term contracts, then review them after a twelve month period, once the business is more established. Whatever you do, budget for a good HR advisor who can:

- Help you explore the best option(s) for your business.
- Draw up written agreements/contracts clarifying duties, expectations, who owns copyright and rates of pay.
- Put statutory policies in place, e.g. Disciplinary, Grievance, etc.
- Clarify the working arrangements with regard to HMRC and employment law, to avoid any tax or employment liabilities

Do this up front as clear documentation can help avoid costly litigation in the event of misunderstandings or breakdowns in any relationships.

Selling and distance selling around the world

In the majority of countries there are legal requirements about the selling of products both online and in person. In the UK, the rules include making sure that your product matches its description, that the description is not misleading, that the product is of satisfactory quality, and that is fit for purpose (Sale of Goods Act 1979). When selling online in the UK, you need to ensure you provide the customer with your identity, your full address, details of the delivery and payment options and details of their cancellation rights amongst other things. The Office of Fair Trading website has in-depth information on all the regulations you need to consider. Online sellers also have to look into cookie regulations, marketing rules and data protection.

TOY SAFETY REGULATIONS

In most countries there are strict regulations for selling products that will be used by children. When selling toys within the UK or the European Economic Area, your products are required to be CE marked to confirm that they meet safety standards. If you fail to comply with this regulation you can be fined or even sent to prison. If you are unsure of whether your product needs CE marking it is best to contact Trading Standards to find out. There are also regulations about chemicals and materials used in children's toys as well as rules governing choking risks.

There is a UK-based company called Conformance (conformance.co.uk) that gives advice, training and self-certification packs for product safety and CE marking. Conformance also has a 'knowledgebase' section on its website which gives answers to many commonly asked questions.

For the requirements of the US Government, The Toy Industry Association.inc have plenty of useful information on their website (toyassociation.org). The legislation you need to be aware of when making toys in the USA is the Consumer Product Safety Improvement Act (CPSIA). The full details can be found online at cpsc.gov.

Australia has various Australian Standards which govern toy safety. The Australian Toy Association website (austoy.com.au) is a good place to start when seeking advice on toy safety.

Another useful resource when it comes to toy safety is the International Council of Toy Industries website (toy-icti.org/info/toysafetystandards.html) which has advice on toy safety standards around the world.

In the USA the Federal Trade Commission is the main agency that regulates e-commerce rules. There is a lot of information on its website about advertising, marketing and selling regulations as well as advice on other financial and legal aspects of running a business. For Australia, the Australian Competition & Consumer Commission is a good place to start your research.

Wherever you live, when selling online you must look into the rules regarding online marketing in your country (such as the Can-Spam in the US), the rules regarding domain registration (try Nominet for UK domains) and labelling laws.

CLOTHING REGULATIONS

As with toys, certain legal requirements must be met when you are producing clothing. Some countries also have labelling requirements. For example, textile products in the UK should contain a label, either on the product itself or on the packing, which indicates the fibre contents of the product. Certain products are exempt, so do double check the up-to-date list of exemptions online.

The Product Safety Australia website has details of the mandatory requirements for labels for clothing, household textiles and furnishings for those either manufacturing or importing into Australia.

In America the Federal Trade Commission (FTC) and the US Customs and Border Protection agency dictate labelling requirements. The main Act you need to be looking at is the Textile Fiber Products Identification Act which can be found on the FTC website.

A lot of regulations apply to children's products in general; whether clothing or toys. For children's clothing there are particular rules about the flammability of the fabrics used, and about hood cords, for example. Many of the useful links given in the box on toy safety regulations (see opposite) will also give advice relevant for making and selling children's clothing.

EU DIGITAL VAT

One of the biggest legislative changes since I wrote the first edition of this book was the introduction of EU Digital VAT in 2015. These new rules mean that if you sell digital products – such as patterns in PDF format, e-books, apps or software – directly to consumers in EU member states other than your own (or from outside of the EU), you have to charge VAT (value added tax) based upon the location of the consumer.

This means you have to gather information to confirm the location of your customer, and charge the correct rate of VAT for their country. You then have to ensure that VAT goes to the relevant country. In the UK you can do this by registering for VAT Mini One Stop Shop (VAT MOSS).

Understandably, this caused widespread panic among small businesses when this was introduced, especially as it was not initially clear how the customer location was to be determined, and whether the retailer would have to become VAT registered, which would have added onerous tax burdens. It put me off introducing the craft business e-courses I was planning to launch and caused several craft businesses to close down.

Since then, it has become a little clearer how small businesses can deal with this change. One of the common ways you can use to process digital transactions is to use a third party website, letting them handle the VAT aspect for you. I have noticed several of the people I buy digital patterns from now use Payhip (payhip.com), for example. Etsy will also add the relevant VAT onto a transaction and remit it straight to the relevant country, saving you having to deal with it. Thus far, it is unclear how digital VAT will be affected when Britain leaves the EU.

GDPR COMPLIANCE

In May 2018, the General Data Protection Regulation (GDPR) became law across the EU. It aims to give individuals more rights over their data and restrict how companies process private information.

Smaller businesses, with fewer than two hundred and fifty employees, will be less affected as they do not have to comply with all the GDPR rules, but it is worth reading up on them in order to check if you need to do anything.

Visit ico.org.co.uk to learn more.

The form of your company

There are different forms that your business can take. Each one carries its own set of legal restrictions and requirements, but also benefits too. Sole traders, for example, have full legal liability for their business which can make it easier to get credit accounts, but does leave you personally responsible for the business debts. It also affords you privacy because your accounts are not publicly published. Other options include limited liability companies or partnerships, which protect the owner from the potential liability of the business (in most circumstances) but often have more stringent accounting requirements.

Activity: The right form for your business

Investigate what company forms are available in your country and decide which one suits your own requirements best.

If you are in the UK, visit gov.uk/set-up-business for more advice on the legal structure of your business.

BREXIT

By 2019 the UK will be leaving the European Union, which could result in legal changes for those living in the UK or Europe. Keep up to date with any relevant legislation using the links at the end of this section.

REGISTER AS SELF-EMPLOYED

Do not forget you need to notify your local tax authority that you are going self-employed, even if you are not making a profit initially. In fact, if you are making a loss this could lead to a tax break, offsetting the loss against any other tax you have paid that year, or carrying it forward to offset against future profit. In the UK you can register online at gov.uk, and must do so by the 5th of October in your business' second tax year.

Your company name

There are many factors, both legal and non-legal, to consider when choosing a name for your business. The name should represent your brand, appeal to the target market, and be unique. If you intend to incorporate you need to check if the name you are thinking of has already been registered. You may also want to check the trademark database too (see page 72 for relevant website links).

There are also restrictions on words that you are allowed to use in your business name. Company names are not allowed to be misleading or suggest illegal activity; nor are they allowed to be too similar to companies that already have established goodwill. Again the websites in the links section will give you advice about what is and is not allowed when it comes to naming your business. Your business name may also be required to reflect the legal status of your business, for instance with the addition of 'Ltd' after the name in the UK, or 'LLC' in the US.

Checking whether the domain names and social media names for your proposed business name are available is not a legal requirement, but well worth doing. You do not want to have to use social media names which are too different from your brand or hard to remember. Normally when someone is searching for a brand on social media they will simply type the name. If that leads them to another company, it can get very confusing. You do not want your customers or prospective customers to be following someone else on social media thinking they are following you.

Activity: Registering your chosen name

Once you have decided on a business name, you should register the domain and social media accounts for that name as soon as possible, to avoid the risk of someone else buying it first.

Once you have registered them, write the links, account names and passwords in your notebook for when you are ready to use them.

DORMANT SOCIAL MEDIA

If you find the name you want has already been taken but is not being used, you can try to contact the account owner to see if they will close their account down or transfer it to you. If they do not respond you will have to get imaginative with your name. You may be able to add your location or the word 'shop' after your business name For example, 'Sew Happy Oxford' or 'Sew Happy Shop' Otherwise you may need to get more descriptive, 'Sugar Sweet Cakes' or 'Sugar Sweet Bakery' instead of just 'Sugar Sweet', for instance.

Trademarks and patents

If you have unique branding or a unique product idea that you want to protect, it may be worth investigating trademarking your logo or patenting your product. The best place to find out whether your idea has already been registered, or how to go about registering it and the costs involved is to visit the intellectual property office website for your country. You can also find out more about protecting your ideas and designs on pages 66–69.

Working with children

If you are planning to hold events that will involve children or teaching children, there are certain legal requirements you have to satisfy beforehand. There are background checks that need to be performed on you and your staff, and there is sometimes a set ratio of adults to children that needs to be observed.

The adult–child ratio can differ based upon the intended activities, any special needs the children have, and the ages of the children. The NSPCC website (nspcc.org.uk) gives you suggested guidelines for the ratio in the UK.

Renting commercial premises

Renting property from which to trade is not the same as renting a domestic property. The lease will be very different, so make sure you read through every clause, and consider getting a solicitor to look over it. The lease will normally transfer several responsibilities over to you during the term of your tenancy, so you need to understand which responsibilities you are taking on, and which will remain with the landlord. You may become responsible for fire safety, gas safety, maintaining electrical equipment, as well as certain repairs and maintenance to the property.

TIPS ON LEASING BUSINESS PREMISES

Annie Barker is the owner of Village Haberdashery (thevillagehaberdashery.co.uk), an online and physical shop. In 2017, Annie moved into new larger premises in West Hampstead.

Signing a lease on new premises can be a daunting experience for a small business owner, but it is also one of the most exciting! I can still remember how proud, terrified and exhilarated I felt when I stood outside my first shop the night before we opened our doors for the first time.

For us, there was a huge difference between the process of committing to our first premises and our second. Our first was a small shop on the ground floor of a residential building that was owned by a family. We agreed to a commitment of one year at a time and it was handled almost like renting a flat.

It was a very different situation with our second premises because we were signing a lease on a brand-new building that had not yet been completed. This came with a whole set of additional challenges and I think it is safe to say that most commercial property lettings will fall somewhere between these two extremes.

A few basic things to know when you are in the planning and budgeting stages is that most commercial leases will be for around ten years. You will be responsible for a portion of the upkeep of the building itself in addition to your unit, and you need to think about Business Rates (taxes) when you are planning your budget.

There are always things to negotiate in any lease, so I recommend consulting a commercial property lawyer who can identify any red flags and help you navigate the legal jargon. In a new building, there are also additional steps to take, including a snagging inspection (making sure there is nothing wrong with the premises) and registering the land and paying stamp duty.

With a brand-new building, your fit out will fall under greater scrutiny than if you take over an existing shop. In our new shop we had to make sure all of the electrical and fire alarm work was completed by certified contractors and the layout met guidelines for wheelchair accessibility before it was reviewed by building control and we were granted our building certificate. When choosing contractors, I recommend hiring the best you can afford because they will make this process easier for you – plus, if all goes well, you will be in your building for a long time!

Taxes and accounts

Taxation and accounts are areas that can seem very daunting when you first start up your business. They sound very complex and change rapidly. This often leads to new business owners simply paying an accountant to deal with it! However, tax and accounts do not have to be as complex as you think. So long as you keep a proper log of what money is going in and out of your business, you have the information you need to do your own tax returns.

Keeping track of your cash flow

When it comes to keeping track of what is coming in and out of your business there are a few things that you need to do:

Set up a separate bank account for your business.

You can run your business through your personal account, but it will make doing your accounts more complicated. Disentangling business transactions from among personal ones, several months after the money was spent, can be very difficult.

Business bank accounts do not need to cost a fortune. As well as making your accounts easier it makes you look more professional to be able to make or receive payments in your business name. For the same reasons, if you are processing online payments, consider setting up a business account with whichever online payment provider you choose to use. See pages 183–185 for more information on selling online and online payments.

Keep all your receipts

The tax office may ask to see your receipts, so you need to keep them safe. In addition, if you ever have a problem balancing your accounts, it helps to be able to go through the receipts and double check each payment amount.

It is easiest if you keep all of your receipts in one place so that you do not have to waste time searching for them if you need them. Keep a big box file with all your receipts in for the current tax year, and at the end of each year put them all in a large envelope and write the tax year on the front of the envelope. You can print out online receipts and store them with the others, or simply save them all in one e-mail or computer folder. If you choose the latter option, make sure to back up the folder regularly.

MY BUSINESS BANK ACCOUNT

I pay nothing for my business bank account. My bank allows me to process online payments and cheques for free (but not to use branch services), which is all I need for my business. Shop around and compare what the different banks offer to see which is best for you.

KEEPING TRACK OF MY ACCOUNTS

I download monthly statements from the various accounts I hold as pdf documents and save them in two different places as back-up.

Log your transactions

This is so much easier if you do it as the money comes in and out, rather than trying to do it all at the end of the month or year. You can do this with dedicated accounts software like Sage or Quick Books, or, if you are more of a pen and paper person, by keeping an accounts book and writing down the transactions as you go. You can buy accounts books with all the columns ready marked in from most stationers.

You can also find free accounts templates online. The Microsoft website holds accounts templates for Excel, and there are a couple of useful ones on the Arts Council website.

Try to establish a habit of updating your accounts around the same time each day, make it part of your daily routine. Use whichever method you are most confident with, and the one you are more likely to stick to. If, like me, your business involves being online quite a lot then a computerised method is probably best. If you are working in a studio or shop away from the computer you may find it easiest to have a paper book and write things down as you go. The main thing is that you need to be logging your transactions as closely as possible to when they happen. Then once a week or once a month have a look over your accounts and make sure the figures add up and that you have not missed any transactions in error, or made any mistakes.

Activity: Pick a logging method

Think about what accounts logging method will work best for your business. Use the useful links at the end of this section of the book to compare some of the different options and see which appeals most to you.

BACK UP FREQUENTLY

Given that a lot of business is now done online, the chances are that many of your receipts and account statements will be online too. Make sure you back up frequently so that you do not risk losing these. Either print them off and keep paper copies, use a service like Dropbox to back them up online, or use a USB stick or external hard drive.

I am a big fan of Dropbox, not only is it free but it automatically synchronizes with your computer so you do not need to remember to back up – it is all done for you automatically. In addition, because the service provides online storage, you can access your accounts and receipts from any computer or device.

You can also get a similar service with Google Drive or Microsoft One Drive.

Know your tax limits

Rather than waiting until the end of the year to see what you owe, look up the current tax limits for your country, how much you can earn before you have to pay tax, and what the tax rate is once you cross that threshold. You can normally find those figures on your government website or tax office website. Check them each year as they tend to change annually.

Take care to read through the notes on the tax office websites for your country because there can be extra costs you need to account for. For instance in the UK, once your tax bill passes a certain limit, you have to pay money in advance towards next year's tax bill (payment on account). You also have to pay National Insurance and, depending on your circumstances and income, you may find student loan repayments will be added to your tax bill. You do not want to wait until you submit your tax return before finding out things like that!

On a similar note, the UK tax thresholds change annually, so you need to check them every financial year.

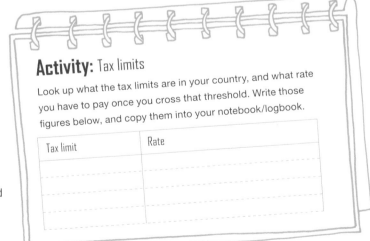

Activity: Tax limits

Look up what the tax limits are in your country, and what rate you have to pay once you cross that threshold. Write those figures below, and copy them into your notebook/logbook.

Tax limit	Rate

I recommend totalling up your figures at the end of every month and checking them against the tax limit. Once you cross the tax threshold, calculate how much you owe at the end of each month and make sure you put that money aside. If you do this throughout the year you do not need to worry about finding money to pay your tax bill.

You might also consider setting up a second business account in which to keep your tax money to make sure you do not spend it. If possible, choose a high-interest account so that you can earn interest on your set-aside funds while you wait to pay your tax bill.

In some instances, the financial requirements are relaxed a little for smaller businesses, for example in the UK sole traders and business partnerships can use Simplified Expenses. This allows you to put through a fixed rate for vehicle expenses and work from home costs.

Smaller businesses can also work on a cash basis when submitting their tax return, only accounting for money actually received or spent in that tax year, and not for invoices issued or received which have not yet been paid.

More information on both of these can be found on the HMRC website (gov.uk).

AVOID LAST-MINUTE PANIC

Bureaucracy can slow things down – in the UK the HMRC can take up to three weeks to send out the necessary information to access and fill out a tax return online, for example, and I am sure there will be similar delays elsewhere. Do not leave things too late!

Accountant or not?

If after reading the above, you still do not think you can handle your own accounts, consider looking into outside help such as local accountants or online firms. Equally, you might decide to learn more about accounts yourself. Most areas have business support including accounts or tax training. There are also accountancy books available and online training courses. Tax offices and government websites are very useful sources of information as well.

If you cannot handle your accounts yourself, it is best to get professional help rather than risk submitting late or incorrect accounts which could result in fines. Try not to leave it too close to the end of the tax year before looking for someone as most accountants will be very busy then and may not be in a position to take on new businesses.

TEACHING YOURSELF ACCOUNTANCY

I attended free courses at my local tax office just before I launched my business, and then did one of its free online webinars a couple years later for a refresher. Both experiences gave me a chance to ask questions as well as find out the current regulations.

You can also ring the tax office with any queries you have; I have done so several times and they are very helpful. In my experience they would much rather you did that than guess what you should be doing and submit incorrect accounts.

SETTING MONEY ASIDE

Whether you decide to set up a separate business account for tax funds or not, it always helps to keep an extra float in your business to cover any unexpected costs like new machinery you need, extra supplies for a large order or an unexpected trip you need to take.

Set an amount that you want to keep in your account at all times, that would cover any possible expense you could foresee. For instance if your business involves you using a sewing machine, keep enough aside to replace or repair it in case it breaks.

Funding sources

There are several ways to fund your business when you start up. In an ideal world you would do it with your own money, but the reality is that most of us require more than that to get going. Below is information on some funding sources you may want to look into if you need extra funds to launch your business.

Bank loans

There are many banks who will provide a business loan, but they will want to see a well-researched business plan that shows your business will make a profit so they can count on getting their money back – plus interest, of course.

Charities

Certain charities will give money and advice to help people start up a business. I received of most the funding for The Sewing Directory from the Prince's Trust who help eighteen to thirty year-olds to turn their business ideas into a reality.

Friends and family

Borrowing from friends and family can be much quicker and easier than approaching a bank for a loan, and the terms are often more favourable. However, do bear in mind that money lending can strain relationships. When I started The Sewing Directory, a third of the money came from a family loan.

Business angels

Business angels match investors with start ups looking for funds. Normally you need to be prepared to sell a share of your business to the investor in exchange for the money. They risk their money in exchange for a part of what hopefully will be a successful and growing business.

Crowdfunding

Crowdfunding is when you raise money for your business by raising money from a large number of people, each of whom provide a small amount of money. Normally the crowdfunders expect some 'perk' in exchange for their investment, commonly this is in the form of product. There are several crowdfunding platforms you can use such as Kickstarter, Indiegogo, Crowdfunder and Crowd Cube.

Government funding

Government grants and loans are available for certain types of businesses (UK only). They vary depending where in the country you are based. To check for any in your area, visit gov.uk/business-finance-support.

> ### WHERE'S MY ANGEL?
>
> Find out more about business angels on the UK Business Angel's Association website: ukbaa.org.uk

Copyright

Copyright is a legal concept which gives the person who created the original work rights over how that work is used or distributed. Not everything can be copyrighted. Ideas cannot be protected and nor can names, but written works such as books, poems and plays can be; as can photographs, drawings, paintings, computer software, sound recordings and more. These, along with trademarks, registered designs and patents, are collectively known as intellectual property or IP.

IP TIPS FROM DIDS MACDONALD

Dids MacDonald is the Chief Executive of ACID (acid.uk.com), an organization that raises awareness and encourages respect for intellectual property.

- Create an IP strategy and ensure that it is communicated within and outside your company. IP communication sends a clear message that 'original design and design integrity equals value' for both the purchaser and the originator!

- Be active when dealing with IP issues. Become 'IP savvy' and create an informed understanding within your team.

- Create an IP portfolio of your design and trademark registrations. Include any patents you may have and guard your trade secrets carefully.

- Clarity of IP ownership is essential, so agreements should underpin most commercial relationships. It is good to know you have the small print to rely on if things go wrong. Never underestimate the risks of sharing a good idea unless you know there are safeguards.

- Choose your battles carefully. Never sue on principle; only if there is a quantifiable loss and a clear IP case to pursue. Consider dispute resolution/mediation as an alternative to litigation. It is good to talk!

Trademarks, registered designs and patents

Unlike copyright, these protections do not occur automatically but are paid-for registration of the visual appearance of your design (registered design), the processes or features that make your design work (patents) or your logo (trademarks). These need to be registered via the Intellectual Property Office website if you are based in the UK or the Patent and Trademark Office if you are in the USA. These sites gives you full details of what exactly can be registered and how to do so. Find the links at the end of this section.

INDEPENDENT DESIGNERS AND THE HIGH STREET

There have been several high-profile cases of high street stores breaching independent designers' copyright. Kate Davies, owner of Kate Davies Designs, found an owl jumper of her design being sold through the high street store Debenhams. After hundreds of her followers made complaints, Debenhams agreed to donate £5,000 to a charity of Kate's choice.

Another well-known case is that of illustrator HiddenEloise and Paperchase. Paperchase allegedly stole and traced one of her illustrations to put on its notebooks, totebags and albums. Her blog post about this went viral, and resulted in Paperchase saying it they would investigate and the items being withdrawn from sale.

A lot of the recent cases have been fought through social media; perhaps as a result of the cost and difficulty that faces a small business pursuing this kind of case through the courts. In a similar case to Kate Davies', Claire's Accessories released a range of necklaces almost exactly like those designed by Tatty Devine at a fraction of the price. Tatty Devine put a post on its blog comparing both sets of necklaces. This very quickly went viral on social media and led to Claire's Accessories trending on Twitter. An undisclosed settlement was reached between the two companies soon afterwards.

Learning to protect your copyright

Copyright is an important issue for any business. The advent of the internet has made it easier for people's designs to be copied. People can now see your products on your website, social media and any online marketplaces you sell through, which makes it easy for them to copy your designs.

Fortunately, the internet also makes it easier for you to find out when this has happened. Companies are commonly notified of breaches to their copyright by their social media followers. You can also use tools like Google reverse image search to see if anyone is trying to pass your designs off as their own.

So how can you protect your copyright? Copyright is established automatically as soon as the item, design or brand is created: there is no need to notify an official register where you can log your designs, but you can join an organization like Anti Copying In Design (ACID).

ACID is a not-for-profit organization which provides help and support in protecting designers' intellectual property. They charge a membership fee in exchange for access to their design databank, initial free legal advice and access to their intellectual property resources. They have IP affiliates in many countries and operate an IP tracker which tracks the sending of any intellectual property or confidential information. They also have the ACID Marketplace, an online safer trading conduit. Designers have the safety of knowing their designs are on the ACID database and are protected by a buyers' charter.

The University of Arts London also has a good copyright site called Own It. This site has a series of useful articles about copyright and intellectual property as well as a legal advice service which is free for some people and available at a nominal fee for others. It also suggests several other places where you can get intellectual property legal advice too. The UK Intellectual Property Office website is a great resource for information on protecting your IP. You could also use the UK Copyright Service. They will register your work and back it up for you, for a fee per work. They can provide independent evidence of when your work was registered.

In Australia, the Australian Copyright Council provides free legal advice services, and seminars around the country, plus a bookshop of useful books. It also has free downloadable advice documents on its website as well.

In the USA, you can register your copyright with The US Copyright Office. Copyright will still exist even if you do not register it with the Copyright Office, but it may help to protect you if you do register.

How can I prevent copying?

Unfortunately the short answer is that in many instances you cannot prevent others copying your work. However, there are steps you can take to minimise the risk.

Notices Include a copyright notice on your site and on products with the year, your name or business name and the copyright symbol © or the word 'copyright'.

Watermarks When putting product photographs online, watermark them. There are several sites and software programs that allow you to do this including PicMonkey, Pixlr and TSR Watermark Image. Pixlr is also available as a free phone app so you can watermark and upload images directly from your phone.

Check the internet Use programs like Copyscape or Google image checker to see if anyone is using your content elsewhere on the internet.

Use the law Legally protect your designs where possible using patents, trademarks and registered designs.

Record your work Keep a record of what you create and when. If your copyright is breached you need to be able to prove that you created it first. Records will help prove your case. Digital methods such as uploading to your blog, or saving digital copies with a file creation date are less useful than hard copies (see box, right) as the dates are easier to manipulate.

Branding Create and use a recognizable logo or other branding so people can check it is your original product and not an inferior copy.

Registration If it is a product or brand name you want to protect, register all the relevant domains to prevent other businesses from being able to use them. These domains can all be linked to feed through to your main website.

Insurance If you think your designs are at a big risk of being copied you may want to get intellectual property insurance. It will cover your legal costs and any judgment costs up to the policy limits.

Impact Aim to make a big impact and to be the best. Things like your business concept are hard (if not impossible) to protect. By making sure you are the most well-known and the best, you will still be known as the person to go to even if people copy your idea and set up competition. Creating and maintaining a high-profile presence means that most people will have heard of you before anyone has a chance to copy your ideas.

THE COPYRIGHT SYMBOL

To get the © symbol when using a Windows PC hold the ALT key and type 0169. If you are using a Mac hold the OPTION key and press G.
The copyright symbol can be expressed by a C in brackets too (C).

POOR MAN'S COPYRIGHT

In the UK you can take steps to protect your idea by depositing a hard copy with a bank or solicitor, or sending it to yourself by special delivery (which gets the envelope date marked) and then not opening the envelope. This is known as 'poor man's copyright'. Note that this does not provide concrete protection.

Licensing

If your designs are proving very popular you may want to look at licensing them to other businesses so that you get paid for them being used. You still retain the intellectual property rights to that design but you give them permission to use it in a certain way. Because the design remains yours you can still use those designs in other ways, subject to the contract you sign. There are three common ways to get paid for your licensed designs:

One-off payment The benefit of a one-off payment for use of your IP is that you know exactly how much you will get paid for the job and when. The downside is that if it becomes a huge hit and sells in very large quantities you do not get any extra money.

Royalties This means you get a percentage of each product sold. Essentially, you share the risk with the company to which you license your designs. If it is a hit you could stand to make a lot more money than with a one-off payment, but if it does not sell well you could earn very little from it. With a royalty deal you will benefit from continuing to promote the products to help ensure high royalties. Make sure this is something you are willing – and able – to do.

Royalties with an advance This minimises the risks slightly for you because you get an agreed sum up front and then royalties if the item sells well enough. Normally you get a lower rate of royalties than if you went for royalties only, and the advance will be deducted from the royalties you earn. Therefore you need to earn more royalties than you had in advance if you want to receive any more payments after your advance.

LICENSING TIPS FROM NEL WHATMORE

The artist Nel Whatmore has licensed her designs to be used on fabric, homewares and stationery (nelwhatmore.com and nelpatterns.com).

- Keep a good digital file of all your paintings that you feel will sell the best. I could say get a good digital file done of every painting, but that would be rather unnecessary and very expensive.

- Never sell the copyright to your work: only the license to use it for a period of time.

CREATING A LICENSING AGREEMENT

A licensing agreement between you and the person or company licensing your designs helps to ensure clarity regarding:

- What exactly is being licensed.

- What it can be used for and where those products can be sold (geographically).

- How much you will get paid, and when.

- How the royalties will be calculated, if applicable.

- How long the agreement will last.

- What will happen if either party wants to terminate the agreement early.

- Whether you can still use that design on your own products or license to another party to use for different products.

- A quality clause to make sure your brand is not associated with substandard products.

The Intellectual Property Office and the Own It website have more information on licensing.

Insuring your craft business

There are many reasons why you could need insurance for your craft business, from insuring the tools of your trade against theft of damage to making sure you have protection in place if one of your products causes injury or illness.

Insurance

It may seem tempting to keep costs down by not being insured, especially when you are only making a very small profit on your business. However, if someone is injured by one of your products or tripped on part of your craft stall at a show or event, you could be looking at thousands in damages. Insurance can provide peace of mind that you will not have to be having to pay out a fortune some time in the future, and it is often surprisingly affordable.

When it comes to finding the right insurance you could approach a local insurance broker who would be able to provide you with quotes from several insurance companies. You can also search online for the type of insurance you want and the country you are based in. I have put some useful links for you in the links section.

There are five main types of insurance that people running a craft-related business need to consider:

Product liability If you supply products then you are responsible for any injury to a person, or damage to their property, which may occur as a result of the use of your product (provided they were using it properly). Product liability insurance can meet the cost of any claims that arise. Depending on the level of harm caused and the amount of people affected, this kind of claim can run into the tens or even hundreds of thousands, so this sort of insurance helps gives you peace of mind.

Public liability Public liability covers any injury or property damage that occurs to a member of the public in connection to your business. If you teach sewing and someone in your class sustains an injury, or trips over some goods you laid out at a craft market, this is the insurance you need. It can be used to defend any claim made against you as well as for compensating any injured party.

Tradesman insurance If you do not have traditional retail premises, you may find that tradesman's insurance may be a better fit for your business. This can provide cover for your tools and premises, and also any liability that may arise as a result of you running your business.

SPECIAL CASES

Exhibiting

Many craft fairs will not let you have a stall unless you can show them your public liability insurance certificate.

Working from home

If you run your business from your house, you need to notify your home insurers because it may invalidate or alter the terms of your existing home insurance policy.

Professional indemnity If you give advice as part of your business – if you are a business consultant or a craft teacher, for example – this insurance will help to protect you from claims of professional negligence. If you offer a service such as social media management you also need professional indemnity.

Employer's liability If you employ anyone to help you with your business, then you need employer's liability insurance. This protects you from claims from employees injured or which became ill as a result of their work while in your employment. This type of insurance is compulsory in the UK and you must have a minimum coverage of five million pounds.

Other insurance you may also want to consider is accident and sickness insurance (to help you pay the mortgage or other bills if you are unable to work), vehicle insurance if you use a business vehicle, intellectual property insurance, and cancellation insurance for shows and events, so that you do not end up out of pocket if they do not go ahead for any reason.

INSURING A FAMILY BUSINESS

If your business is not a limited company, you may be exempt from the requirement for employer's liability insurance.

For more information please look at the Employers' Liability (Compulsory Insurance) Act 1969. This can be viewed online at legislation.gov.uk.

EXCLUSIONS AND EXCESSES

Exclusions

It is important to note that all insurance policies have exclusions, so make sure you have a good look through your policy to understand what is and is not covered. For instance most policies will not cover claims that arise as a result of your negligence, or if you fail to comply with health and safety or product safety laws. Some policies may only cover selling at events and shows and not online; or only cover trading from commercial premises, not from home. Always double check the small print.

Excesses

Most insurance policies will require you paying an excess/deductible if you claim. This means you are responsible for the first part of any claims payment. If you accept a larger excess, it will often give you cheaper insurance premiums. However you must make sure it is an amount you would be able to pay if you did have to make a claim.

USEFUL LINKS

Toy safety

CE marking information: gov.uk/ce-marking

UK trading standards: uktradingstandards.co.uk

Product safety advice (UK): conformance.co.uk

UK product safety regulations:
gov.uk/guidance/product-safety-for-manufacturers

British Standards Institution: bsigroup.com

Australian Standards: standards.org.au

Australian toy association: toyassociation.org

Product Safety Australia: productsafety.gov.au

Toy safety advice (USA): toyassociation.org

US toy safety legislation: cpsc.gov

International toy standards:
toy-icti.org/info/toysafetystandards.html

Clothing and labelling regulations

Clothing and footwear regulations (UK):
gov.uk/guidance/clothing-footwear-and-fashion

Product safety including clothing (UK):
gov.uk/guidance/product-safety-for-manufacturers

Trading Standards Institute advice on labelling (UK): gov.uk/product-labelling-the-law

Regulations, including 1007/2011 on textile labelling (EU): eur-lex.europa.eu

Relevant UK legislation: legislation.gov.uk

Labelling requirements (Aus):
productsafety.gov.au

Federal Trade Commission (USA): ftc.gov

Customs and Border Protection (US): cbp.gov

Further reading on toys and clothing:
etsy.com/teams/6861/keeping-up-with-cpsia

Selling regulations

Domain registration (UK): nominet.org.uk

Federal Trade Commission (US): business.ftc.gov

Small Business Administration (US):
sba.gov

Australia Competition & Consumer Commission: accc.gov.au

Australian Government Business:
business.gov.au

Health and safety

Health and Safety Executive (UK): hse.gov.uk

Occupational Safety and Health Administration (US): osha.gov

Safe Work Australia: safeworkaustralia.gov.au

Business structure

UK Companies House: gov.uk/government/
organisations/companies-house

Australia: asic.gov.au

USA: sba.gov

Business names, trademarks and patents

Companies House (UK): gov.uk/government/
organisations/companies-house

Intellectual Property Office (UK): gov.uk/
government/organisations/intellectual-property-
office

Small Business Administration (US): sba.gov/
starting-business/choose-register-your-business/
choose-your-business-name

US Patent and Trademark office: uspto.gov

Australian Securities and Investments Commission: asic.gov.au

Trademark and patent database (Aus): ipaustralia.
gov.au

Renting commercial premises

Advice for commercial tenants (UK): gov.uk/
renting-business-property-tenant-responsibilities

A sample commercial lease agreement: lawdepot.
co.uk/contracts/commercial-lease-agreement-uk

Information for commercial tenancies and retail shops (Aus): commerce.wa.gov.au

Accounts

Accounting software:
sage.co.uk; quickbooks.co.uk; accountz.com; godaddy.com/email/online-bookkeeping

Accounts templates:
artscouncil.org.uk/advice-and-guidance-library/management-account-templates; templates.office.com

Tax office (UK): gov.uk/government/organisations/hm-revenue-customs

Australian Tax Office: ato.gov.au

Dropbox: dropbox.com

Copyright and licensing

Copyright advice (UK): gov.uk/government/organisations/intellectual-property-office

Anti Copying In Design: acid.uk.com

Own It: own-it.org

Copyright Council (Aus): copyright.org.au

UK Copyright Service: copyrightservice.co.uk/

Copyright Office (US): copyright.gov

Tatty Devine blog post: tattydevine.com/blog/2012/02/can-you-spot-the-difference

Katie Davies blog post: katedaviesdesigns.com/2012/07/12/thankyou-knitters

Watermarking images

TSR Watermark Image: watermark-image.com/

Pixlr: pixlr.com

PicMonkey: picmonkey.com

Canva: canva.com

Insurance

Useful guide to insurance on The Crafts Report website: handmade-business.com/craft-business-insurance

Advice on insurance for artists: cerfplus.org

Artist insurance Australia: artsure.com.au

Market and trade exhibitors insurers (Aus): aami.com.au

Craft people, businesses and club insurance UK: craftinsurance.co.uk

UK firms that offer craft insurance: gmisl.co.uk; simplybusiness.co.uk; craftcover.com; tradesmansaver.co.uk; directlineforbusiness.co.uk; cmtia.co.uk; co-opinsurance.co.uk

YOUR LINKS AND NOTES

You can use this space to keep a list of links to websites and services you find helpful.

PRESEN

TATION

PRESENTING YOUR BUSINESS

This section focuses on the visual side of your business, including branding, product photography and visual marketing. The visual impact your business makes on your potential customers is incredibly important, and ensuring your brand and products are presented well can be a critical factor of success.

Visual presentation ties in to many aspects of your business, from advertising to social media and web design. As the saying goes, 'a picture is worth a thousand words'.

Branding

When you are launching your business, think about the impression you want to make with your branding. Identify who you need to appeal to, then reflect on what message you want to send to that target audience.

Consider the core values of your business and how you can communicate those through your branding. Do you want to be seen as fun and quirky? Sensible and trustworthy? Innovative and creative? Cool and trendy? Your aims are to make your business recognizable through your branding, and to appeal to your target audience at the same time.

BE DISTINCTIVE

Take a good look at your competitor's branding before deciding on yours in order to avoid any potential confusion. In addition, bear in mind that most large brands have trademarked their logos: make sure yours is not too similar.

Colour

Different colours can trigger different responses in your audience. For instance, red suggests energy, yellow happiness, green nature, while blue symbolises trust and loyalty. The colours of a brand are often what will stick into people's memories. The blue and yellow of Ikea is instantly recognizable to most people, just like the red and yellow of McDonald's. Colour makes an instant impact, so make sure you think through your choice properly.

Vibrant clashing colours can put off people who want something more subtle and sophisticated, whereas muted browns and greys will probably not appeal to people looking for a vibrant brand.

Getting the colour wrong can instantly rule out a large number of potential customers. The gender and age of your potential audience can influence your colour choice. Many women prefer subtle soft colours such as pastel shades whereas men are often more attracted by bright bold colours. However, bright pink may put off as many men as it attracts. Similarly, striking black and white can be too boring for a younger audience. Focus on your intended audience to make sure the branding you choose will appeal rather than deter them.

There are also the practicalities to consider. You want colours you can easily recreate on different platforms, whether printed on paper or viewed online. Cost can be an issue too: if you are planning to print a lot of flyers, for instance, it is often cheaper to print in black and white than in colour.

IDENTIFYING COLOUR ONLINE

Colours used online are represented by what is known as a hex colour code. This code consists of a six-digit string of letters and numbers, and it specifies the precise colour. The digits represent the red value, green value and blue value of the colour. For example the hex number for blue is #0000FF; as the shade of blue varies the code will change, so navy blue is #000080.

Knowing the hex colour code of your branding makes it much easier to ensure consistency across your brand.

If you see a colour online that you like but do not know the hex number you can use a colour picking tool like ColorZilla to find out. This installs a tool on your browser bar that allows you to pick colours from any site whenever you want. There are web addresses for a few colour pickers in the links section on page 102.

Blue – #0000FF

Navy – #000080

Picking colours

Start by choosing a main colour for your scheme, then establish complementary colours that work well together with your choice. The easiest way to do this to look at a free online colour wheel tool like Colour Scheme Designer. This allows to you experiment with various colour combinations until you find the one that suits your brand.

Another useful site for choosing your brand colours is Design Seeds. This site extracts colours out from an image to create a colour palette. There are numerous images and corresponding colour palettes on the site for you to browse for inspiration. Many of them are combinations you probably would not have come up with by yourself. If you look on the sidebar of the site there is the option to pick palettes based upon their dominant colour. This can be useful if you have a rough idea what colours you want to go for, but need a little more help deciding on the specific combination.

USING A COLOUR WHEEL

There are three ways you can use a colour wheel (see right) to choose your colour scheme.

- **Analogous colours** These are the adjacent colours on either side of your main colour. Blue and pink are analogous to purple, for example.

- **Complementary colours** A complementary colour is the hue directly opposite your chosen colour on the wheel. Purple is the complementary colour to yellow, for example.

- **Triads** Draw an equilateral triangle in the middle of the colour wheel, with your first colour on one of the points. The other two corners of the triangles with give you your other two colours to use. Using purple as your starting colour would result in orange and green being on the other points of the triangle, for example.

Activity: Choosing colours

Make a list of the key words you want associated with your brand and then think about which colours would best epitomise those words. Then using a free online colour tool like Colour Scheme Designer or Design Seeds, experiment until you find the exact hues that you want to represent your brand.

Make a note of the hex numbers of those colours so you can re-create the exact same hues across all your branding.

Colour name	Hex colour code

Lettering

Consider the typeface or font you will use. This covers those fonts you will use in your main logo (see opposite), but also on your website and in promotional materials. These do not all need to be the same font but aim to create a cohesive style across all of your branding – too many different typefaces risks diluting this effect.

As with colours, you want your typeface to represent the spirit of your brand. There are fonts in a variety of styles – modern, vintage, quirky and traditional. When choosing a font, make sure that is it easy to read. Ideally you want something with well-defined lettering, and good spacing between the letters to make sure people do not struggle to read it. As great as some of the novelty fonts look when reading just a word or two, they can be very hard going when trying to read an entire page of them.

SERIF VS SANS SERIF

You may have noticed that fonts are classed into two categories, serif and sans serif. Serif fonts have small finishing strokes on the end of the character and sans serif do not. See the examples below:

SERIF FONT
SANS SERIF FONT

It is generally thought that serif fonts are easier to read in print, and sans serif on screen.

Activity: Choosing your fonts

Experiment with a few typefaces to see how they look in different sizes, and across different media – online and in print. Do remember to see how the numbers look too.

Once you have decided which fonts you want to use make a note of them below, or in your notebook.

Logo

Once you have decided upon the colours and typeface you will use, you need to think about how you will combine them to create your logo. Will your logo be just lettering, just an image, or a combination of the two? Will it have a design unique to you? It helps to consider where you will be using your logo when considering the design. If it is going to be on small labels, your logo should not be too detailed or involve a lot of text. If it will be the centrepiece of your advertising and promotional materials and your website design, ensure it is eye-catching. An ideal logo can be easily recreated in a variety of sizes – large for posters or a shop sign, but also on a smaller scale for letterheads and business cards.

If you are unsure which colours, fonts and logos will resonate best with your target audience, then ask them. You could create a few different versions of branding for your business and conduct some market research to see which they like best, or show them a selection of colours, fonts and business keywords to see which appeal most to them.

COMPLEXITY

A logo does not need to be complicated. Simpler, iconic designs are often more effective. Think of the Nike swoosh, the Apple logo, or the Twitter bird: all are instantly recognizable and easy to use in different situations.

LOGO DESIGN

In addition to professional programs like Photoshop or Adobe Creative Suite, there are plenty of free design programs, such as Pixlr or PicMonkey, that you can use to create your logo. There are also several logo creator websites that will help you. Search for 'logo maker' and you will get a selection of sites from which to choose.

However, if graphic design is not your forte, then outsource it. A poor logo can make even a very good creative business look unprofessional. It is critical to get your logo right, so leave it to the professionals if you are not sure what to do. Many graphic design and illustration services have surprisingly affordable rates: there are graphic designers on services like Fiverr.com who will design a logo for as little as $5. Check the reviews to see what other people think of those services you are considering approaching.

Activity: Creating your logo

Using your research into colours and lettering, work on ideas for your logo. If you do not want to do it yourself ask around for recommendations of graphic designers and illustrators. You can always do a rough sketch on paper and then send it to someone to digitize and tidy it up for you.

As an alternative to having a single logo, consider making two; one a shorter or smaller version of the other. The Facebook logo and 'wordmark' below are a good example of a pair of logos used for different purposes:

Message

Branding is not all about appearance: the principles behind your brand are just as important. Some of these principles can be conveyed in your visual branding, but they are also portrayed in the way you do business and the way you interact with your customers.

Creating a strong set of brand principles will not only help you stand out from your competitors but will also help to make your customers feel loyal to you. If your brand message resonates with them they are much more likely to return to you again in the future.

Write a list of words that you want people to associate with your business, and plan how to demonstrate those key words through the way you run your business. Think about how can you communicate these principles through your branding, through your interactions with your customers and through your products or service. For example, if you want to be perceived as being helpful, go that extra mile to make sure you assist your customers wherever possible. If you want to build a reputation for being reliable, put systems in place to ensure deliveries are sent quickly with a low error rate.

Think about what you can do to make sure you deliver what you promise. Customers will learn what your brand principles are and come to expect them from you, so make sure you do not set standards that are impossible to keep up. It is much better to over-deliver than under-deliver.

Strapline

A slogan or strapline for your business that can be used in your promotion can help to communicate your message. It should summarize what your business stands for, what it provides, and how it will help fulfil the customer's needs.

If you are struggling to come up with a strapline, ask friends, family or customers how they would describe your business or business concept to another person. They might help you come up with something really creative and original. However, do not try to make it too obscure or unusual. A subtle play on words might make a clever or amusing slogan, but if some of your potential customers do not understand it, it will not benefit your business. Equally, your slogan should not be too vague or too 'off the wall'. Remember that it needs to tell people what your business is about – or at least give them a hint and make them want to learn more. A good strapline will help you connect with existing and potential customers, and encourage them to look further into what it is you do. If people can instantly tell from your strapline that you offer what they want, then you are onto a winner!

> ### MY STRAPLINE
> The strapline for The Sewing Directory is: 'Making it easier to find great sewing resources.' That short sentence encapsulates the core principles of my site. Can you summarize what your business does in just a few words?

Applying your branding

Once you have finalized the message you want to convey with your branding, and how you are going to do it, think about how to apply your branding to your business. Places you can apply your branding include:

- **Your website**

- **Business cards**

- **Flyers**

- **Adverts**

- **Banners or posters for shows or your shop**

- **Packaging and labelling**

- **Headed paper**

- **Your social media accounts**

The fronts of my current business cards for The Sewing Directory.

PROMOTIONAL MATERIALS

Free trials

There are many companies, such as Avery, Moo and Vistaprint, that allow you to create your own promotional materials by simply uploading your logo and choosing a colour scheme that matches your branding.

Most of these companies offer new customer deals with free trials, discounted products, or sample packs. Make the most of these offers to experiment with your branding and determine what works best for you.

Business cards

Get good quality business cards where possible, even if you pay a little more. As the first thing you give to potential customers or contacts, they need to make a good impression.

Brand consistency

When you have settled on your brand identity you need to ensure you keep it consistent so that people learn to recognize it as your business. People may see information about your business in several different places but if your branding is the same throughout, they will come to realize it is the same business they are seeing.

Often your business will evolve over time and you may want to come back and review your strapline, and branding every year or so to make sure it is still relevant to your current business. As an example, I changed my strapline after I had been trading for a couple of years.

Finding a balance between developing your business and keeping true to your core principles is a rewarding challenge.

MOO BUSINESS CARDS

It is tempting to go for bulk over quality; I did that when I first started. However, I have since found it is worth having business cards that 'wow' people.

Personally I like Moo best for this. It lets you use a range of images so that you can tailor the card to the people you are giving them to, plus it has some very high quality finishes. You can also create product labels or stickers through its site as well.

Take a look at the inspiration section of the Moo website for some great branding ideas and useful tips.

CONSISTENT BRANDING TIPS

Torie Jayne is a lifestyle blogger at toriejayne. com, author of the books Craft Show & Sell *and* Stylish Home Sewing, *and has recently launched her own brand of homeware products.*

One very easy way to maintain a consistent look for your brand is to pick a colour (or two) that you will incorporate into all of your visual materials. My brand colours are duck egg blue and vintage washed-out pastels. Integrating your brand colours in your logo, landing pages, product, and more will help you achieve the highest impact.

This does not mean that all of your visual materials have to look exactly the same, but it does mean that you should strive for visual cohesion. Think about the props you use in your photography and visual identity and try to keep them in the style and colours of your brand. Keep your visual identity and key messaging consistent and you will effectively develop and strengthen your brand, helping your business make a far stronger, long lasting impression.

Photography

I cannot emphasise enough the importance of your product photography, particularly when you are selling your products online. Unlike in a shop, where people can see and handle your products to examine the quality, online they are fully dependent on the photographs that you give them. Photographs really are the key to selling your products. No matter how amazing your products might be, if you are displaying them in poor quality photographs, you will struggle to get a sale.

In the art and craft industries this seems to be where many people fall down. So many stunning products are let down by poor photography, which unfortunately puts off many potential customers. With so much competition online, good photography can really help make your products stand out from the competition's.

Even if you do not sell products, you will still need to have some good photographs to help promote your business – images of yourself, your work space and your team to send to people who want to write a feature on your business; or stock photographs you can use on your site and social media. The advice in this section will be just as useful for those photographs as for product photography.

The good news is that you do not have to be an expert photographer to produce good quality images. This chapter includes lots of useful guidance and tips which will help you to improve your photographs. Digital cameras are most common nowadays, so most of the information in this section has been written assuming you are using one.

Image credit: Roddy Paine Photographic Studios.

FURTHER READING

If you would like to learn more about improving your photography I recommend reading
The Crafter's Guide to Taking Great Photos
by Heidi Adnum. This book is an in-depth guide to both producing and editing art and craft photography.

COMMON PHOTOGRAPHIC TERMINOLOGY

Diffusion Scattering light in several directions. You can diffuse a camera flash by putting fabric or paper over it. You can diffuse light from a lamp or natural light by using a reflector.

DSLR Digital single lens reflex. Unlike a digital compact camera, where the viewfinder only estimates what the sensor is seeing, DSLR cameras have a mirror that reflects the light going into the camera's sensor to the viewfinder, so the user sees exactly the same image as the sensor.

Resolution This refers to the amount of detail recorded by an image. The higher the resolution the more detailed and clearer the image. Digital cameras measure their resolution in megapixels (MP): the higher the MP, the more detail the camera can record. High MP cameras can take larger images without the picture quality deteriorating or becoming blurry.

DPI Dots per inch. The DPI measures the density of dots per inch of a digital image when printed. Printed images are made up by a series of very small printed dots; the more dots per inch, the clearer and more detailed the image.

Exposure The amount of light collected by the camera in a single photograph. Most cameras let you adjust the amount of light collected by the camera by adjusting the ISO speed. When working in low light you can increase the ISO on the camera to get sharper photographs.

Pixel size The size of a digital image is often referred to in pixel size, or 'px'. When booking an online advert the person hosting the advert will tell you what size image is needed to fill the space – 180 x 150px, for example. An advert made to those dimensions ensures there will be no loss of image quality from resizing, and no need to crop the image to make it fit the space.

JPEG/GIF/PNG File formats for digital image files. There are hundreds of different image file types but those three are the most commonly used on the web, and will be suitable for most uses.

Equipment

Camera

You do not need to rush out and spend hundreds or thousands of pounds on a high-end camera to take good photographs. You can produce good images with the majority of cameras and even with your phone. Most mobile phones include a digital camera that can produce images that are suitable for viewing on webpages. Some have very high quality cameras on them which produce images as good as most digital compacts. However, the camera on your phone will probably not produce high enough quality images for press photographs (see page 88). If your mobile phone images are not high enough quality you may want to look at getting or borrowing a camera too.

MY CAMERA

I recently upgraded my camera to a Sony Cyber-Shot DSC HX400V, which cost around £300. It has a good quality optical zoom (50x) which allows me to zoom right in on details like stitching when shooting tutorials. It also has manual settings to allow me to experiment with aperture and shutter speed.

It is worth thinking about what you require from your camera, and what you will be using it for before buying. For me, the zoom was a key feature as close up photographs tended to blur on my old camera.

One of my site contributors takes and edits all her photographs on her iPhone and they look great and are perfect for web use. However, do check the size and image quality of pictures from your phone if you intend to also use them in print. If you are going to be printing a lot of large detailed images you will want a high-resolution camera. High-resolution cameras used to be very expensive but as technology improves the price comes down.

You can pick up a decent digital compact camera fairly affordably. Most of these have pre-set modes and you can essentially 'point and shoot' as soon as you take it out of the box. It is worth reading through the manual, visiting the manufacturer's website or searching for instructional videos to learn about the full capabilities of the camera. These are great if you are a beginner or do not want to get too involved in the technical side of photography.

If you have a little more budget you could go for a DSLR camera. These are more expensive cameras that give you a lot more control over the settings, and work better in low or varying light conditions. If you are keen to learn more about photography, these cameras will give you a lot more chance to experiment and will usually result in higher quality images. You can also change lenses on a DSLR, giving you more creative options.

If you are unsure of what camera to go for, ask around to get feedback from other people on the cameras they use. If there is anyone whose photography you admire, contact them to find out what camera they prefer to use. You can also ask on forums or social media for recommendations, or take a look at review websites.

Other useful equipment

Tripod A tripod keeps your camera still so avoids any blurring and giving you a sharper image. You can buy these cheaply, or you can improvise by resting your camera on surfaces. The heavier your camera, the stronger and sturdier your tripod will need to be.

Backdrops The background to your image can make a big difference. It can just be your wall, or you can buy or make fabric or paper backdrops to use especially for your photography. Just remember that you do not want your backdrop to distract people from your product.

Light tent These are great for creating a brightly lit image with a plain background. Light shines in from the top and then bounces off the sides onto your product in the centre, giving a more even exposure and resulting in less shadow. If you use a plain background, it means all the focus of the photograph is on your product.

You can buy pop-up light tents with interchangeable backgrounds online for very little. There are also numerous tutorials online about how to make your own using a cardboard box. There is a link to one in the useful links section.

> ### REDUCING CAMERA SHAKE
>
> Kneel down and rest the elbow of the arm supporting the camera on your leg to steady yourself. This is a quick alternative to using a tripod – but not as comfortable!

Image size and quality

Is important to remember how you plan to use your photographs as this will dictate the quality you require. To check the image size, file size and quality of an image on your computer, right click on the file and select 'properties'.

Images for the web

Image size and quality can be a lot lower for web images than images which will be used in print – in fact, small web images are a benefit: they take up less server space, load more quickly when people view the web page, and you can upload them to your site or shop a lot faster too. You normally need a file size of around 100kb with a width of around 1000 pixels to cover the full width of a page. Most cameras will produce images a lot larger than this. You can put your camera on its lowest settings to reduce the image size. Alternatively, you can reduce images shot at a higher quality by altering the size or compressing the file on your computer. There are many free image compressor sites online which will do this for you, such as compressnow.com, or you can use image editing software on your computer to do it yourself.

Images for print

In my role as a freelance journalist, a common problem I face when featuring people's products is that their images have been taken with their websites in mind and are neither large enough, nor good enough quality to use in print. Magazines usually require images with a minimum resolution of 300 dpi and a file size over 1MB. Journalists often have tight deadlines and cannot wait for you to re-shoot images. If you do not have a good enough image when they call, you could lose out on valuable coverage!

When taking images for your website, adjust your camera to its highest quality settings, take some print-quality pictures, and store them all in a folder called 'Press'. This ensures you have the images ready if a journalist wants to feature your business or products in print. Once they know you supply high quality images, they are more likely to come back to you for future features.

By storing all of the high resolution images you take in a separate dedicated folder, you are less likely to accidentally compress the image or to try and upload the large image to your website. It will keep them separate from your lower quality, smaller web images.

Activity: Organizing images

Create a press folder on your computer and go through your current photographs, checking the size/quality and moving any suitable for magazine use to your press folder. If you do not have any suitable images, take some.

MANAGING YOUR PRESS IMAGES

Be careful which images you delete from this folder – you never know when they will come in useful. There are a few I deleted which would have been ideal for a recent article a magazine wrote about me. I was kicking myself for not having kept them! If you are short of space on your computer then put them on a USB stick or CD ROM and keep them somewhere safe for when the press come knocking!

Lyndsey James teaches crafters how to take great photographs, and is often found speaking at business and craft events about photography for retail. A photographer herself, she is also a retailer and founder of Photo Boards® (photoboards.org)

There are a few key elements that can be the difference between an average photograph and one that really grabs a reader's attention: light, clarity and backgrounds.

Light

Always search out the natural light in a room, even if you are tempted to turn on the lights or use your camera flash. Soft natural daylight from a window will dance across your subject, highlighting texture and detail that would otherwise be lost if you use an overhead or harsh direct light.

Clarity

Have you ever wondered how professional photographers always get their shots looking so clear and crisp? It's all down to ISO. Dig out your camera manual and switch your ISO from the AUTO setting to a specific number. Controlling your digital ISO is like choosing which film type to put in your camera – higher numbers produce a grainier effect and lower numbers a smoother effect.

Grain/noise can be a beautiful effect when controlled, but if left on AUTO ISO, your camera/phone will often select a very high ISO number by default, giving your photographs a very grainy appearance and dramatically reducing tonal detail. Manually setting your ISO to 400 or lower (I love to use 100 or 200) will ensure that the clarity of the colours and tones in your scenes are not lost. You might need a tripod to stabilise your camera because a lower ISO setting means slower shutter speeds as the camera becomes less sensitive to light.

Backgrounds

Background choice is an important one as your background will really help to set the scene. Photographing your subject on a wooden background could suggest a rustic, homely setting, for example, while switching it onto marble instantly suggests glamorous chic. A simple switch completely changes the appearance so build your backdrop collection and you can fake any scene! Photo Boards® are great for faking small scenes and thanks to the design, you can easily move your set up to the best light.

Light

Light is one of the essential components of good photography. One of the most common problems with craft photography is dark images, where it is impossible to properly see the colour or the detail in the products. Here are some suggestions for how to get good lighting for your photographs.

Daylight Daylight produces a broader and more even light source than artificial light. Natural light is ideal for product photography, but avoid strong direct sunlight as it casts harsh shadows. Try photographing your products next to a large window; using a net curtain to diffuse the light if it is too strong. Even on a cloudy day you will likely get more light outside than you will inside. In fact, an overcast day is better for your photography than a bright sunny day as it will produce less stark shadows.

Lamps/spotlights Artificial lighting produces a more intense and narrower light than daylight, and now that most of us have energy-saving bulbs in our houses, it is much harder to get a good photograph using a regular light. LED panels deliver a consistent high level of light and tend to be portable, so you can take them anywhere you want to shoot.

It is best to buy a desk lamp which allows you to move the head, or use a spotlight – either one designed for studio shoots, or a portable one if you often photograph in different locations – so that you can angle towards the area you are shooting. Use directional light to highlight certain aspects of your products and create interesting shadows on other parts. Try lighting your products from different angles to see the different effects you can produce.

Light tent As mentioned on page 87, you can buy or create your own light tent for your photographs. The sides of the light tent diffuse the light giving a more even spread of light and softer shadows than direct lighting. You can also use a neutral backdrop ensuring that the focus is on your product and not on anything around it.

Flash The camera flash can often be very bright and can overpower the shot making it look very white. However you can soften that light by diffusing it. This can be done by placing something like tissue paper, white fabric, paper or thin white plastic over the flash. This spreads out and softens the light so it is less harsh on the item you are trying to photograph.

Reflectors You can make your own reflectors by wrapping foil around cardboard to increase the light when taking photographs. Try using crumpled foil so it will bounce the light all around, or if you do not have foil you can use white card. You then need to point your light source at the reflector, and angle the reflector to shine on the item you are photographing.

MY LAMP

I use a photography spotlight (with umbrella) plus a handheld LED light for my photographs as there is little natural light in my sewing room. If it is a bright day then I tend to just use the LED light for an extra boost of light.

Shadows, reflections and a true image

When photographing artwork, make sure the light is not casting any unwanted shadows or reflections on your work. Ideally, you want bright soft lighting, such as natural light. Hang or prop your artwork up and try to set the camera up opposite at about the same height.

Aim to ensure the colours in your image are as close as possible to the colours in your photograph. Look at the screen on your camera and adjust the colour and exposure settings on your camera if the colours do not look the same.

PICTURES OF YOU

It is worth taking a few good pictures of yourself, your work area and any behind-the-scenes type pictures for the 'about us' section on your site, and for anyone who wants to interview you.

To the right is a good example of a generic picture which can come in useful for different purposes. It is a photo of Lisa Comfort who runs a sewing café called Sew Over It (sewoverit.co.uk) in London.

This image is friendly and welcoming and the background shows what Lisa does. This picture would work well on the 'about' page of her website, accompanying a press feature about Lisa and her business or on her social media accounts.

If you have a few of this kind of image you will find they can be multipurpose.

Image credit: Sew Over It.

Background

There are three main choices for backgrounds for your photographs.

Plain Using a plain background makes it easier to use the image for different purposes. You can add text around the product for promotional images or you can cut around the image and combine a few product images together to make one new image. This is not so easy to do with textured backgrounds or if all the images have different backgrounds.

You may want to experiment with different coloured backgrounds to see which makes your products look the best. Generally a muted white works better than a bright white one, it is not so harsh on the eye. The same applies for black, a dark grey can often work better than a bold black. If your product has a lot of detail it is best to go for a plain background so that the focus remains on the product. Once you have found the background you like, stick with it to ensure consistency.

Textured Using a textured background such as fabric, wood or bricks can make an image more interesting than a plain background; but be careful that it does not detract attention from your product. Some textured backgrounds can really complement the product, haberdashery items photographed on fabric, for example; or country chic style products photographed on distressed wood.

If you do not have the background you want, you can buy textured backgrounds specifically for photography. Alternatively you could try buying a roll of wallpaper or a length of fabric with an interesting texture and hanging them behind where you are photographing your products.

Lifestyle This is a staged background intended to show your products in use. This helps the potential buyers imagine how they could use your product. For instance you could photograph your cushions on a chair, one of your paintings hanging on a wall above a fireplace, or your Christmas decorations on a Christmas tree. For jewellery, clothing, bags or shoes it is useful to see what the product looks like being worn as well as against a plain background. Similarly for home decor products, it is good for potential purchasers to see them where they would be in a house. Not only does it help the buyer think about what the product would look like on them, or in their home, but it also gives a good indicator of scale. You can even take this a step further and create a background around the theme of your products even if that is not where your product will be used.

Lifestyle photographs help your products to tell a story. However, be careful that the background does not detract from your product. If you are going to have other items in the photograph, try to ensure they are yours where possible. That way if anyone likes one of the other items it will still lead to a sale for you. For instance, if you photograph a ring you have made in a jewellery box surround by other jewellery items, make sure those other items are yours too. Tell people in the product description that they can find the other items elsewhere on your site.

A SENSE OF SCALE

It can be hard to tell the scale of an item when there are no other items in the shot. Clearly indicate product size in your description or include something else in the shot which indicates scale.
I have noticed a lot of fabric photographers include a spool of cotton, or a coin to show the scale of the print.

These example images were all taken by photographer and founder of Photo Boards Lyndsey James (lyndsey-james.co.uk). Read her photography tips on page 89.

Rings design © Dino Daisy 2018.

Plain

The plain white background draws all your attention to the product being photographed and makes it really stand out.

Textured

The textured background brings interest to the photograph and makes the contrast between the product and background less harsh than the plain background. However, its subtle colour and texture still keep the focus on the product itself.

Lifestyle

The lifestyle shot brings in other interesting elements and adds more colour to the image which can make the overall image more striking. This particular image helps to show the inspiration behind the designs. You can also use lifestyle images to show the product in use.

Jewellery designs © Sarah Jane Whittaker 2017.

The rule of thirds

If you want to make something in your photograph stand out, it is best not to place it in the centre of your image. Instead imagine the image was divided into thirds both horizontally and vertically by lines. When people look at an image they naturally tend to look at these points rather than at the middle of the image, so placing the focal point at one of the points that the lines intersect makes for a more pleasing photograph.

Multiple photographs

When selling your products online, you ideally want to use a combination of different photograph types. This will show off your products to best effect.

The focal point of this photograph – my son's face – sits where the grid lines intersect.

- At least one shot of the item on a plain background, with the full focus is on the product.

- If your product is available in different variations or colours, include a group shot showing the different options that are available.

- A lifestyle shot of the item in use.

- Close-up shots of any details. These photographs should show your product from as many different angles as possible – even inside. This lets people see your product in its entirety as they would if they were physically handling it in a shop.

GROUPS OF PHOTOGRAPHS

These shots, of a Rajput turquoise spinning ring by Charlotte's Web (notonthehighstreet.com/ charlottesweb), show a good example: a large central lifestyle shot to show as much of the product as possible, surrounded by close-up details on plain background so the customer can clearly see the object from all sides.

Image credit: Charlotte's Web.

Laura Strutt is the former editor of **Craft Business** *and* **Sew** *magazines. Having made the break from journalism to work freelance, she has written a number of crafting books and shares makes, how-to-guides and handmade inspiration on her blog (madepeachy.com).*

Photography is increasingly important for creative businesses – it can be used to showcase a finished project, support a blog post, make a clear how-to guide, sell handmade designs, as well as boost your social media following and presence on Pinterest. Here are some tips for getting photographs that will help promote your business online:

Be clear

A photograph is telling a story; be sure that the main subject is apparent. Decide on whether to create studio shots or styled shots – this will help you to decide what you need in the image to support the overall picture. Ensure that you understand the settings on your camera so that all elements that need to be in focus are sharp.

Lights, camera, action

Lighting is crucial. Photographs taken in poor lighting conditions, for example at night or under electric lights, often appear dull and gloomy. A lightbox can be beneficial. Even a piece of white card to re-direct light back to the main subject are quick and cheap options for improving lightning. If you do not have access to a lighting kit, aim to photograph items in good natural light.

Keep it simple

Styled shots – those showing the object in use or *in situ*, with a setting and/or complementary props – are often the most complex to shoot. It is all too easy to overfill a shot and lose the overall aim of the photograph. Be sure to keep all surfaces, materials and tools in the frame, clean and free from lint or fingerprints. If you plan to add props to a shot, do so gradually so as not to overcomplicate the image.

Filters and effects

It can be very tempting to add lots of filters and effects to an image. However, do so with caution. Manipulating the image in this way can often reduce the clarity of images needed for tutorials, and can be misleading on images used to sell items. If in doubt, avoid additional filters and effects; you will soon notice your own signature style becoming apparent in your shots.

Editing your photographs

Once you have taken your photographs you may want to do a little touching up to make them look even better. It may seem like a lot to worry about, but once you get used to the editing programs and what works best for your photographs it will take less than a minute to really enhance your images. There is an abundance of free editing software available that will allow you to make most of the common edits I recommend below, such as PicMonkey or Pixlr (both available online), or even Microsoft Paint, which comes pre-installed on most Windows computers.

If you are doing extensive photo editing, you might like to invest in a professional program like Photoshop, but this can be an expensive option. One great advantage of using such programs is that there is an abundance of useful tutorial videos available online, mostly for free. The Photoshop website and YouTube are the best places to find these videos.

As with all of your branding try to stick to a consistent style with your images to help make your brand more recognizable. Once you have created and edited your images make sure you give them relevant names so that you remember precisely what they are. Most importantly do not forget to back them up! You do not want all that hard work to be lost.

The following pages explain some of the common edits you might want to apply to your photographs, along with pictures of examples where appropriate, all based on the image below.

FREE SOFTWARE

Because most paid-for software has abundant support online, and because I use free photo editing software myself, this section will concentrate about what you can do with free programs. There is a list of free editing software and associated links in the useful links section of this chapter (see page 110).

This image, of Kona cotton fabrics from Plush Addict (plushaddict.co.uk), provides the basis for the edited images on the following pages.

Main image:
Re-sized (enlarged). Note the
pixellation and loss of quality.
Inset: Re-sized (reduced).

Re-sizing (1) This edit will change the size of your image, which is useful to ensure that you do not put unnecessarily large images onto your website. You can usually type in the exact number of pixels you want your image to be and whatever software you are using will re-size it for you. Sometimes you have to reduce by percentage instead so there can be some mathematics (or a little guesswork!) involved. Do note that increasing the image size will reduce the quality resulting in the image looking blurry and low quality.

Cropping (2) If there is a bit too much space around your product, or you want to cut out some unnecessary distractions from around the edge of the image, cropping allows you to cut out the part you want and get rid of the rest.

Rotation (3) If your photograph came out horizontal when it should be vertical (or vice versa) you can do a 90-degree or 180-degree rotation to correct the orientation. You can also do a freehand drag rotation to correct a distracting tilt or intentionally pull your image around to a more quirky angle.

Do bear in mind that directional lighting can look a little odd when the image is rotated. If the light is even throughout the picture you can minimise this problem.

This image has been rotated by 180°.

Text (4) This very useful tool allows you to add your product name, a description, tag line, message, price or enticement to buy to your image. There is a huge selection of fonts to choose from. Remember to use one of your chosen fonts to ensure brand consistency.

Watermark (5) Adding a digital watermark helps to protect your images. This can be done by either uploading your logo, or adding your business name or website as text to an image. Once you have it in the right position you can then fade it a little so it enables people to see the image beneath the watermark. You do not want the watermark to obstruct people's view of your products.

BRAND YOUR IMAGES

I always add my web link to my images as part of my branding. That way, if people share the images on social media, people can see the original image came from my site, and already have the address.

Overlays (6) An overlay is something added over the top of your image. When you put text straight onto an image it can be a little difficult to read unless you have an area of plain background to put it on. Overlay a white box, then fade it out a little so you can still see the image behind it, and then add your text on top. It makes the text stand out a lot more, and is easier to read.

You can also get themed overlays to add things like hearts, banners, buttons, or seasonal designs. For example, if you have a photograph of your jewellery that you want to promote for St. Valentine's Day, instead of re-shooting the image with heart props nearby, you can simply add a heart overlay to the image. You can also add your own overlays so you can upload your logo and add that to the image.

Borders (7) Adding a border can be a nice way to frame your image. Experiment with the different borders available to see which best fit with your style. Do not forget you can alter the size and colour of the borders too. Once you have found one that you like, stick with that one to ensure brand consistency.

This image has a banner and text overlay, plus a logo overlay in the top left-hand corner.

Exposure (8) Altering the exposure settings will allow you brighten a dull image, or tone down an over-exposed photograph. It also allows you to increase the shadows or bring out the lighter parts of an image.

You can also adjust the contrast. Increasing it will make the colours darker and bolder. Lightening an image can wash it out a little, but you can increase the contrast to make the colours more vibrant again.

Colour (9) You can change the colour saturation of an image, increasing it to bring out the colours more or decreasing it to tone down the colours. You can adjust the colour temperature too, making it warmer (more yellow), to make an image more summery or to give it a romantic, candlelit feel; or colder (more blue), for bright blue skies or wintry images.

This image has been lightened. To avoid a washed-out look to the edited picture, I subsequently increased the contrast.

The colours on the left have been warmed, and cooled on the right. I have exaggerated the effect in these images so you can see the difference. You would not normally adjust the colour to such an extreme!

The right-hand side of this image has been selectively blurred to draw attention to the left-hand part, which remains in focus.

Main picture: focal black and white effect applied to the top right corner. Inset: sepia effect and frosted edges.

The dotted background has been edited out and replaced with a fabric texture.

Blur or sharpen (10) Adding a subtle blur effect across an image can make it seem a little dreamy or abstract; while sharpening can help if you have accidentally blurred your image. You can also use these tools selectively so you can apply them to certain parts of your image: sharpening your product and blurring the items in the background ensures the focus is on your product.

Effects (11) Various different effects can be applied either to the whole image or to just part of it. One common and effective change is to desaturate (remove the colour) most of the image in order to draw attention to the one part you leave in colour. On PicMonkey this effect is called Focal B & W. You could use this to make a certain part of your product stand out, or your product stand out from everything else.

There is also a focal blur effect which has a similar effect of highlighting one specific part of an image, making one part of the image clear and the rest blurry.

There are other effects you can apply to the whole image such as sepia to give it a vintage look, frosting the edges of the image, softening or boosting the image, or giving it a variety of colour washes to change the tint of the image.

Textures (12) If you wanted a textured background for your picture but did not have one, you could add your own after you have taken the photograph. You can either upload your own texture or use one of the selection they have available including metal, water, paint and fabric.

FABRIC SALES SHAREABLE

This image is a good example of a edited 'shareable' – an image designed to catch the eye and bring traffic to a website.

It was created to go on a page on my website that has details of the latest fabric sales. Beginning with one of my own fabric stock images for the background, I added a frosted effect around the outside so the edges of the image were not so harsh. I then used two overlays – a rectangle at the top left and a ribbon at the bottom – to make the text stand out from the background. I also added my weblink (URL) so that if people share the image without crediting me or linking back, people can still find my site from the image.

I share this image regularly on social media to encourage people to visit this page and find the latest fabric sales and offers.

Activity: Choosing your editing software

Decide which editing software you want to experiment with and upload an image. Try out as many of the different editing tools as possible to experiment with different effects and combinations. Once you know what they all do, write down your favourites to come back to in the future.

AUTO CORRECT/ WIZARD

Some software has an 'auto fix' option which is a combination of a few different effects to bring out the best in your image. I have to say personally I have not found these to be as good as doing it yourself but if you are in a rush it could be worth a try.

What else you can use your images for?

As well as using product photographs on your site or online shops there are many other ways you can use your photography to promote your brand.

Social media Social media platforms are perfect for promoting your brand with good quality images. Certain platforms like Pinterest, Facebook and Instagram really work well for visual marketing. Remember to include your business name or web address on the images so that if they get shared all the viewers also see your brand name.

Stock images It is useful to use your own images as stock images when writing blog posts, content for your site newsletters or guest posts for other sites. It saves you having to pay for stock images (see pages 105–107) and gets your products out in front of more people.

Business cards What better way to promote your products than to have images of them on the back of your business cards? It is much more attractive than just a logo. Some companies, like Moo, allow you to use different images on each of your business cards at no extra cost.

Catalogues As you build your range you may one day want to produce a catalogue so people can see your full product range at a glance.

To generate press coverage Magazine editors and website owners/bloggers, are often on the lookout for visually attractive content to share with their readers. If you send them a press release, there is more chance they will use it if it is accompanied by really professional looking eye-catching images.

On leaflets Instead of just using text, make your leaflets really visual by using some of your best images with a small amount of text on them.

Send them to potential stockists Spark the interest of potential stockists by sending them your images printed onto postcards.

SHARING ON SOCIAL MEDIA

Add a slogan or quote over your image to make it more shareable.

VIDEO

Photographs are not the only thing that can help you reach more people with your brand message; video is a fast-growing tool too. Not only have you got YouTube and sites like Vimeo but now even traditionally photograph-orientated platforms like Flickr and Instagram let you upload video clips. Facebook, of course, also lets you add video to personal or business pages.

You could use video to show customers behind the scenes, to show clips of you making your products, to speak directly to them (perhaps a welcome message on your site) or to share advice on how to use your products.

You can learn more about creating and using video to promote your business on pages 140–149.

Visual marketing

Visual marketing is the use of images to communicate a message about your business. The images you use can come in a number of formats such as jpg files, video, PDF, slide or print, and can contain a wide variety of content – text, photographs, diagrams and icons – so the definition of visual marketing is actually a lot wider that it may seem at first. You can create visual content that suits you, your business, and your audience. The key is to get visual.

Why use visual marketing?

People are visual. Social media is visual. Visual content is highly shareable and resonates in a way that words alone often do not. Visual content adds variety to your marketing, creates brand recognition, and helps your business stand out!

The best way to get started is to take something that you already know resonates with your audience and make it visual. A quote, a helpful tip, a list, some instructions, something funny or entertaining – choose something that fits with your brand and will appeal to your audience. Use a free tool such as PicMonkey or Canva to create an image using that text. You can include a photograph or just use a plain background – the key is to keep it really simple, as simple images look the most professional. Brand your images using your brand colours, use a typeface that matches your brand vibe, and be sure to include your name or website address. Finally, share the image with your audience using all of your social media platforms – plus your blog and newsletter too.

BOOST YOUR SKILLS

With photography being so important to a craft business, it is worth taking the time to learn as much about it as you can. If you like to learn online visit photocraft.org for e-courses in photography and styling for crafters. You can also join their newsletter for free weekly photography tips.

Etsy has a collection of useful guides to photography on its blog (etsy.com/blog) as do Craft Blog UK (ukcraftblog.com) and Folksy: (blog.folksy.com).

Many people teach craft photography. Try looking at your local craft class studio to see if they offer courses. In addition, many colleges and universities run general photography courses and classes, so have a look on their websites to see what is on offer.

Image sources

Good quality images are essential to your business, but sometimes you do not have the time or resources to be taking your own. Luckily there are many kinds of images available for you to use on your site or social media.

If you are writing articles for your site or blog, building your website, looking to create shareable images, or need images for adverts, there are several places where you can source images, some free and some that charge.

Stock image sites

Images on stock sites are usually taken by professionals and are high quality. The sites are easy to search and usually have hundreds, if not thousands, of images available for most keywords you search. They also have vector graphics available too. Stock image sites are mostly paid-for, either charging a fee per photograph or on a contract basis – usually monthly – which allows you to download a certain amount of images. I have listed some of the main stock sites in the links section.

The benefits of using stock image sites are that the images will be good quality, there is a huge range available (saving you time searching lots of sites), and you do not usually have to credit the image. Most stock images do not need to be credited to either the photographer or stock site; however, I have found that a few do, such as paparazzi photographs.

MAKING THE MOST OF A STOCK IMAGE CONTRACT

Monthly contracts can work out well if you use a lot of images, or if you are setting up a website and need lots of images at once. In the latter case, you could sign up just for a single month, download as many images as you think you will need and save them in a folder. You can then upload them to your site as you complete it, subject to the stock site's terms and conditions. They usually specify images must be used within a set period after purchase.

This approach can work out cheaper than the pay-as-you-go rate if you are looking for a large number of images in one go.

BUSINESS INTEGRITY

Your product images should always be actual images of your products as made by you; otherwise you are misleading your customers. You should never use images of other people's products or stock images and pretend that they are your own.

MY PREFERRED STOCK IMAGE SITE

Personally I use Shutterstock because I have found it has a good selection of craft-related images, and works out cheaper than most other sites to download individual images. It has over twenty million images available in total.

Shutterstock charges up front in batches of twelve images; but you can download them individually as and when you need them, so long as it is within twelve months of the purchase. It offers a monthly payment option, too.

The downsides of using stock sites are the cost, and the fact that other people could be using the same images as you, they are not unique. Also you can often find that the pictures have a distinctive 'stock image' look, which means some people can tell you are using stock images and not your own.

If you plan to use stock images, always take the time to read through the terms and conditions and the licensing terms. Some companies require you to purchase an enhanced licence if you plan to print their images on your products, for example. The terms can vary from site to site so make sure you read them for each site you plan to use.

Some stock image websites offer free trials, or allow you to download a certain number of images for free so this can be useful if you do not have a budget for images.

LOOK BEFORE YOU LEAP

Most stock photo sites allow you to search their database and view the images, with a watermark on them, before you join. Try searching a few to make sure they have the type of images you are looking for before you sign up.

Free image sources

There are also many places where you can get free images to use. Normally you are expected to credit and link back to the original source in exchange. A lot of the free stock photograph sites are funded by advertising for the paid stock sites. Do double check before clicking on an image or you may find yourself being transported off to another site and being asked to pay before you can download the image. They are indicated as being from a different stock site but on your first visit it can be a little confusing.

Creative commons sites

Flickr Creative Commons is a collection of images that people have shared under various creative commons licences. The exact licences vary so you need to read through before using the images. Some images are allowed to be used for personal use but not for commercial use. Others allow any use but require a specific accreditation and back link. The images are sorted by licence type and, once you choose a category, you can then search by keyword.

The benefits of Flickr Creative Commons are that there millions of images to choose from, and it is easy to find relevant images because a lot of crafters use Flickr. The downside is that you need to take the time to read and understand the different licences, and make sure you correctly credit the images.

Wikimedia Commons is a similar site with a large number of creative commons images available.

MY PREFERRED FREE STOCK IMAGE SITE

I use Pixabay for free stock images. They have a good range and no restrictions on use. I have uploaded some of my own images to the site for others to use, to help support this useful resource.

Free stock sites

There are many free stock images sites where you can download images at no cost. Most require registration and often have conditions imposed on the use of the images. These sites include:

Morgue File A free stock site, made by creatives for creatives. These images are intended to be used 'in the creative process' for artists or crafters creating their own work. Therefore you cannot use them as standalone images but have to adapt them or incorporate them into one of your designs.

Pixabay Pixabay allows you to download its images to use as you wish, whether altered or in their entirety and for commercial purposes. It does not require credit, but says it would appreciate a link back.

Stock Xchng A source of royalty-free photographs that can be downloaded to use as you choose, whether for commercial purposes or personal. There are some limits: you cannot sell or redistribute the image itself or use it as part of a logo or trademark.

Open Photo The licences on these photographs vary. All are free, but some require accreditation to the original photographer. It is clearly indicated under each photograph what the licence is and whether you need to credit the image or not.

Public Domain Photos These images require a hyperlink back to the page of the site where you downloaded the image if you are using them online.

Death to the Stock Photo If you sign up to this site you will get e-mailed ten free high-resolution stock photographs every month. The images are based around a different theme each month: 'technology', 'bricks and mortar', or 'coffee shop', for example. You do not need to credit the photographs, nor link back to the site, but the owners say they appreciate it if you do.

STICK TO THE CONDITIONS

When using any free stock images, always read through the licence and make sure that your usage of the image is within the licence.

VINTAGE IMAGES

Copyright on images expires a certain number of years from creation or publication, depending on the date the original work was created. This is good news for any small craft business. In the UK, all images are automatically copyrighted, and remain protected for seventy years after the creator's death; after which the copyright expires and the images enter the public domain, making them usable by anyone.

This means that there are many (though not all!) beautiful vintage adverts, drawings and photographs that are free for you to use. One website, thegraphicsfairy.com, has over four thousand predominantly craft-based vintage images free for you to download.

Other image sources

Individual owners

Another potential source of free, non-stock images are those you come across in online searches on individuals' websites. Those images are copyrighted to the individual owner, so if you see one you want to use you need to contact the person whose photograph it is and ask them for permission to use it.

The majority of individuals do not mind their image being used when it is promoting their product and sending people to their shop. Legally, however, they can insist you take the image down if they do not want you to use it, and in extreme cases you could find yourself being billed for having used the image without consent. As a result, it is best to ask permission wherever possible in order to protect yourself from potential problems in the future.

In reality, a lot of people will use photographs without prior permission, instead crediting the person to whom it belongs. For instance when bloggers write a post on 'my favourite handmade fox-themed products' they do not tend to contact the owner of every single image they are featuring and ask permission. They will take the image from their site or shop and include a link back to the relevant website or shop in the blog post.

Build your own image collection

The ideal solution is to start building your own stock image collection for use in your visual marketing. Keep a camera close to hand and take photographs whenever you can. When you are planning your website or blog content, think about what images would fit well with it and see if you can take those images before you write the post. Build up a collection of generic images of your craft supplies, your workspace, nature shots, office shots, pictures of your creative process and so forth. If all else fails see if you have any product photographs which vaguely tie in with the subject you are writing about and use those to illustrate your post.

BEWARE!

You could find that by taking an image from someone's site without consent you could actually be downloading a stock image.

Stock image companies regularly run image searches to see if anyone is using their property without permission. In this situation the stock image companies may end up charging you a lot more than the original purchase price of the image.

COMBINING PROMOTION

While conducting marketing training for T&G Woodware (tg-woodware.com), a kitchenware company, I asked the employees to write a blog post with their ten favourite chicken recipes, which they would find on the internet. Rather than illustrating it with photographs of the food, from other people's websites, I suggested they used photographs of their own chicken tea cosies with a product link embedded in the photograph description. Not only did they not need to seek permission to use the recipe images, but they could also subtly promote their products too.

Creating other images

Of course, not all of the images you use in your visual marketing have to be photographs. If you are artistic you can draw or paint your own images, and even if you are not artistically inclined, there are several sites which will let you create your own graphics, adverts, infographics, and shareable images for free. These can all be used to spread your brand message, and if you create them yourself you are saving money too.

Images that you have created yourself have the advantage that they are unique and specific to you – and ideal for the purpose!

Use your images creatively

It is important to make sure you get the most possible use for your images, especially if you are paying for them. Do not limit yourself to only using the image once. Think of different places you can use it, such as your site, blog, social media platform, newsletters, flyers, or adverts. By altering it a little, you can use it in more places without people realizing they are seeing the same image. Photo editing software can help you add text, graphics or special effects to the images; to change the colours; to combine or crop them; or any of a hundred other changes that will help to keep them fresh.

KEEP YOUR BRAND IN MIND

Remember that you want to keep your branding consistent, so consider this carefully when choosing your stock images. Do not just go for an image because it is free or cheap; it is worth paying to get something that is perfect for your visual brand.

Activity: Learning the tools for visual marketing

Trial and error can be the quickest way to learn. Take a look at some of the recommended sites overleaf and set aside some spare time to play with them. Experiment and see what you can make and which interfaces you find easiest and most rewarding to use.

Make sure you bookmark those sites – or write them down either below or in your notebook – in order to return to them in the future and create more great images for your business.

USEFUL LINKS AND FURTHER READING

Branding

The psychology of colour:
helpscout.net/blog/psychology-of-color

Colour meanings:
color-wheel-pro.com/color-meaning.html

Colour scheme designer: paletton.com

Design Seeds: design-seeds.com

Colour pickers: colorzilla.com; colorpicker.com;
iconico.com/colorpic

Wordmark, allows you to test fonts: wordmark.it

Free Fonts Database: fontlibrary.org

1001 Free fonts to download: 1001fonts.com

Fiverr: fiverr.com

Useful branding site: bigbrandsystem.com

Useful guide to branding: designcouncil.org.uk/
news-opinion/power-branding

Free design and editing software

PicMonkey: picmonkey.com

Paint: getpaint.net

Gimp: gimp.org

Pixlr: pixlr.com

Canva: canva.com

Commercial design and editing software

Photoshop: photoshop.com

Adobe Creative Suite: adobe.com

Logo Maker: logomaker.com

The Logo Creator: thelogocreator.com

Branding products

Instant Print: instantprint.co.uk

Moo: uk.moo.com

Avery: avery.co.uk

Vistaprint: vistaprint.co.uk

Photography

**The Crafter's Guide to Taking Great Photos by
Heidi Adnum:** book available from
searchpress.com

Image compression site: imageoptimizer.net

Image compressor: compressnow.com

Digital photography school, lots of useful tips:
digital-photography-school.com

Light tent tutorial: digital-photography-school.com/
how-to-make-a-inexpensive-light-tent

Photography backdrops: photoboards.org;
creativitybackgrounds.co.uk

Photography tips and e-courses: photocraft.org;
photography.nationalgeographic.
co.uk/photography/photo-tips

Advice for photographing art:
saatchionline.com/artschool

Craft photography tips: ukcraftblog.com/2011/10/
craft-photography-tips.html

Photography tips: picturecorrect.com

**Program for removing the background from
images:** Clippingmagic.com

Visual marketing

Video platforms: vimeo.com; youtube.com;
flickr.com/explore/video; instagram.com;
facebook.com

Commercial stock image sites:
shutterstock.com; gettyimages.co.uk;
istockphoto.com; bigstockphoto.com

Free stock image sites: flickr.com/
creativecommons; commons.wikimedia.
org; morguefile.com; pixabay.com; sxc.hu;
openphoto.com; publicdomainpictures.net;
deathtothestockphoto.com

Copyright free vintage images:
thegraphicsfairy.com

Image creation programs

Infographics: visual.ly; piktochart.com

Word clouds: wordle.net

Collages: picmonkey.com

Banner adverts: bannersnack.com

Moving adverts: ms-gif-animator.en.softonic.com

YOUR LINKS AND NOTES

You can use this space to keep a list of links to websites and services you find helpful.

SOCIAL

MEDIA

USING SOCIAL MEDIA

One of the areas that has changed the most since I wrote the first edition of this book is social media. This is a constantly evolving arena, with new platforms being launched and others becoming defunct all the time. The focus of the platforms themselves also changes – what they consider to be the most popular form of content, and therefore which formats they will ensure reach more people.

Why use social media?

Most business owners are hard pressed for time and adding social media into an already rigorous schedule can seem like a daunting task. It is not just something you can do once or twice a month when you remember, it is a commitment. Social media works best when you are regularly and consistently updating. Social media is fast-moving, and if you only post something once a week you will only reach a very limited amount of people.

Finding a balance

With that said, you do not have to constantly be online and posting. Yes, many big businesses do but that is because they have entire social media teams whose only job is to keep that company's social media updated. If you are a one person business, or even a small team, it is not going to be realistic to be doing social media full time.

My business is run by two people both working part time so we cannot spend hours every day on social media. However, what do is make sure we have a clear social media schedule so people know when to expect posts from us. Plus, we make the most the ability to pre-schedule posts, so we can prepare most the week's posts in advance freeing us up to focus on other things during the week. More on that later in this section.

The first question you should be asking is why should I use social media? How will it benefit your business? One of the biggest benefits is that it gives you direct contact with your customers, and potential customers. It provides somewhere that they can ask you questions and you can tell them about your business, new products, inspiration behind your designs, upcoming events and sales etc. It can also help to build relationships, not just with customers, but with other complementary businesses and even with the press. Social media is by nature very interactive; you will often meet many more people through social media that you will in real life, even if you have a busy shop, or attend many shows.

THE CHANGING FACE OF SOCIAL MEDIA

Back in 2014, when I was working on the original edition of this book, the focus was just switching to visual media. Facebook would give your posts more reach if you used an image in your post, and visual platforms like Pinterest and Instagram were just taking off. We were being encouraged to share photographs rather than just text. Visual marketing was becoming a buzzword: it was all about the images.

Fast-forward four years and the focus has evolved beyond just static images to video. YouTube is immensely popular with 1.5 billion users logging in monthly to view content (techcrunch.com June 2017). Platforms like Facebook, Instagram and Pinterest have all incorporated video, and give more reach to posts that use video. Taking inspiration from apps like Snapchat, they have begun to encourage people to share video stories. Like Snapchat, Instagram's 'Stories' are video clips that disappear after a limited time period. Both Facebook and Instagram have increased the emphasis on live streaming video; encouraging you to show people what you are doing right now, while allowing them to interact with you and ask questions. On Instagram, Stories are given a boosted status above standard images, appearing at the top of people's feeds. Videos on Facebook often reach more people than images and for many people auto play when they appear in their feed, luring people in.

Video ranks increasingly well in search results. You will notice that every search you make using Google will include two or three videos – generally from YouTube, which is owned by Google – on the front page. YouTube is now the second largest search engine, after Google itself, with many people going straight to YouTube and then typing in the information they are looking for.

In the first edition of this book, I touched on video but it became clear to me in the years since that there needed to be a greater focus on video in the second edition. Businesses need to understand the benefits of using video to promote their business and where to start.

That is not to say that this part of the book will focus solely on video. There are many businesses out there successfully using social media without using video at all. Do not be alarmed if video is not your thing, you can still harness the power of social media to provide a direct line between your business and your potential customers.

Providing value in your social media posts

Social media is a marketing platform, but you need to bear in mind that people do not want to receive an endless stream of self promotional posts. You need to provide 'value', something that will make people want to follow you and keep checking your posts. You need to keep their interest, and ideally encourage them to share your posts so they reach other people, growing your following.

Value

Value, in social media terms, is something useful or of benefit to your followers. That could mean tips and advice, it could mean projects and inspiration. It could also include details of sales, helping them save money, events in which they might be interested, or problem solving. Do you have a product that can help save them time and money? Can you give some advice that would make their life easier in some way but is also related to what you sell? Can you share news about what is happening in your part of the industry?

If you teach crafts, give people a little taster of what they could learn in your classes: share a useful tip or a technique and add that they can book onto a course with you if they want to learn more about the subject. Share photographs of your samples, or show followers what people have made on previous courses in order to tempt them to make a booking.

If you make handmade products or art, then show examples of how your products can be used or displayed in order to convince readers that the product will fit perfectly into their homes. People like to know the story behind your designs, so tell or show them what inspired you. Sharing the back story of your product can create an emotional connection to your creation.

The process of making your artwork will also interest some of your followers. Share photographs of the making stages in order to build anticipation of the final design. If you take commissions, share pictures of the things you have been commissioned to make, and then let people know how to commission you.

SETTING THE TONE

Personally I think posts on business accounts or blogs are best kept mainly to business, but that does not mean there is no space for an occasional bit of general chit-chat. In my experience, those kinds of posts tend to have a very good response rate too!

PROMOTION

There is no point writing a post and not telling people it is there. Put a link on your social media, mention it in your newsletter, tell your customers face to face... just let people know!

PROMOTING YOURSELF AND OTHERS: THE BALANCE

Followers will expect that you will talk about your own products and offers through your social media platform – but it bears repeating that over-saturation may annoy or drive some people away. Keep self-promotional posts to a quarter of less of your updates – use the rest to give value to your followers, or to promote complementary businesses or events you think will be of interest to your followers.

Although it may feel odd to promote others on your social media, it can be a great way of ensuring you are not always talking about your own business. It does not make good business sense to promote direct competitors, but promoting complementary businesses is a great idea. For instance, if you sell quilting fabric but not wadding, you could recommend a place to buy wadding. Not only is that useful information for your customers but hopefully when they then get customers asking about where to buy fabric for their quilts they might send them your way.

Be careful not to go so far down the path of promoting others or providing their useful information that you forget to mention your own business. In your interactions through social media, aim to strike a balance between promoting yourself and others, and also show clearly what products you make or service you provide.

TAGGING

Tagging a person or business on social media normally involves putting @companyname in your post. This alerts them that you have mentioned them. On certain platforms, typing the first few letters of other business' name will automatically bring up the business.

Which platform to use

The key thing to remember when choosing which social media platforms to use is that your content needs to reach your target audience. It is much easier for you to go to them than to try to make them come to you on a platform they do not already use. It may take a bit of customer research to find out where your customers spend their time online.

You also need to consider what kind of content you plan to share. If you want to share video-based content, then platforms like YouTube, Facebook, Vimeo and Instagram would work well for you. If your update will be more text-focused, then Facebook and Twitter would probably be the best combination. If you have lots of information to share then SlideShare could work well for you as it allows you to share slideshows and infographics. LinkedIn is becoming a place where people share in-depth articles.

You do not need to have a presence on all platforms. Not only would that be very time-consuming, but it would also be almost impossible to keep on top of, especially when running a small business. I would suggest identifying two or three platforms which you feel would best reach your target audience and which are most suited to the form of content you want to present. Start with those and you will always have the option to expand onto other platforms in the future.

I have given information on several of the main social media platforms, but they are not the only options. You should do your own research to determine which would be best for your business.

CONTENT RIGHTS

Check the terms and conditions of each social media platform to see what you can and cannot do on said platform and what rights you are giving them over your content.

MY PINTEREST

Pinterest has rocketed to the top of my social referrals list on my website analytics – even though I have significantly fewer followers there, it sends me more traffic than Facebook and Twitter combined.

SOCIAL MEDIA TIPS

These tips are from Alex Veronelli, brand manager of Aurifil Threads (aurifil.com), an Italian company whose renown amongst quilters worldwide is largely due to its great internet marketing campaigns.

- **Be yourself** People prefer to engage with people rather than brands: it is much more personal. Profiles with a face, a name and a last name give better performance than those with logos. Once the relationship is established, it becomes easier to steer the audience towards the brand.

- **Listen** A regular search of the tags related to your brand is due in order to figure out what your product's users are saying about it, and to discover the content related to your products.

- **Promote others** Do not be selfish. The very best content for a brand's page comes from what the others say about it. Of course we say great things about our own brand, but it means much more when others say it. Do not let the voice of your customer be left by the wayside, but instead share and highlight it. They will be also grateful to receive traffic and readers coming from your page.

- **Pay attention to engagement** Do not measure your social marketing performance purely by the number of followers but by how they engage with your business.

- **Always on and everywhere** Social networking does not stop for breaks, weekends or holidays. Answers should be always given, ideally within twenty-four hours.

Facebook

Facebook is one of the best-known social media platforms and is used by a lot of people – over two billion worldwide. It allows you to share text, images, links and video updates. You can have a personal profile, which allows you to control who sees your posts, a group (which you can make private or public) or a business page which is public.

Once the company went public a few years ago, a much heavier focus was placed on adverts. The 'reach' of posts on business pages was reduced to try and persuade companies to pay to make their posts visible by more people. According to Locowise, a social performance measuring company, the average reach for Facebook posts in 2015 was just under three per cent of the page's followers. So for every one hundred people following you, fewer than three of them see each post.

Despite this, many people still use Facebook, and the chances are that a large percentage of your target market will be on there. Despite the dwindling reach of posts, it is still good for interaction and business. If your posts hit the right note, the few people who see them will comment or share which will lead to more people seeing the posts. It is also worth paying to boost important posts to ensure you reach more of your followers. Facebook business pages often rank well in Google, coming up when people search for your business name.

Another benefit of Facebook is that they allow you to create very precisely targeted adverts, because they gather so much information about their users. You can use that to your advantage to make sure you only advertise to people who will be interested in what you offer.

PAPER PANDA'S TIPS FOR USING FACEBOOK

Louise Firchau set up Paper Panda (paperpandacuts.co.uk) in 2010, and has built a Facebook following of over 250,000 people.

Since 2010, I have built my business making typographical lyrical papercuts from recycled paper to the point that I can now teach and sell my original papercuts alongside a range of papercutting supplies and kits, homewares and greeting cards. I've also written a book, _Paper Panda's Guide to Papercutting_. Facebook is a great promotional tool that has helped me to bring all these different threads together. To use Facebook to grow your business you should:

- Find your own USP, you need something different to what is already out there.

- Reply to as many people as you can and chat with them.

- Rather than trying to gain likes, try to engage with people.

- Work hard, it really can be 24/7 sometimes.

- ...and of course – network, network, network.

You Tube YouTube

Website metric company Alexa ranks YouTube as the second most popular website in the world, second only to Google, and ranking above Facebook, which holds the third slot. Almost five billion videos are watched on YouTube every day!

In the craft industry YouTube is largely used to show people how to make things, to demonstrate techniques, projects and ways of using craft products. Unlike networks like Facebook, Instagram and Twitter which combine text, images and video, it is solely video orientated. One big advantage it has over many other social media networks is that, as mentioned earlier, people also use YouTube as a search engine too.

YOUTUBE TIP

On YouTube you can create a 'suggested video' pop up to direct people to other relevant videos you have made. There is a link to a video showing how to do this at the end of this chapter.

Twitter

Twitter may be dwarfed by Facebook and YouTube in terms of numbers of users, but it is still a popular and growing network. It is primarily text-based, with updates limited to two hundred and eighty characters or fewer, although you can also attach links and images. Twitter recently decided that images would not count towards the character limit, which encouraged users to be much more visual. Although it is not traditionally viewed as a video platform, you can share both live and pre-recorded video on the site.

Being limited to so few characters can be a little frustrating and it is a fast-moving network, but it is great for making new contacts and your following seems to grow a lot quicker on Twitter than on Facebook. I find people seem to be a lot chattier on Twitter too. This leads to more conversation, but because the lifespan of a tweet is quite short, I find I get fewer clickthroughs to my website from Twitter than from networks like Facebook or Pinterest.

Pinterest

If you are in a visually-led business like the creative industries, Pinterest is a great platform to use. Describing their service as a 'visual discovery engine', Pinterest is an online pinboard that allows you to collect useful links in a visual manner, rather than as text bookmarks. You pin your chosen image from a page so you can find that page again at a glance.

You sort your pins by theme, into individual boards. You have the choice of whether to make them public – so other people can see and share your pins – or to keep them private so only you, and those you invite, can view them. There are over 175 million active users and Pinterest is constantly adding new features to make it beneficial for businesses.

Business-focused features include analytics; promoted pins; product pins, which give real time information on pricing, availability and where to buy your products; app pins, which allow people to download your app from within Pinterest; and rich pins, which allow you to add extra information like recipes to your pins.

> ### PINTEREST TIP
> Remember: people will likely pin images from your website, so make sure they are of good quality and have a relevant image description as that description will automatically carry over into the pin description box on Pinterest.

TORIE JAYNE'S TIPS FOR USING PINTEREST

Torie Jayne, a lifestyle blogger at toriejayne.com, has 1.25 million Pinterest followers.

A selection of Torie Jayne's boards.

Torie Jayne

Living Room Ideas
178 Pins

Hallway Ideas
44 Pins

Kitchen Ideas
274 Pins

Pretty gardening
221 Pins

Summer House
63 Pins

- Pin consistently: at least five times per day.

- Design images at the proper size: The best aspect ratio for Pinterest images is 2:3 or 1:3.5, with a minimum width of 600 pixels.

- Create and pin images with text.

- Add a subtle logo or brand name to the bottom corner of the images that you create.

- Write keyword-rich descriptions and boards using positive sentiment and detail. Descriptions are limited to one hundred characters or fewer – make the most of the space.

- Give the reader something to do. If there is an action they can take, share the next steps and add a link to somewhere useful.

- Add a link to your pin descriptions.

- Use multiple images within a pin.

- Categorize your boards. This will make your pins more easily found and will potentially result in more people following you.

- Increase brightness and saturation of your images before pinning. Pinterest darkens images slightly when they are pinned.

- Verify your website domain and include a link in your bio.

- Link your Pinterest account to your Facebook and Twitter accounts.

- Find friends: The quickest way to get followers on Pinterest is by finding and inviting people you know. Pinterest makes it easy to find friends through Facebook, Twitter, Google and Yahoo accounts.

Instagram Instagram

Instagram is a photo-sharing app which works from your phone or mobile device and allows you to add filters to enhance your photos, and text to accompany the image. These filters are very useful if you are not the best at photography. They can make even a dark, dingy photograph look good.

Instagram has over 700 million users and 95 million photographs are uploaded to the service per day. It is particularly popular within the craft industry, because ours is a very visual industry. Businesses use it to share photographs of products, behind the scenes pics and videos, offers and sales, pictures of things they or their customers have made and inspiration.

It was purchased by Facebook in 2012 and has since adopted some of Facebook's traits, including regular adverts and an algorithmic home feed (meaning it picks which posts you get to see rather than showing you all posts by all the people you follow). Hashtags are very popular and used by users to help find relevant content. There is limited functionality when using the computer version of the app.

#HASHTAGS

Hashtags are a search tool, mainly used on Instagram, Twitter and Pinterest, which allows people to find relevant content. They provide a quick shortcut to help search social media or find related posts. To create a hashtag you simply type the hash sign # in front of a word of phrase. To create a valid hashtag, there must be are no spaces between the hash and the words. As an example, here is a hashtag I created for a recent quilt-along event:

#fancyforestQAL18

People taking part in the quilt-along added the hashtag to their photographs; and anyone clicking the hashtag could then see how other people were getting on and get ideas, tips and inspiration from their posts.

You can also use hashtags to add extra information into your post. If, for example, you share an image of a dress you have made, you could use hashtag to tell people which pattern and fabric you used. For example #monetadress #atelierbrunette. These hashtags help to tell people that the pattern was Colette's Moneta Dress and the fabric is an Atelier Brunette fabric.

TIPS FOR USING INSTAGRAM FROM TATTY DEVINE

Tatty Devine is the go-to brand for original, fun, acrylic statement jewellery.

Founded in the heart of East London in 1999 by Rosie Wolfenden MBE (left) and Harriet Vine MBE (right), all their jewellery is still designed and handmade in-house by a passionate and skilled team.

All of Tatty Devine's collections are sold online and in their two London stores in Covent Garden and Brick Lane. New designs, as well as iconic pieces from their archive, are highly coveted and collected by a loyal fan base from all over the world and discovered by new customers every day.

- **Tell a story** Instagram should not be a heavy sales push, remember that you want people to genuinely engage, so tell the story behind your brand and products. We often feature snaps of our jewellery-making process to give our fans a behind the scenes look into the world of Tatty Devine.

- **Point and shoot!** Do not just rely on model and campaign shots on Instagram, as this is where you can get really creative! We often shoot members of team Tatty to show off how they are styling their look that day. We also use colourful flat lays, close-up details and candid shots to really make our Instagram feed pop.

- **Plan ahead!** Search for major exhibitions, holidays, anniversaries, events, national and international days throughout the year – it is a great way to see if you can showcase related products on these days and be relevant.

- **UGC!** User Generated Content (UGC) is earned content created and shared by customers and fans. Customers are more like to purchase a product after seeing how a product is used or worn in a real life scenario, as this allows customers to picture themselves in a similar way. Real images are more trustworthy and authentic. Regramming images of your customers using your product is a great way of saying thank you to your customers, too.

- **Hashtag!** Take ownership of a hashtag! Are your customers using and engaging with your brand name as a hashtag? Utilize this and remember to tag all of your imagery with this hashtag. You can take things a step further by creating a new hashtag to drive and encourage more UGC. For example, we launched the #MyTattyDevine hashtag as a monthly competition, with the best image per month receiving a £25 voucher to spend online.

Examples of the range of images from Tatty Devine's Instagram account.

Flickr

Another popular photo-sharing site amongst creatives, although many abandoned Flickr in favour of Instagram. People with shared interests can form groups on Flickr to share photographs of what they are making. You can also comment on images and start conversations in the comments to build relationships.

Uploading photographs with a creative commons licence, giving other people permission to use them and link back to you, can be a good way of reaching more people with your brand/product images. Flickr was acquired by Verizon in 2017, so it will be interesting to see if they make any substantial changes.

vimeo Vimeo

Vimeo is another popular video-sharing site, a competitor to YouTube. This platform has been becoming more popular within the craft industry. It may not attract as much traffic as YouTube, but do not be fooled into thinking it is a small site. It attracts over one hundred and seventy million unique visitors per month.

Like YouTube, you can use Vimeo to share instructional videos on how to use your products, clips of you making your handmade products or to share tips and techniques that you use. Vimeo has been described as a smaller, more niche, version of YouTube. If you want help deciding which one to use there is a good comparison on the Hootsuite blog. Find the link at the end of this chapter.

Linked in. LinkedIn

LinkedIn is not just a chance to share your C.V.; it is very good for networking within your industry. You can connect with people you meet at shows and events, build your network of contacts and keep them updated with news of your business. There are several good craft groups on LinkedIn where people share tips and advice.

LinkedIn has 500 million users and they have been developing into a more active social media site, by getting influencers to share long-form articles rather than brief updates on what their business is doing; and publishing them online with the LinkedIn Pulse service. These longer articles tend to lead to much more interaction and shares, plus they send the popular ones to their subscribers in their weekly digest e-mails. It can also help to establish businesses as thought leaders in their industry.

Dos and Don'ts of social media

Whichever platform – or platforms – you choose to use, there are some general principles of using social media which carry across. Shown here is a summary of what I consider to be the unofficial rules of using social media for business.

DO

✔ Take the time to reply to comments and queries. Social media is about interaction. Responding to your followers promptly will encourage that.

✔ Post links to articles, projects, news stories and events that will interest your audience. A reputation as a good source of knowledge will attract more followers.

✔ Update regularly, but leave a gap of at least half an hour between updates. Aim to stick to a regular schedule so people know when to expect updates.

✔ Tell people about your offers, sales and new products – but in moderation and interspersed with other updates.

✔ Ask questions and try to encourage interesting debates relevant to your area of business.

✔ Share good quality images. Posts with images often attract more interaction than those without.

✔ Promote businesses complementary to your own. It can help you build relationships with other businesses, and they may return the favour.

✔ Address negative comments to show your customers that you do acknowledge and deal with complaints in a professional manner.

✔ Take the time to check your spelling and grammar to help make your account look professional.

✔ Allow your personality to shine through. With small businesses in particular, people want to get to know the owners and feel that they can relate to you.

✔ Think before you post. Once in the public arena, some things cannot be unsaid.

✔ Experiment with using video to promote your brand, videos tend to get much more reach than text or image only updates.

DO NOT

✘ Engage in arguments. Remember that everyone can read your comments, so keep it professional at all times.

✘ Only post links to your own site, or post the same links over and over. It will bore your followers and make them stop following you.

✘ Suddenly post ten updates in a row because you have not had chance to update for a week or so. That is a very fast way to lose followers because you will fill up their feed with your posts, stopping them from seeing anyone else's – very annoying!

✘ 'Spam' people with endless updates about your business. People to not want to be marketed to all the time; so mix your self-promotional posts with posts about other things.

✘ Debate contentious issues which could result in you losing followers. It is generally best to avoid voicing strong views on religion or politics.

✘ Use poor images. Potential customers may think that poor images equals poor quality products. On a related note, never try to pass other people's images off as your own.

✘ Bad mouth competitors – it makes you look petty and could even result in libel action.

✘ Ignore or delete complaints. It will irritate the complainant more and could lead to them bad-mouthing your company on other platforms that you cannot control.

✘ Use swear words, slang or a rude tone. It will give a bad impression of your business.

✘ Over-share personal information, or moan about your personal problems. People do not like negativity.

✘ Post when you are angry or over-emotional. Think about it and come back to it later when you are feeling calmer.

Setting up your social media presence

Although the social media platforms all work differently, there are certain things you need to do across them all to get up and running. I will not go into the 'click here and select this option' kind of specifics because social media platforms regularly update and move around the options so it will likely have changed by the time you read the book. Instead, I will address the general things you need to do to get your social media accounts running, plus some tips for the individual platforms you may use.

Decide on your social media account names

To avoid confusion, you should pick one name which you use on all platforms so that people can easily find and connect with you. Sadly, it is not always as simple as just using your business name. Your account name should be kept short, memorable and related to your business, so if your business is called *Becky's Delicious Cakes and Pastries*, for example, you might try an account name like Becky's Cakes on social media. Most platforms require you to have a one word username, and there are usually restrictions on the number of characters you can use, so that would then become Beckyscakes. So when people want to tweet you, or tag you on Facebook for example they can just type @beckyscakes which is much easier than typing the full business name. When looking for your social accounts they know to just type the platform link followed by beckyscakes e.g. facebook.com/beckyscakes to find your page.

Another consideration when picking your username is that some names will already be taken. If @beckyscakes is already being used you might then try @deliciouscakes or @beckyspastries instead. Do check all the platforms you think you will want to use even if you are only setting up one or two of them initially. It is best to register with those sites and get that username saved before anyone else can. Most platforms will not transfer usernames over to other people even if those names are not being used, or have become inactive. This can cause a problem if you want a name that is already taken but is not being used, you are unlikely to have any success asking the platform to transfer it to you. Instead, you can try to track down the owner of the inactive account and ask if they would close the account down fully, so that you can then register the name.

You can look for the owner by seeing if they are active on other social media platforms, by searching for their website and sending them a message or by sending a private message to the account on the off-chance they still check their messages from time to time.

> ### NO SPACES
> Although you can use underscores to add a space between words, people will often forget. It is also harder for people using smartphones to type, so ideally you want to just join the words without a space. My social media name, for example, is @sewingdirectory

Create an avatar and biography

At the top of most people's social media pages, and next to any comments they make, you will spot a small photograph or image. This is called an 'avatar' and represents that person online. In time your customers will come to recognize you from your avatar, so you want to make sure it is something that represents your brand. It could be a logo, a product photograph, or your face. To keep a sense of cohesion, aim to use the same avatar on all platforms so that people can see at a glance that it is you. Most platforms use square or round format avatars. They appear quite small on people's screens so you want something simple and eye catching without too much detail. It is best to avoid using much text and concentrate on the visual impact instead.

As well as being asked to upload an avatar when creating a new social media account you are normally asked to write a biography, or bio, too. Most platforms enforce a short character limit, so keep your bio precise and tell people about your business in two or three lines. The goal is to give people enough instant information that they can decide whether to follow you and/or whether to visit your website. Communicate the key points of what you sell or what service you offer and, if possible, add a link to your website so that people can get more information. If you are a local business make sure you include your location in the biography so people can quickly see if they are near you.

One key thing to remember is that social media networks tend to rank well in search results, so if you are able to get a few of your SEO keywords into your biography this could help. However, I would not do it at the expense of a natural sounding biography.

The Sewing Directory

www.thesewingdirectory.co.uk

The Sewing Directory is the UK directory of sewing businesses. Follow us for free sewing patterns, projects & techniques. www.the-sewingdirectory.co.uk

3.9k	**76**	**1.1M**
Pins	Boards	Monthly views

A sample Pinterest biography – my own, in fact! Note the avatar is relatively small on this platform.

Annie
@VHaberdashery Follows you

Classes, supplies and inspiration for Modern Makers! Shop online or in West Hampstead, London. Click the link to shop our feed! #thevillagehaberdashery

⌖ West Hampstead, London

🔗 thevillagehaberdashery.co.uk/shop

This Twitter biography demonstrates the obvious relationship between the account name '@vhaberdashery' and the shop's name 'The Village Haberdashery'.

HEADER IMAGES

In addition to your avatar and bio, on some platforms you also get the option to add a header image. This is a larger rectangular image that stretches across the top of your social media account page.

The header image is often the first thing people see when visiting your page so make it count. A striking image with a little text to say who you are and what you do is generally best. However, you may wish to use it to promote sales, special offers or events.

sewcurvycouture   Following ▾ ···

1,676 posts   **11k** followers   **494** following

Julia Bremble Corsetiere Waist technician specialising in modern corsetry for modern people. Bespoke & made-to-order corsets and vintage inspired special occasion wear. sewcurvycouture.com

An excellent, to-the-point biography and clear, striking avatar combine to make the business' aims and products clear. This example is from Instagram.

Brand identity

As discussed in the Branding section of this book (see pages 76–83), once you have decided on an identity for your brand, you should aim to keep it consistent across all platforms, from your shop to your press advertising, social media platforms to packaging. If you chose certain colours, specific fonts or an ethos to help identify your brand, try to use them in your social media presence too.

There are several ways of doing this:

Consistent backgrounds You could use backgrounds for your images which represent your brand. Tilly and the Buttons is a company which does this well. Take a look at her Instagram account: instagram.com/tillybuttons.

Brand colours You may wish to make sure that the subject of most, if not all, of your images show your brand colours. Have a look at Torie Jayne's Pinterest account for a great example of this: pinterest.co.uk/toriejayne.

Text and type You can overlay images with text that represents your brand. Sew Me Something do an excellent job of this. Visit their Instagram account to see what I mean: instagram.com/sewmesomething.

As you can see from these examples from Sew Me Something, the same typeface and layout have been used in all their images. Together with the distinctive arrows above and below the text, these elements help to tie the pictures together and create images that are instantly recognizable as being theirs.

Torie Jayne

1,244,742 **234**
Followers Following

toriejayne.com
UK / Designer, crafter, baker and interior stylist. Author of 'Craft, Show & Sell' & 'Torie Jayne's Stylish Home Sewing'. Known for my signature pastel style.

Follow

Guest bedroom ideas
140 Pins

Torie Jayne is well known for her pastel colour palette and light, airy pictures. Across her social media – even on Pinterest, when pinning other people's images – she makes sure she sticks to her aesthetic. Her pictures always contain either duck egg blue, pale pink or lilac with a white/pale grey/pale blue background. She also tends to add a watermark or copyright notice to her images as well with her brand name or logo on.

Next steps

Once you have created your social media accounts, the next steps rely on two things: content to post and people to read those posts. When thinking about what to share on social media, check back to the do's and don't of social media (see pages 126–127) and how to provide value in your social media posts (see pages 116–117) for some ideas. I have also written down a list of prompts for you below:

Show who is behind the business People love to know who they are doing business with. Try profiling your company owners and staff on your blog, share pictures of them at shows or in the shop on Facebook. Let people know about the history of the company, celebrate milestones with them and make them feel a part of your business. It is a lot easier to relate to a person than to a faceless business.

Your products and offers It is expected that you will talk about your products and offers; just be careful to keep it to a minimum so you do not spam people. Facebook is ideal for sharing pictures of your new products; blogs give you a place to tell people what is coming soon (or has just arrived in stock); and tempting one liners on Twitter – 'Wow, look what just arrived!' – will get people clicking to see more. On Instagram, you can share videos showing new stock or a quick tip or technique.

Related products and services If you sell fabric, then share projects and tutorials that show people what to do with the fabric they buy from you; or discuss sewing magazines and books. These things are complementary to your products, and will help to engage your followers. If your followers like sewing, the chances are that they also buy sewing magazines or books and read sewing blogs. This gives you common ground with them beyond your products alone. If you have the time, try and find projects made from or with supplies that you sell, so if someone loves the fabric featured they can buy it from you. When posting a link to those projects, you could say this would look great made up in a particular fabric, and link to it on your site.

Promote others As outlined earlier, it is nice to promote others, and it has tangible benefits for your business too. If you know sites in your niche that have some great free tutorials, then share them. It will be useful to your followers and could lead to that other site promoting you in return. Becoming known as a good source of information and inspiration will naturally bring you more followers both through social media shares and word of mouth.

Tips and 'How-to' guides People always appreciate good advice. If you sell beads, tell people about different storage options, different beading techniques or write a tutorial to share with people. If you stock art supplies explain the difference between the different types of paint and when best to use them. Demonstrate techniques, or interview artists to get advice to share with your followers.

Industry news & events Keep an eye on key industry sites and magazines so that you can share details of upcoming shows, new products, craft television shows and industry news with your followers. If people know you are a good source of information, they will keep coming back to you. If you will be at the event, let your followers know where they can find you. Even if you will not be exhibiting, shows are a great chance to build face-to-face relationships with people who have been following you on social media.

General chat As the name suggests, social media is all about being social. Think about what you would discuss with someone you just met in real life – the weather, what was on television last night, what is in the news, and so on and so forth.

Planning ahead

When you are first starting out on social media, it can seem daunting to keep coming up with ideas for new posts. For this reason, it is worth taking the time to plan out your first few weeks' worth of posts before you begin. This will ensure that you do not feel panicked, and can focus more on interacting and growing your following. You can take photographs in advance, make notes on what you want to share, or even pre-schedule the posts ready (see the Schedule It box, right).

Ideally, you want to establish a schedule of posts from the start, so that your followers know what to expect from you. It will also help you to fall into a routine. If you are short of time, then you may wish to start with just three or four posts a week. On the other hand, if you are keen to build your social following as quickly as possible and intend to be quite active on social media you could do two or three a day.

SCHEDULE IT

We look at pre-scheduling in more detail a little later on; for the moment, it is enough to know that many platforms can be set to automatically post updates written earlier.

PROMOTING YOUR BUSINESS WITH FACEBOOK

These tips are from Mat and Monica from the fabric shop Frumble (frumble.co.uk), which has a great mix of photographs and questions that get a good interaction rate on their Facebook page.

- **Post regularly** Try to post a little bit every so often, but be careful not to get carried away and let Facebook take all of your time. Our favourite kind of posts are the ones that engage our fans in a way that lets them continue the conversation with their own momentum, bouncing ideas off one another. This way the interaction builds up more reach for the post.

- **No hard sell** One of the main reasons most businesses have a Facebook page is to sell more things, but you have to be careful not to always be pushing your latest items onto your fans. Try not to always talk about your own business, but make sure you engage people too. Not all posts should be business related – mix them up with posts that reflect your page's personality to show that you are a person running a business and not a business chasing the sale.

- **Share the love** Facebook is a social network that thrives off sharing. If you have fans whose work or posts you appreciate, make sure you share them with your fans. This will add something different to your page and also often help out the other pages too.

- **Did you get the picture?** When you add a picture to Facebook it appears in your fans' newsfeeds along with hundreds of other updates and photographs. An original, good quality, eye-catching image is the best way to get noticed. Consider investing in a good camera and a photography course to enhance your skills if you do not feel very confident behind the lens.

Building a following

There is no point spending hours every week on social media if no-one is reading your posts. So, from the very outset, you want to be expanding your following.

Close contacts A good starting point is to follow people you already know in real life – your customers, friends, other local businesses and so forth.

Magazines Think about the magazines you may one day want coverage in and follow them. Interacting with them on social media could lead to a feature in the future. If nothing else, you will be able to see when they put a call out for contributors, last minute advertising offers or requests for products to be included in their features.

Handmade selling platforms It is worth following the big handmade selling platforms like Etsy, Folksy, and Not on the High Street. They often share selling tips which could be useful to you. In addition, some of the items they share could be made by your competitors, so it helps you to keep an eye on then too.

Competitors Speaking of competitors, it is worth following them as well so you can see what is going on in your area of the industry. Seeing how people react to their posts can help give you valuable knowledge on current trends. Also bear in mind that the people who follow your competitors would also probably be interested in your products. So why not work your way down your competitor's followers list and follow some of them too?

Follow your heroes Think about businesses/people you admire and want to learn from, then find their social media accounts and follow them too. Track down those complementary businesses we discussed earlier and follow them too. Next, find any sites which have useful projects, tips or tutorials that you want to share with your followers. That way, instead of having to take the time of find things to share, they should just pop up in your feed.

Aim for quality It is not the number of followers that counts when it comes to social media, but the quality. You could have thousands of followers, but if they are not interested in what you offer it will be of no benefit to your business other than boasting rights. Much better to have a hundred engaged followers who order from you, than a thousand uninterested followers who are just after your giveaway prizes. Ultimately, social media is part of your marketing plan: you do it because you want some of the people you reach through social media to buy from you.

Activity: Building strategy

Using the ideas opposite, try to find ten or so new accounts at a time. It is worth taking the time to look over their last few posts and seeing if you can interact in any way. When you interact with people they are more likely to follow you back. You have to overcome the 'do not talk to strangers' advice you may have been given when you were young and chat with as many people as you can on social media, especially when first starting out and trying to build a following.

You will find that some people will automatically follow you back (thereby growing your follower numbers) simply because you follow them. Others will wait until they have seen you comment on their posts a few times or they have spotted a post of yours that they like. Interaction is a great way to build your following faster.

GROWING ONLINE: THE IMPORTANCE OF BEING EARNEST

Do not try to force people to follow back by sending messages like 'I have followed you; please follow me back'; it just looks desperate. Equally, do not comment on someone's account to say 'new like from @soandso'; that also appears like you are trying to make someone follow you back. Be genuine, try and build real connections with people. This approach, while slower, will benefit you much more in the long run than someone following you because they feel they have to. Respond to what they are posting, compliment their work, ask questions, offer help or advice if they are asking for it and they will soon see you are trying to build a genuine relationship with them.

Another big no-no is posting links to your products or website on other people's pages. This is spam, and people will likely block you if you do it repeatedly. Unless the account owner asks for people to share links on where they can find a certain product, do not do it. That person/business has taken the time to build their own social media following – why should you benefit from that by posting your links on their page? Think of it as a real life shop, you would not walk into someone else's shop and start shouting about your products. That would be rude and disrespectful, and it is much the same if you do that on someone else's social media page.

Advertise and promote to your existing audience

You will want to let people know about your new social media presence as this will help you increase your followers and post reach too.

Identify yourself You could do this by including your social media username in any advertising you do, saying something like 'find us on Facebook, Twitter and Instagram @sewingdirectory'. It is prompting people to track you down and hopefully if they like what they see they will follow you too. This is also where it comes in useful to have the same username on all platforms, you can include it in the advert rather than leaving people to guess what the name is.

Campaign You can advertise directly on the social media networks themselves with a campaign to attract new fans. These tend to be cheaper than adverts directing traffic to your site, because you are keeping people on their site.

Hand-outs You can create flyers or business cards with your social media details on and hand them out at shows, networking events and include them in your customer's orders. You should also make sure to include links to your social media accounts on your own website. Most people make sure these are placed near the top of their site so they are easy to find.

Posters If you have a physical shop you could put up posters with your social media details on. Do not forget to use your newsletter to let people know too. In fact it is a good idea to keep the social media links on all your newsletters so new subscribers can easily find them.

THE SOCIAL SEWING DIRECTORY

I have always been very active on social media. I started with three posts a day, which soon grew to four, and when I took on a business partner, we ended up doing five posts a day. As an online-only business it was particularly important for me to be building traffic from several sources from the outset, and social media is my second highest traffic referrer, after Google. However, this amount of updates is not realistic for most small businesses, especially those who are not on a computer all day. Find the amount that is comfortable for you and does not leave you stressed trying to keep on top of it.

Giveaways

One popular method of attracting fans to a social media account is to run a giveaway. Encouraging people to comment on or share one of your posts will help the word spread about both your giveaway and your account. You could ask people to follow your account to be eligible to enter the giveaway.

However, you must be careful when running a giveaway to not breach the social network's rules. For example, Facebook do not allow you to ask people to share a post to enter a giveaway, as they do not want people's feeds being full of giveaway posts. Many people do breach this rule, but Facebook can close your page down if they catch you breaking the rules and then all your hard work would be lost. Personally, I do not think it is worth the risk.

Giveaways can be a very successful way of growing a following, which is why you see so many companies doing them, but you do need to make sure you have properly planned them to get the maximum benefit. Firstly, you must be clear about the prize that can be won, what the participant should do to enter, any geographical restrictions and when the giveaway ends. You also need to make sure that none of those details breach the regulations of the sites you are running the giveaways on.

The next important thing to think about is the prize. You want it to be interesting enough to attract a lot of entries, but not so large that you attract tons of entries from people who are not actually interested in your business. There are many forums out there where people compete to win the most prizes. They post links to any competitions they spot and you suddenly get hundreds of entries from people who have no intention of buying anything from you in the future.

One way to avoid this is to keep the prize really relevant to what you do. If, for instance, you run a knitting shop, offering wool and knitting patterns as a prize is unlikely to appeal to people who do not knit. Those items would be useless to those people so they probably would not think it worth their time entering. If you offered a hundred pounds' worth of high street vouchers, they could be used by anyone, whether they knit or not, and you could end up with hundreds of new followers who do not knit so therefore will not be buying your yarn or patterns any time soon.

Another way to ensure you are reaching the right audience with your giveaway is to ask an entry question which requires knowledge of your niche to enter, or to ask people to make something with your products or place an order with you to enter. Then you are rewarding your existing customers, or encouraging new customers. At the very least, you are getting entrants who know something about the niche you operate in who could become customers in the future.

FACEBOOK'S RULES

Check the full rules for running giveaways on Facebook here: facebook.com/page_guidelines.php

Other useful things to know

Sharing Most networks have a way for you to share other people's posts. On Facebook you will find a share button under the post, on Twitter you can re-tweet (the arrows in a circle button under the post) and on Pinterest you can pin other people's pins onto your own board. A big part of social media is about sharing other people's content. It is best to use the share options so that it still credits the originator of the post. If you just save the image or text and then upload it to your own account as a new post you are then taking credit for it and could be breaching someone's copyright. So when you share make sure you do it properly and ensure the original poster is credited.

Private messages Most social media platforms have the option of sending a private message. This is a message that only you and the person you are sending it to can see, not all your followers (unlike your other social media posts). Try not to mix them up or it can become embarrassing when something you thought was private can be seen by everyone!

Mentions On the majority of social networks if you use a person or company's name with the @ sign in front it is known as a tag. This means the person you mention gets notified you have mentioned them, great for when you are sharing projects or tutorials from other people's websites or recommending complimentary businesses. It also allows you followers to click on that tag and be taken to that person's account. So, it can lead to new followers for them. Likewise when people mention you some of their page fans may click over to your account and follow you.

Saving posts If you spot a post that interests you – perhaps something you want to share in the future or come back and read when you have more time – many social platforms give you a method on saving it. On Twitter, you click the heart under the post to favourite a post, while on Pinterest you pin it onto one of your own boards. On Instagram, you click the little flag symbol under the post; on Facebook click the arrow on the top right of the post, then click the flag symbol to save it; and on YouTube, click the + button to add a video to one of your playlists.

MAKE IT EASY TO SHOP

Make sure people can easily buy any products you feature on your social media accounts. Firstly, make sure you include links to those products wherever possible in your posts, and make sure the link to your shop/site is in your profile. Another idea is to have a specific page on your site featuring the products you have recently shared on social media. See misformake.co.uk/pages/social for an example of this.

Link Tree

Link Tree (linktr.ee) is a program that allows you to direct people to multiple links when they click the link in your social media profile. This is useful if you sell in multiple places, as you can share all those links at once. You can also promote several things at once. This is especially useful on Instagram where you can only have one clickable link in your profile and none on your posts.

Scheduling social media

It can feel like social media keeps you tied to your computer when you would rather be getting on with creating. However, you do not have to add your posts one by one scattered throughout the week. You can batch write them, and then schedule them to go live at the time you specify. If you do it this way you can set aside an hour or two to write your whole week's worth of social media posts and then just check your accounts every day or two to respond to any replies, comments or messages.

Although there are programs which allows you to schedule posts for multiple networks at once, such as Hootsuite or Tweet Deck it's worth noting that Facebook prefer you to schedule your posts on their site. Their algorithms can mean that posts scheduled on other programs appear less in your follower's newsfeeds, giving them a lower reach. To pre-schedule a post on Facebook write your post as normal. Then click on the downwards arrow next to the word publish on the bottom right of the update box and select schedule. You then pick a date and time for you post to go live.

For prescheduled Twitter updates I use Hootsuite which is free to use. I like that it shortens your links, I tend to write my updates in Hootsuite first, shorten the link and then copy over to Facebook when scheduling. As with Facebook Hootsuite allows you to add images, or video plus text and then pick when you want the post to go live. With pre-scheduled posts you can always alter them or set them to publish at a different time if you wish too. Twitter have recently just added the option to pre-schedule direct on their site but I have not tested it out yet. At the time of writing this you need to have a Twitter Ads account in order to be able to pre-schedule.

For Instagram it is a little trickier, you cannot specify when you want a post to go live but you can write posts in advance and save them as drafts to manually put live in the future. To do that you write your post, choose your filters, add your text and tick any networks you want to cross post to. Then instead of publishing you click the back arrow twice and it will pop up asking you if you want to save as a draft, or discard your post altogether. Once saved as a draft you drafts can be accessed by pressing the plus sign as if adding a new post but when viewing your gallery of photos scroll up and you will find all your drafts.

There is a choice of apps to pre-schedule your Pinterest posts such as Viral Tag, Viral Woot and Everypost. Do beware that some of these require payment to use although most offer a free trial first. With YouTube when you select 'upload' to add a new video select 'schedule' from the arrow that appears next to the word 'public' on the select a video to upload page.

Video

Video can give you much more reach (i.e. more people will see your posts) than text- or image-based posts. As mentioned at the start of this chapter, video on social media is becoming increasingly popular. It is no longer confined to certain sites like YouTube and Vimeo: you can share videos on Facebook, Instagram, Twitter and Pinterest, amongst other networks.

It is worth noting that there is a difference between live video updates – that is, ones that are uploading as you film so you cannot edit them – and pre-recorded video, which you can edit before putting live.

Live videos are particularly good for chatting with your audience in an informal manner, giving them the chance to ask questions and you to respond to them live. You can also use them to show people what you are up to at that moment in time. Examples of this including sharing footage of a show you are attending; taking viewers on a tour of your workroom; or showing your works in progress. You need to be quite confident and well-prepared before shooting a live video, as you will not have the option to remove parts or re-take bits where you make a mistake.

If you want more opportunity to check your video and make edits before showing it to the world then pre-recorded video is the better option for you.

My friend Claire-Louise Hardie (see right) has worked as the sewing producer on the BBC Television programme *The Great British Sewing Bee*; presented dressmaking shows for The Sewing Quarter; and has filmed both her own sewing e-courses and a selection of useful YouTube videos. She has kindly provided the video-making advice for this part of the book.

HOW TO USE VIDEO TO PROMOTE YOUR BUSINESS

Claire-Louise Hardie is the owner of The Thrifty Stitcher Sewing School in London, sewing producer of The Great British Sewing Bee *and author of* The Great British Sewing Bee: Fashion with Fabric. *She also runs online sewing courses through her website: thethriftystitcher.co.uk*

Over the following pages, I explain how to film your own videos. Once you've read through my advice, you need to think what kind of videos you could make and how to use them to best promote your business – the list below will give you some starting points.

How to use products

A great way of using video is to show people how to use your products – especially useful when you sell crafting tools: a good video could lead to hundreds of product sales. If you pick a tool which does not have much help and support online, then you are likely to get even more views because of the lack of competition. Do not just limit yourself to technique videos; what about projects too? Then you can feature several products you sell all in one video.

Position yourself as an expert

You can also use video to show your expertise. This works well if you are a craft teacher. You can show your potential customers that you know what you are talking about, and that you teach in a clear, easy to follow manner. If, for example, you run a workshop on sewing with knit fabrics, you could film a video featuring your top five tips for sewing knits and then, at the end of the video, encourage people to book onto your workshop to learn more.

Q & A

You can use video to answer questions that you are commonly asked. You can also ask people to comment with further questions, in order to give you content for your next Q & A video too.

Behind the scenes

Helping people relate to you as a person, rather than just as a faceless business, can really help grow customer loyalty. Why not share videos of your workspace, footage of you talking about your business and why you set it up, introduce them to the other people you work with, even share clips of you making your products or an average day in the shop or studio.

Desirability

A well-shot video can really make people want to buy the items featured. It gives you a chance to show your products from all angles, *in situ* and on a white background, in use, close up, from a distance – and more. That would require a lot of photographs, but a brief video clip can show all that and more. Use your video to make people feel like they must buy the items you have featured.

Video for creative businesses

There is no denying the importance of video in your marketing arsenal. These days, it is essential to have video to promote your creative service or product. As a small business owner, making videos may seem like yet another skill to learn or another expense to pay out to a professional, stretching your budget even further. It is possible, however, to make some really good quality DIY video content yourself with a minimal outlay. Here are some tips to get started:

Decide on your story

We are bombarded with high-quality video content, so your customer is used to being engaged by videos. Before you think about what camera you need or how you will edit your videos, sit down and think about your ideal customer. What problems do they have that your product will solve? How can your product or service solve their problems, and what will that feel like to your customer? The best video content tells a story. Although your video is not necessarily an advert, you are making it to sell or promote your products. Check out a couple of ads on YouTube and see how they are telling stories. The John Lewis Christmas ad campaigns are a great example, as are the recent 'Should have gone to Specsavers' campaigns.

Planning at this stage is essential, as it will inform all other decisions later on in the process, and will save you masses of time. Once you have identified a story you would like to tell in your video, start a storyboard. This is a sort of brainstorming process that's used by film makers from adverts to soaps, and is a way to get your ideas into some kind of order.

Once you have got a rough outline of the story you want to tell, you can break down the 'scenes' and work out what space they need to be shot in, and what props you might need. Having developed the story a little more, write a rough outline script – nothing fancy, just some word prompts you can use on the day. You now know exactly what scene or scenes you want to create, so the next step is to think about some of the logistics and kit you might need if you are planning to shoot it yourself. You can of course use a professional videographer, but these can be pricey.

> ### ENGAGE THE VIEWER QUICKLY
>
> Viewers make the decision to keep watching a piece of video content or not within the first three seconds, so you should make the opening visually appealing or impactful.

Cameras

It is possible to shoot really good video with a smartphone, provided the camera is reasonably modern and you have a decent amount of memory available. Most smartphones allow you to touch the screen to focus on something, set exposure and so forth, so you can create interesting footage with varied depth of field. When combined with a remote clicker, the timer function on most smartphones means that you can easily film solo.

If you want to do close-up cinematic-style shots, it may be worth investing in a digital camera with a recording time longer than twelve minutes. There are many options available, so ask in-store for some advice, and go with the best camera within your budget.

If most of your video content is likely to be live streaming, your best option may be a webcam. These vary in price and functionality, so research the one that best suits your needs. An external webcam usually has superior picture quality to the camera built into your computer, and you can use it together with a tripod to get better angles than if you were looking at a fixed computer camera.

Camera accessories

If you want your video to look professional, you will need to invest in a tripod. ball-head tripods are purposely designed for video. You can get tripods with extra functionality like horizontal arms for overhead shots.

> **CHEAP TRICKS**
>
> For sliding shots like panning across a selection of products, or zooming slowly into a detail you can do your own budget version using a skateboard. You can also zoom in by unclipping one leg of a tripod and tilting both the tripod and the camera together.

Sound equipment

No matter how good your story is, it will mean nothing if you have poor quality sound. It is essential to get a microphone or 'mic', as the quality of the built-in microphone on a phone or camera is not good enough. Whatever mic you choose, it is a good idea to reduce the chance of any ambient noise. This may therefore affect where you to choose to film. Filming close to a main road, with lots of traffic and sirens, will not help your audio! If you are filming in a public place like an office, you may need to ask your colleagues to avoid speaking. Fans and generators all create low level ambient noise so you will need to switch them off or avoid being close.

Microphones

- **Lavalier mics** These clip onto a lapel/neckline and are a good option when filming a talking heads style video, or if you are shooting someone moving about in a room. You can get a reasonable model from around £30 ($40). To get a good result, the mic needs to be around 12–15cm (5–6in) away from the mouth and uncovered, so note that it will be visible on the wearer. If shooting outside, you will need a fluffy cover to stop wind noise.

- **Directional microphones** These attach to your camera pointing towards the subject. They are good for picking up speech in amongst noise, but do not record great surround sound. Basic shotgun mics start at around £30 ($40), but do your research before purchasing.

- **Handheld recorders** These digital recorders can be a good option if your subject is static, or you have a pair of hands spare to hold the recording device. They are a versatile option, especially if shooting outside in public places.

Recording devices:

Apart from the hand-held recorder, you will need to attach your mic to a recording device. You can plug into your smartphone, although you may need an adaptor. If you are recording with a camera and a lavalier mic, there are apps you can use to record your sound. If using a directional mic, you will be connected directly to your camera to record the sound.

CLAPPING FOR SYNCHRONICITY

When you start filming, make sure to clap. This creates a noise spike, which will make it easier to edit and synchronize the audio to the visual. This was the function of the iconic clapper board! After your clap, state which section or scene it is, and what take you are on: 'Beading, scene 1, take 2', for example. This will help in the editing process: as it will help you sort through your footage – you will likely have a lot to process. If you use an external editor, this will also help them to identify each segment.

Lighting

Murky, poorly-lit shots are not the best representation of your business! Lighting is an art all of its own, but the good news for a small business is that you can achieve a lot with inexpensive kit, especially if you can use natural lighting.

- **Reflectors** These are really useful in natural light to help fill in shadows; a great investment that will not break the bank..

- **LED light panels** These panels, which can be battery powered or mains operated, attach to a camera and can enhance filming even in natural light. They help to light up the face, providing what is called a 'key light' (see below). If you are filming over a long day, they can be used to maintain consistent lighting as the sun moves.

- **Artificial lighting** Soft box lights/diffused lights: you will need to get to grips with the three-point lighting system to maximize using artificial lighting. The three basic lights are:
Key-light This produces the most light, and shines on your subject.
Fill-light This 'fills' in any shadows left by the key-light.
Back light A light that beautifies the image with a soft glow on the back of the subject's head/shoulders.

Video editing

Unless you are doing live broadcast on social media channels, you will need to edit your footage. Great editing is invisible, but without it, you will not have a cohesive finished film. If you are looking to do it yourself, here are a few options

- **Basic editing** Imovie or Windows Movie maker are limited in functionality, but readily-available.

- **Screenflow/Camtasia** Both of these programs (Screenflow on Mac, Camtasia for Windows) are designed for screen recording, but have built-in editing facilities which include better functionality.

- **Adobe Premiere Pro** This is a powerful editing programme, which works well with other Adobe products like illustrator or Photoshop.

- **Final cut** Another powerful pro-quality editing suite.

If you are time-poor or not technically-minded, consider outsourcing this job. Having wasting hours trying to teach myself and doing a poor job editing my own footage, I employ an editor. I still shoot myself, but then hand on to a professional editor, who adds in lovely graphics/transitions and music. To find an editor, try People Per Hour where you post your job and people apply. You could also try a film school as recent graduates or final year students will be looking for work. You could also try and get a recommendation from someone who has used an editor.

LOOKING OUT

When shooting in natural light, make sure your subject is facing a window, not away from it.

FREE MUSIC

Did you know You Tube has a channel of copyright free music that you can add to your videos? Browse the tracks here: goo.gl/YmnOAx

Preparing to shoot

All of the logistics are in place, you know what you are planning to film, your location is sorted, and you have sourced all your props and kit. You should now think about the actual filming process. Here are my top tips:

- **Make-up** If you are the main focus of the video, make sure you look the best version of you. Your face can look washed-out or featureless without make-up. A touch of contouring around your cheek bones, will help give your face some definition, and a little colour on your lips will ensure they do not get lost on camera. Similarly, accent your eyes with a little mascara. Have some powder or blot paper on hand during the filming as shine is not a good look!

- **Dress rehearsal** Whilst you have done a lot of preparation for your video, it is really worth having a trial run as unexpected problems invariably pop up. This offers you a chance to correct light or sound issues.

- **Learn about line of sight** If shooting in an interview style, have the subject look at an interviewer rather than directly to camera. Think about the way reality competition shows are shot when they talk to the contestants. Position your subject to one side of the frame.

- **Use a variety of shot types or sizes** To create a visually interesting piece, a mixture of close up, medium and wide frame shots are usually used. Make sure to film different versions of the same thing so you have more options in edit. Better to have too much footage than not enough to tell your story well.

SAY CHEESE

Practise smiling while you talk, and try and keep your voice light and animated if you are talking in the video. It may feels odd at first, but it will ensure you do not sound flat and uninteresting.

KEEP ROLLING

Keep shooting for around ten seconds after your dialogue or action finishes, as this will help when editing. The same rule applies if you need to start over. Do not rush back into repeating the words or action. Pause, take a beat and then start again or your second attempt may also be unusable in edit.

ENJOY YOURSELF

Try and be playful, and have fun with your video. You may not have a big budget, but you can still be innovative and creative as a small business owner. Think about playing with slow motion, or hyperlapse. Try and develop your own style and signature.

LIVE VIDEO STREAMING TIPS FROM RACHEL PINHEIRO

Rachel Pinheiro is a creative industry professional and digital influencer, find her at houseofpinheiro.com or at instagram.com/houseofpinheiro.

For businesses that are interested in engaging with their audience, there is nothing better that live streaming. It is my favourite tool as it offers real time feedback and a unique opportunity to build rapport.

There is no single formula for successful streaming. It is a combination of personality and planning. There are areas you can control to improve the experience, especially if you are nervous:

- Firstly, practice, practice, and then practice some more!

- Some social media platforms; Facebook for example, allows you to set a privacy setting that means only you will be able to watch it. Take the opportunity to verify not only your performance, but the quality of streaming and audio. The biggest reasons people stop watching are poor quality of audio and speed.

- Since you can stream from your phone, table or computer, try adding a microphone and shooting your stream in a location with natural light to improve the quality.

I get asked a lot about duration and frequency of videos. The simple answer is that it depends on your objective. A short video of three to five minutes delivers a message more effectively. Longer videos will allow 'late' followers to catch up but you will lose the attention of the early engagers. Whatever you decide, it is important to have a structure of start, message, closure line and end of broadcast.

One main subject for broadcast is ideal. Short and often is my recommendation. Try to keep your videos less than ten minutes in length. A weekly schedule of short video updates of three to five minutes each will achieve a lot more than half-hour long videos published intermittently.

During the broadcast, make sure you introduce yourself and the theme. Set the rules on how the session will run. It is very important to acknowledge viewers by name, and to have a flow. Ask viewers to add comments and use reactions if they agree or disagree with the statements. If possible, have another person to read and feed questions to the presenter. If you are running a Q&A, ask the questions in advance so that there is time to think about the responses.

After the broadcast, if your broadcast will stay live, make sure to edit it to reflect the points discussed. Also ensure you keep comments session open and reply promptly to any that arise.

After your shoot

Post production

Once you have got everything filmed and edited into a timeline, you will need to think about adding graphics, titles and music.

Music It is really important to have some music over most videos. Music can really help to tell the story, or convey a mood or feeling. Your music choice should not be over-powering, and you will need to ensure it is not too loud. Think movie score: you are aware that it is there, but it does not interfere with the film itself. There are lots of places where you can get inexpensive royalty-free music, and you can even get music created especially for you. It is not advisable to choose something that is covered by royalties, as this could cause you issues with platforms like YouTube who can block you for copyright abuse

Graphics It is good to have a video header and footer. These are graphics that will be synonymous with your brand. It could also be the thumbnail used wherever your video is embedded. If you can use graphic software like Photoshop, you can create this yourself. Alternatively, the online platform Canva will allow you to create graphics without having graphic software. Since the graphics are important, you may choose to outsource this job.

Exporting It is likely you will want to use this video content on multiple platforms. Different platforms have different dimensions, so export your video multiple times to the size specification of each platform you plan to use.

Measuring the results

Most social media platforms, especially when you have a business account, offer some form of analytics which allows you to measure the reach and engagement levels of your posts. Do not forget to keep an eye on these to see which kind of posts prove most popular so you can do more of these in the future.

You can also use these statistics along with your web stats to monitor the overall effectiveness of your social media marketing.

BUILDING A SUCCESSFUL YOUTUBE CHANNEL

Find sewing expert and author Debbie Shore's YouTube Channel at youtube.com/user/thimblelane, or visit her website: debbieshore.tv/ to find out about her books and products.

I started my YouTube channel in 2011, as a way of sharing project ideas with like-minded people from around the world. Now, it is a very important part of my work life, a window to the world of sewing through which peer approximately 20,000 people a day. It is a place where I can promote my books, website and social media platforms, and receive invaluable feedback from viewers.

Content

There are several key factors to a channel being successful, the first being content. Choose a subject that you know, and make it interesting for the viewer. Research other videos on YouTube with similar content and try to create something with a different angle. Do not be tempted to copy other people's work – there is no point, those videos have already been done!

Equipment

It is worth investing in a good video camera and lighting. Although sunlight is very flattering, it is not consistent, so having control over your lighting is preferable. I use four Excelvan lights, and two Canon HFG30 video cameras; although one camera would be sufficient to start with. I use one camera for overhead or close-up shots, and one for myself in vision, then cut between the two when editing.

I use a radio mic to give clear sound to my videos: echoing and background noise can be off-putting to the viewer. An overlong video will lose viewers, so I edit out any unnecessary content, and if I need to stress instructions or measurements I add text to the screen.

I use Sony Vegas Pro 14 editing software – and to be honest, I find this the most enjoyable part of the whole filming process!

Attracting and engaging visitors

- **Be happy!** A smile engages the viewer, and a cheery presentation makes for pleasant viewing. Watch your videos back before uploading them. Do not be overly critical, but make sure you are happy with their content and overall look.

- **Visuals** You will need a thumbnail that really stands out to bring the viewer's attention to your video above others which are similar. A clear picture of your project with large type that can be read on smart devices. Look at other thumbnails and see which ones stand out, this is important as you do not want your video to be overlooked.

- **Make it easy to find** When uploading your video include key words in the title, what would the viewer search for? The titles of most of my videos include the word 'sewing' and my name as these are my most popular searches. You can list 'tags' which again are words that the viewer searches for, for my videos I would include 'sewing', 'sew', 'needlecraft', 'project', 'pin cushion', 'home décor' and anything else that is relevant to the video content.

- **Reward subscribers** Once you have uploaded your videos, you need to entice subscribers and importantly, keep them watching and keep them subscribed, so ask them! There is no harm in

pointing out in the introduction to your video that subscribers will be the first to be notified of latest videos and suggesting they click on the 'subscribe' button. Alternatively you could add a 'subscribe' annotation by going to the 'end screen and annotations' section of your video manager. End screens are useful tools to invite your viewer to view another video, or create a play list of several videos to keep them on your channel.

- **Ask questions** Did you know that you can add a poll to your video? Whilst in your video manager click on 'cards' then 'add card' then 'poll' – then ask the question! What would viewers like to see more of? There will be multiple choice answers which can be useful to gauge if you are getting it right.

- **Respond** Take time to read any comments and messages, I reply to as many comments as I can, even if it is just to say 'thank you for commenting', this makes for a more personal relationship for your viewers and their opinions can be invaluable.

Monetizing and monitoring

Although you can monetize your videos, do not expect to make any substantial amount of money from advertising for quite a while. With that said, the pocket money generated comes in handy!

Use the analytics for your channel to their best advantage. Here you can monitor where in the world your views are coming from, how many subscribers you have, what percentage of views come from subscribers and nonsubscribers and their watch time. Take note of traffic sources, if you see a particular web site linking to one of your videos it may be worth getting in touch with them to form a collaboration.

There is so much useful information about your channel and its viewers that can help it grow, if you need further advice there is bound to be a YouTube video to help you.

Online communities and content marketing

Content marketing and online communities are big buzzwords in online promotion. You can do both on your own site, or can host them elsewhere. These are long-term investments in terms of both time and money, but can result in your having access to a large number of people who are your target audience and who are loyal to you and your brand.

There is also a great sense of satisfaction knowing that you have brought so many people together!

Online communities

Building an online community is creating a place for people with similar interests to gather and interact. You can build a community around your site, through your social media, through your blog and by e-mail. I have built a great community around The Sewing Directory and after a few years of interacting online, I held sewing meet-ups which gave people a chance to get together face to face to sew and chat about sewing, fabric, and industry gossip. There are many people who have followed The Sewing Directory from the start and, as a result, have now connected not just with me but each other as well.

Another great example in the sewing industry is the American website Sew Mama Sew, which has built a great worldwide community of sewing bloggers who participate in sewing challenges, worldwide giveaway days and in 'sew-along' events and swaps.

Pattern company Burda have created a community website (burdastyle.com) which encourages people using their patterns to share photos of what they have made, pattern hacks and tips. They also have a forum where people can ask for advice, organize sew alongs and report issues with pattern instructions.

Building an online community has many benefits, it shows people that you care about them and their interests. It helps them to see you as a valuable resource and the lynch pin to the community. You bring people together and build a loyal following around you and your brand. It also establishes trust and helps you build relationships with potential customers.

I have put links to all the mentioned sites at the end of this section. Visit them and think about whether you could create something similar around your business. Even if you decide not to, if there is already an online community in your part of the industry, consider becoming a part of it in order to help raise your brand profile, to network and to keep up with what is popular in your industry.

Content marketing

Content marketing involves creating great quality content that will attract visitors to your site and help build awareness of your brand. The majority of the content should be on your own site and blog but you can also use it to guest post on others in order to establish yourself as an expert in your area and send traffic to your site.

The key to creating good quality content is to identify what specifically your customers want and is hard to find elsewhere. There is no point writing something that has been covered elsewhere unless you can put a unique spin on it or cover it better than has been done anywhere else.

Your content needs to be compelling, to help people and to be shareable. You want people to read it and think 'this is great, I must tell so-and-so about it, or share it on my social media'. Good quality content will encourage the reader to read more of your content and look through your site. This will hopefully lead to them signing up to your newsletter, following you on social media and eventually purchasing whatever you are selling.

WANT MORE?

There is more on creating good content below in the blogging section on pages 152–162 and in the SEO section on pages 184–194.

CONTENT MARKETING TIPS FROM SUSAN MOELLER

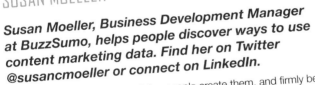

Susan Moeller, Business Development Manager at BuzzSumo, helps people discover ways to use content marketing data. Find her on Twitter @susancmoeller or connect on LinkedIn.

I love great messages and helping people create them, and firmly believe in the value and ability of social media to enrich lives, to sell products, and to make people laugh.

Great content reaches new audiences and creates business opportunities. To be successful in today's crowded content landscape, two skills are crucial. The first is to recognize a niche that is not saturated with content, so that you can be the most important publisher in that space. The second is the ability to create genuine and mutually beneficial relationships with others in industries more saturated with content. Collaborating with other leaders gives you the chance to grow your audience much more quickly than you could alone – and it's more fun!

Blogging

Your blog is a platform to tell people more about you and your business: what you make, what you love; and also to share advice, tutorials and inspiration. Unlike most social networks you are not limited to just a few lines or one image. This is where you can create great content that shows off your expertise as well as your creations.

On-site or off-site blog?

You have two choices when setting up your blog. You can make it part of your website or you can host it separately to your website. This decision will depend on what you want from your blog. There are many sites which will host your blog for free including Blogger, WordPress and Tumblr.

The obvious downside to having an off-site blog is that an on-site blog is easier for people to find – make sure you that there is a clear link from your main site to your blog and vice versa. I chose to host my blog separately, on the hosting site Blogger, for a variety of reasons.

Search engine optimization From an SEO point of view, I knew Google would index my blog before my website, so separate hosting would drive traffic to the site via my blog while I waited for my site to rise in the rankings.

Backup If there is ever a problem with my website, my blog is still usable. I once had a big competition ending, and server problems with my site which meant it was down for a few hours. Instead of using my website, I posted the winner of the competition on my blog and shared that link on social media. Once the site was live again I copied the details over to there.

The personal touch Around half of my posts on my blog are about The Sewing Directory and sewing, but the remainder are about me: my goals, hobbies and news. I shared the process of writing this book on my blog, I shared the progress of converting my garage into an office, the sewing projects I have been working on and my business goals each year.

Communication Hosting my site on Blogger means I have a Blogger account which makes it easier for me to comment on other blogs, and it includes an automatic link back to my blog in those comments.

> ### MY BLOGS
> I started on off-site blog for The Sewing Directory while my website was being built in order to build some early followers for the site. I did the same with my social media too. Neither is inherently better, so experiment to see which you prefer and which works best for your business.

> ### A FRIENDLY PLACE
> I feel like I can be both more relaxed and personal, and less corporate, on my blog than on my website.

COMMUNITY BUILDING

These tips come from Kristin Link from the popular community site, Sew Mama Sew (sewmamasew.com).

Community is the name, reciprocity is the game. When we re-launched our site in 2013, we sent a letter to our contributors that included this slogan. Although the cheer-inspired sentiment may sound corny, they are words we really do try to live by. Being part of an online community is a lot like being part of a family, so it is important to be mindful of what you can give and not just what you can get.

- Participate in social media. Follow it, pin it, like it, comment on it, favourite it, and share it. Most of the social channels make it easy to give people a virtual fistbump, which you should do every day.

- Invite guests to your blog and sing their praises! Even if they are not business owners or for-profit bloggers, they will appreciate being appreciated.

- Take advantage of opportunities to meet people in person. Connecting faces with online handles is good for your community and your soul.

- Always respond to requests for interviews, guest posts and blog hops. Graciously oblige whenever possible.

By paying attention to how you can help other people grow their businesses or their blogs, you are sure to get plenty of respect in kind.

PURELY ONLINE COMMUNITIES

You could set up a site dedicated solely to creating an online community. The aforementioned Burda Style and Sew Mama Sew websites are great examples of this, as are sites like Craftster, Cut Out and Keep and The Fold Line.

Ravelry is a knitting community site based around a forum layout. In addition to the chat forums, it lets members sell their products through the site too.

Creating your blog

Once you have chosen where your blog will be hosted, start thinking about the design of the blog. Your blog should:

- Be uncluttered and use white space (see page 183 for information on white space).

- Be easy to navigate and easy on the eye.

- Have a biography to tell people who you are and what you do. You could add a strapline into your header image to do this.

- Include social media links.

- Include a newsletter sign-up link.

- Include a link to your main site, or shop if hosting off-site.

- Include options for people to follow or subscribe to your blog.

- Have popular topics or posts on the side to encourage people to look at other posts.

- Have branding that fits with the rest of your business.

There are many blog templates available for most blogging platforms; most of them are free too. Your blog should be an extension of your company even if it is hosted off-site. Stick to your branding. Use a similar colour scheme and the same logos and avatars – that way people will know it is part of your business.

You can search for widgets to add to your blog which do things like track visitor numbers, show what countries people visit from, allow you to showcase products in your online shops, adding social media feeds, and more. Most can be added by copying and pasting an html code onto your blog – you do not need a lot of technical knowledge to do that.

Most blogs have the option of adding a blog header across the top. This is a great place to show your logo, include a link to your site or shop (if your blog is off-site), showcase some of your products and tell people what you do. You can add a text motto or strapline into the image to communicate more information. This header image is the first thing people will see when they visit your blog, so make it count.

Activity: Blog design

Analyse the popular blogs in your part of the industry and think about what elements of their design and layout you would like to incorporate into your own.

- Do they have a great breakdown of the content on their sidebar?
- Have they got a bold header image which tells people what the blog is about?
- Do they make good use of white space?
- Are their images outstanding?
- Are their blog posts really easy to read and digest?

Look at blogs outside of your industry for design inspiration too.

MAKE IT EASY

Make sure the 'follow' options are near the top of the page to encourage people to subscribe to your blog.

DESIGN TIPS

The information on setting up a website on pages 174–185 includes tips on design. These principles can be applied to your blog, too.

Writing blog posts

Cornerstone content

Once your blog is designed and live, start filling it with great content. It is good to have a mixture of different kinds of posts on your blog. The main thing you will need to put time and energy into is the what is called 'cornerstone content'. These are the really good articles which make people come back for more and attract traffic from search engines. They form the foundations of your blog.

Craft blogs often include how-to guides, great projects or some really in-depth expert advice, such as how to choose a sewing machine, for example. Cornerstone content does not represent the kind of posts you will be writing every week. They take more time, more research and a lot of effort.

However, if you can create one of these killer pieces of content every few months, it will encourage people to subscribe and help grow your blog. After you put so much into writing these posts you want to make sure you promote the hell out of them! Promote them on social media every few months, highlight them on the sidebar of your blog, modify them to offer as guest posts on other blogs, mention them in your newsletter, update them regularly for SEO purposes. Keep them working for you for years; do not just view them as a one-off. I have a few articles on my site which each get several thousand hits a month. When you get a single piece of content bringing you over 50,000 hits a year you will realize it was time well-spent.

Play to your strengths. If you are really good at choosing colour combinations for the craft supplies you stock, write an in-depth guide to colour theory and how to choose colours which work well together for your craft projects. Of course you can research and write about subjects you do not know well, but if you already have a certain amount of knowledge it will save you time.

SHORT & SWEET

Try to create a short descriptive web address (URL) for your cornerstone posts, this makes them easier to share. For example, 'thesewingdirectory.co.uk/dressmaking-techniques' rather than 'thesewingdirectory.co.uk/how-to-sew-your-own-clothes'

LET PEOPLE TALK

Make sure you have activated the comments section so that people can comment on your blog.

Activity: Cornerstones

Spend some time reading similar blogs to yours. Identify information that ties in well with your business which has not been covered well elsewhere; or that you could talk about in more detail. Make a note of these ideas as these will form your cornerstone content.

Create an ongoing list to which you can add ideas. Set aside a day to work on something really detailed, then pick one from your list of ideas and write a blog post.

Other content

Other content you can share on your blog includes:

Your business news Share information such as new stock coming in, opening hours, staff, events, or changes to the business. This goes back to letting people know who they are buying from and helping them to form a relationship with you.

Your projects Sharing your own craft projects and challenges works well. Show people what you have been making, what you plan to make, and even what you are struggling with. If you find you are working so much you do not get much time for making, then share pictures of your supplies, of your workspace, what you have been buying recently or what you plan to make in the future.

Inspiration Ideas are another good topic for blog posts. Share the source of your inspiration. Tell your followers about some really great blogs you want to recommend. Are you a Pinterest addict? Is there a particular magazine that you find always gets you fired up? Write about these things, share them with your followers, and ask them where they get their inspiration.

Personal posts Posts about my business and sewing make up roughly half of my blog, but I do write some personal posts too. These posts help your followers relate to you; and sometimes there are things you just want to share.

HELP!

Asking for advice or showing you are struggling with something really makes people relate to you. They can see that you are just like them and it builds common ground. It also has the benefit that it will encourage more interaction as people reply.

TOO MUCH INFORMATION

Be wary of 'over-sharing' – giving away too much personal information. One craft blogger told me someone turned up at her children's school one day to meet her because they had worked out which school it was from her blog posts!

Remember that anything you put on your blog, website or social media is entering the public arena, where it becomes impossible to control. As with all places that you use for business, keep negative posts to a minimum. Using your business blog for a big rant about your interfering mother-in-law or noisy neighbours is bad form – and, needless to say, never use it to bad-mouth your customers or suppliers.

Quick tips and techniques These are different from your cornerstone content as you may just want to cover something brief and not write a huge in-depth article – perhaps a new technique you have learnt or think your readers would benefit from, or a useful crafting tip you have come up with.

It is handy to draft some of these posts and keep them ready for when you do not have time to write anything fresh as they are not time sensitive and do not have to go live straight away.

Lists These work well as blog posts. Collect information from several places and combine it all into one post. For example: 'Twenty ways to drive more traffic to your Etsy shop', 'Five simple tips to speed up your card making', or 'Eight essential tools for jewellery making'. These kinds of posts always appeal.

Interviews Sharing an expert's talents, advice and views is a great way to attract new followers to your blog. The interviewee will often tell their own followers about it, which sends extra traffic to your blog. If you are worried about over-promoting your own business, conducting an interview will both give useful advice to your followers and mean one less post you are writing about yourself.

Reviews Reviews can form great blog posts. There is now so much choice when it comes to craft magazines, books and supplies, that any advice you can give to help people choose will be appreciated. Contact publishers and ask to review one of their books on your blog – most are glad of the publicity and many will send review copies for free.

SCHEDULING

Some blogging platforms allow you to schedule your posts. If so, write a batch of posts and schedule them to go live on different days.

KEY INGREDIENTS OF A POPULAR BLOG POST

- Substance: something really worth reading.
- A catchy headline.
- Great images.
- Subheadings and bullet points to break up the text.
- Good promotion of the post.

Shareable images

A really good shareable image to use on social media and Pinterest will help your blog post spread more quickly. Include the name of the blog post and the link to your blog in the image. Here are a few examples of the shareable images I have created for my posts.

BLOG READERS

Running your own blog means being involved in the blogging community. Most of us do not have the time to spend hours reading and commenting on other people's blogs and looking for trends, and this is where blog readers come in useful. They stream the latest updates from your favourite blogs into one place so that you do not need to hop from blog to blog – you just load one page and find all the updates there.

Blog readers are very useful when it comes to looking for content to share on social media. You can sort the blogs you follow into categories: separating business blogs from sewing blogs, and your customers' blogs from other blogs. Once split into categories, you should be able to easily find relevant posts on any topic you wish; which you can then use to help write your own blog posts.

See the links section on page 163 for some popular blog streaming programs you can use.

FEEDLY

I use the blog reader Feedly. Its magazine-style layout makes it feel like reading a big free craft periodical full of ideas and inspiration; and it also synchronizes with smartphones and tablets.

Attracting followers

Once your blog is live, encourage people to read it and – ideally – subscribe so that they see all your posts. Part of getting new followers is promotion. As with social media, when you set up a new account or blog you need to let both existing and potential customers know that it exists.

Enticement to click When promoting your blog post, make sure you include an enticement to click through to read the full post. Perhaps share a quote from the post, or ask a question and say 'to find out the answer, click here'.

Reach out You can reach existing customers through e-mail, social media, your site or face to face when they are in your shop. Using online advertising such as Facebook adverts or blog adverts on other relevant blogs is a good way to attract a new audience.

Interact Another great way to get followers is to interact with other blogs. Follow other craft blogs and interact on a regular basis. Read their posts and comment on their posts in a thoughtful, genuine way where you can. Share posts you enjoy on social media, and tag the blogger so they know you have done so. Interact with other bloggers on social media to start to build relationships. There is a really active craft blog community – get involved and you will start attracting people to your blog in no time at all.

Guest blog Guest blogging involves writing a blog post for another blog or website. In return, they credit you and include a link to your site. Ideally you want to use your best content for guest blog posts – if the post is brilliant, you are less likely to be turned down by the site to which you offer the content; and you want to impress people so that they click through to your website.

BECOMING A GUEST BLOGGER

When deciding where to guest blog, aim for blogs that are a little bigger than yours but have a similar target demographic. Ideally you want to build a relationship with the blogger in advance before approaching them to offer them the guest post. You can do this through interaction on their blog, on social media or by responding to their newsletters and by sharing their content.

When you approach them make sure you let them know the benefits for them, why you think their audience will enjoy your content and why they should give you space on their platform. Make the content as useful and engaging as possible, not self-promotional.

BUILDING A BLOG AUDIENCE

Tilly Walnes from Tilly and the Buttons (tillyandthebuttons.com), has been featured in **The Guardian** *and* **The New York Times,** *is the author of two dressmaking books and runs her own sewing pattern brand. Here are her tips on building an audience for your blog.*

- **Be niche** Be clear and very specific in choosing what your blog is about and who it is for, otherwise it will most likely drown in the vast ocean of the Internet. If you try to appeal to everyone, you are going to struggle to appeal to anyone. Decide who your niche target audience is, write your blog to speak to those people directly, and you are much more likely to develop a loyal following.

- **Be purposeful** It is tempting to write about whatever pops into your head that day, but it can make for a random-looking blog. Potential subscribers will have no idea what to expect in their inbox if they click 'follow' so probably will not risk it. Instead, work out the purpose of your blog, what you are trying to achieve with it, and develop content that reflects your objective. For example, Tilly and the Buttons aims to help and inspire young women to start making their own clothes, so I write posts with this mission in mind.

  Develop regular strands to make your blog more considered, and showcase previous posts in these strands on dedicated pages so that they do not get lost in your archives but instead can be read and re-read for years to come.

- **Be social** Blogging is about having a conversation, so get friendly with other bloggers, by chatting on Twitter, contributing to group blogs and blogging projects. Moreover, be social on your own blog too. Being social is not only about talking, it is also about listening, and people want to be heard – so ask your readers questions, have a discussion, and use their input to help you write your blog. This will make your blog much more engaging for everyone.

Encouraging interaction

The key to courting interaction is making sure people read your post. Use a catchy title to tempt people to click to read it, and promote it on your social media too. Include questions in the post to encourage responses in the comments. Writing engaging content will make people want to join in and comment. Giving a new twist or alternate view on something is likely to encourage debate. Take the time to respond to commenters so they know their comments are being read and are appreciated.

Consistency is critically important. Produce regular good quality content to keep people coming back for more. Try not to set impossible standards. Promising an in-depth blog post every day is something you may well come to regret. One really good post a week is better than writing five low-quality rushed posts.

It helps to do some advance planning and draw up an editorial calendar for your blog. This helps ensure you do not find yourself short of content, and you can plan a regular schedule of different types of post. Put aside a couple of hours a month to read through other blogs in your industry for inspiration, brainstorm post ideas for your own blog and then schedule them on your calendar. Schedule when they will go live (remember that most blogging sites allow you to schedule those posts to all go live at different times) and also when you plan to write them too. Many people find it quicker to write in batches, and setting aside some time means you can turn off all distractions like social media and really focus on your writing.

GIVE BACK

Leaving comments on other blogs encourages people to take the time to leave comments on yours too.

SERIES

A lot of bloggers run a regular series. Many bloggers take part in Wordless Wednesdays, for example, where their posts contain no words, only a photograph; the idea being that the image says it all.

CAPTCHAS, SPAM AND SECURITY

Dealing with spam is an unfortunate reality of running a blog. Captchas are one system of preventing spam. They generate random combinations of words and letters that readers have to type into a box before they can reply to a post.

Although they rule out computer-generated spam, they can put people off. I have found disallowing anonymous comments got rid of nearly all of the spam from my blog without requiring people to complete captchas.

USEFUL LINKS AND FURTHER READING

Social networks

Facebook: Facebook.com

Twitter: twitter.com

Pinterest: pinterest.com

YouTube: youtube.com

Vimeo: vimeo.com

Instagram: instagram.com

Flickr: flickr.com

LinkedIn: linkedin.com

Social networking tips

Instagram tips:
socialmediaexaminer.com/
instagram-for-business-tips

Advice for using Flickr: flickr.
com/bestpractices/

**10 ways to optimize your craft
business YouTube channel:**
http://bit.ly/2gMlanv

Comparison of Vimeo and YouTube:
blog.hootsuite.com/vimeo-vs-
youtube-business/

Grow a social media following:
impactbnd.com/blog/grow-
social-media-following

Facebook etiquette:
contemporaryhandmadealliance.
blogspot.co.uk/2011/07/
facebook-etiquette.html

Getting interaction on Facebook:
buildalittlebiz.com/blog/how-to-
get-more-interaction-on-your-
facebook-page.html

**Facebook's advice for
businesses:**
facebook.com/business

Pinterest marketing:
copyblogger.com/pinterest-
marketing

**How to use Twitter for
marketing:**
blog.hootsuite.com/twitter-
marketing

Guide to Instagram for bloggers:
blogtyrant.com/the-ultimate-
guide-to-instagram-for-bloggers

**How to embed a suggested
video on YouTube:**
youtube.com/watch?v=l0-
5rc6mvYk

**26 ways to use video for social
media marketing:**
socialmediaexaminer.com/26-
ways-to-use-video-for-your-
social-media-marketing

**How to use Instagram for
business:**
blog.hootsuite.com/how-to-use-
instagram-for-business

**How to shoot great videos on
your smartphone:**
bit.ly/2uxSN0l

**How to take good photos with
your phone:**
later.com/blog/how-to-take-
good-instagram-photo-with-
your-phone

**10 elements of a successful
social media profile:**
blog.kissmetrics.com/
successful-social-media-profile

**How to get tracking shots with a
tripod:** http://bit.ly/2vXMdTo

Social Media Management Apps

Hootsuite: hootsuite.com

TweetDeck: tweetdeck.twitter.com

Buffer: bufferapp.com

Viral Tag: viraltag.com

Viral Woot: viralwoot.com

Everypost: everypost.me

Blogging tips and advice

Useful social media tips:
everythingetsy.com/2013/02/10-
social-media-tips-to-make-you-
a-rock-star

Social media scheduling apps:
authormedia.com/how-to-put-
social-media-on-auto-pilot

Blogging platforms

blogger.com

wordpress.com

wordpress.org

tumblr.com

typepad.com

Blogging tips and advice

**Lots of useful blog related
advice:**
hernewleaf.com/primp-my-blog

10 great blog headlines:
visual.ly/10-blog-titles-drive-
massive-traffic

Many great craft blog tips:
ukcraftblog.
com/2011/09/blogging-tips-and-
tutorials-craft-blog.html

How to get more followers:
poppyloves.co.uk/2013/02/top-
tips-how-do-i-get-more-blog.
html

**Common blogging mistakes to
avoid:**
jeffbullas.com/2011/04/13/are-
you-making-these-20-mistakes-
on-your-blog

Ways to make money blogging:
problogger.net/moneymap

Blog readers

feedly.com

bloglovin.com

feeddemon.com

reederapp.com/ios (for Macs)

newsblur.com

netvibes.com

163

SELLING

ONLINE

THE ONLINE MARKETPLACE

Selling online is a good way to start a new business. It saves you the expensive overheads of a shop, removes any limit of a single geographical area, and you can fit the hours around the rest of your life. However, you do need a willingness to learn and a good USP to make you stand out from the many other online businesses. Selling online is not as simple as just setting up a website or shop and sitting back to wait for the orders to come in.

Before selling online, it helps to have or build a knowledge of search engine optimization (SEO) and online marketing. The ability to set up a simple site yourself will help keep costs down, and an understanding of web analytics will help you to grow your business. Photography skills and branding knowledge (see pages 76–83 for more information) will help your shop or site stand out.

Learning the ropes

When I started The Sewing Directory I knew nothing about online marketing, SEO or analytics, but was prepared to put in the time to learn. These areas are constantly evolving and it really helps to keep on top of trends.

My aim for this part of the book is to explain the basics, but I suggest following some of the websites and blogs in the useful links section (see pages 220–221) to keep up to date with any changes. This will help you to stay one step ahead of your competitors and make sure that you are using your time as efficiently as you can.

KEEPING UP TO DATE

It does not take a huge amount of time to keep up to date on SEO, analytics and online marketing. Putting aside an hour or so a week to read up on any changes will ensure that you can keep your site ranking well in the search engines and that you are not wasting time on something that will not return any benefits. I would much rather spend an hour a week than pay someone else to do it on my behalf.

Legal requirements for selling online

There is some legislation you need to be aware of when considering what to include on your site. Below is a brief summary of the UK legislation and rules you need to consider. Use the links on pages 72–73 to find the relevant requirements for other countries.

Distance selling regulations and e-commerce regulations

You must provide your customers with the following information:

- Your identity.

- Description and price of the goods being offered.

- Details of delivery and payment options.

- Full address. If you are trading from home you are obliged to give your home address.

- When they can expect to receive the goods.

- Information about your customer's cancellation rights.

- Your e-mail address and VAT number, if registered.

- A way to store or download your terms and conditions.

Sale of Goods Act

Under the UK Sale of Goods Act 1979, your products must:

- Match their description. Anything you say about the product (in advertising, on your site/shop) must be factually correct and not misleading.

- Be of satisfactory quality: free from any defects, safe to use and in good working order.

- Be fit for purpose.

Customers who have purchased online/by phone/by mail order can cancel up to seven days after they have received their goods, even if the product is not faulty. However, this does not apply to personalized or tailormade items. It is worth looking through the full details of this act to find out more about your customer's refund rights.

> ### LATEST RULES
>
> For more detailed or up-to-date information on any legal requirements for selling online in the UK, visit the Office of Fair Trading website (oft.gov.uk).

Privacy and Electronic Communications Regulations

These regulations cover a couple of different areas of which online sellers need to be aware.

Cookie law Site visitors must be notified if you use cookies (see page 169) on your site, be told what they are for and must give consent to their use. Many sites do this through the use of pop-ups, or by a clearly indicated cookies notice on their site. The cookie law is an EU directive, so it is only enforceable within the EU. However, despite this, many countries outside of the EU have also chosen to comply too.

Digital marketing You can only electronically market people who have consented to receive promotional communications from you. For example, by signing up to your newsletter or ticking a box to consent to future marketing when buying your products. The CAN-SPAM Act governs the rules for commercial e-mail in America. For the British rules, visit the Gov.uk website for more information.

Data Protection Act 1998

When handling your customers' data, you must ensure that you take measures to keep their information safe so that it cannot be used unlawfully. You must get consent to store customers' details and tell them how they will be used.

Companies Act 1985

If you have your own website and are a registered company, you must make sure that the company's registered address and the company number are included on your website.

Nominet

Nominet governs the registration of .uk domain names. It can suspend or cancel the domains of anyone who does not comply with their rules. The main rule to be aware of is that companies or individuals using their websites to trade cannot opt out from having their names and addresses published on the WHOIS database, but private individuals can. Find out more by visiting nominet.org.uk.

Online marketplaces

If you just want to get going, or are not sure if you want a website yet, you can try an online marketplace first, then build your own website at a later date. Online marketplaces are a good place to start when just starting out as you do not have big set-up costs or the time or hassle of designing your own website.

First steps: where to sell

Popular sites like Etsy and Folksy have a lot of advice and guides on how to use their sites. You can also find many 'off-site' guides to those selling platforms too. However, whichever one you choose, there will inevitably be a lot of competition from other users, so you need to be ready to compete against hundreds if not thousands of other craftspeople and creatives.

Smaller sites may have a lot less traffic but also have a lot less competition. Ideally it is worth listing your products with two or three different platforms (if allowed by their terms and conditions) and compare sales over a set number of months to see which works out best for you.

There are many smaller sites you can use to sell your handmade products, but the main online marketplaces for handmade businesses are listed below. The statistics noted are taken from their respective websites or press releases.

Etsy Etsy (etsy.com) is the biggest of these platforms and probably the best known too. It has hundreds of thousands of sellers all around the world, many of whom who run full-time businesses purely on Etsy. There is no denying Etsy gets a lot of traffic and makes a large amount of sales. According to data from digitalcommerce360.com, Etsy has more than one and a half million sellers and twenty-five million customers with total sales for the first quarter of 2016 totally over $629 million!

Since the company IPO'd – that is, made their shares public for the first time, in an Initial Public Offering – in 2015 and appointed a new chief executive officer in March 2017, there have been lots of changes happening. Keep an eye on their blog and forums for details of new changes being implemented. Unfortunately, Etsy's popularity means there will be a lot of competition for you. You need to put a lot of time into your SEO, your marketing and your product research to make sure you stand out amongst the other shops.

> ### ETSY ADVICE
> There are literally thousands of places you can get advice on selling on Etsy. On page 220, I have listed a few links to more information.

Folksy Folksy (folksy.com) is a UK-based equivalent to Etsy. Only UK residents are allowed to sell on Folksy, and as a result it is the most popular UK site for selling handmade gifts and supplies. As its tag line says, they are focused on 'Modern British Craft'. As of April 2018 there are more than 134,000 items for sale on Folksy and nearly four thousand sellers; combining to draw three and a half million page views per month. Folksy is significantly smaller than Etsy which means less competition but equally less traffic too.

Not On The High Street A more exclusive marketplace, Not On The High Street (notonthehighstreet.com) is not open to all sellers. Instead, it chooses what it considers to be the best creative small businesses to sell on its platform. It may approach you or you can submit an application to them. If accepted, you agree not to sell on any similar online marketplaces.

Not On The High Street gets two million unique online visitors per month and promotes the site on television as well as online and in print. The site itself is very visually appealing and has very good quality images. It charges a one-off joining fee rather than listing fees per product. Like Folksy, the site is currently limited to UK sellers, although at the time of writing it plans to expand to international sellers.

DaWanda DaWanda (dawanda.com) is a German platform which covers many European countries. The word means 'something extraordinary, unlike any other'. It is a large site with over 200,000 shops and around three million products. The website gets on average thirteen million visits per month.

Artfire Artfire (artfire.com) is a US-based site which charges a monthly fee for selling products. As of July 2017, there were over half a million products listed for sale on its site.

CHANGING COSTS

Selling costs for the sites shown here are subject to change. They all have their selling costs on their websites so just pop over to their sites and check out their 'sellers' sections or FAQs.

How to sell using an online marketplace

Once you have settled on which online marketplace(s) you want to use, how can you make sure that your shop and listings have a good chance of being found and how will your products stand out amongst the others?

Be unique A good way to compete against all the other shops is to offer something a little different. If you are the only person offering a particular item, you do not have to worry about the sale going to someone else, but if hundreds of shops offer an identical item, the buyer will often simply choose whoever is first in the search results. If your product is not completely unique, think of reasons why people should buy your product as opposed to one of the others, and include them in your product description. See the information on USPs on page 22–25 for further details.

Photography As discussed in the chapter on presentation (see pages 74–111), good photography will really make your products stand out. Use clear, bright photographs that show your products from several different angles, show the products in use and giving an indicator of size. Make the most of being able to upload several photographs per listing and do not just stick to the one shot. Remember that you can use editing software to enhance your photographs too.

Shop front Personalize your shop front. Use a banner with your branding and fill in your profile with your back story (use this as you would the 'about us' section on a website). Complete the welcome message with details of what you offer, any special offers or new products. If you have a blog, website or social media accounts, include details of these in your profile too so prospective customers can find out more about you. Use your shop title as a tag line, a chance to tell people about your business in a few words.

Get your pricing right On many marketplaces you are competing with hundreds, if not thousands, of other similar products. Trying to compete on price is a big mistake. People are often sceptical of cheap items and you will find there is always someone willing to undercut you. Read the pricing tips on pages 28–33 for more information.

Reviews Encourage customers to leave feedback. Having several positive reviews will allow people to see that you have sold many items and have lots of happy customers – always an encouraging thing to see when you are deciding from whom to buy.

Great customer service If people are very happy with your service not only are they likely to become repeat customers or leave a positive review, but they are more likely to spread the word and tell others about your shop.

> ### PLAY TO YOUR STRENGTHS
>
> One advantage you have over mass producers is that you are selling handmade products, so make sure the word 'handmade' appears several times in your shop.

> ### SELLING WHOLESALE
>
> Do not forget there are also online platforms which can help you to sell your products in wholesale quantities to shops and boutiques. The Indigo Fair (indigofair.com) or Hubba (hubba.com)

Get the right category There can be a lot of different categories to choose from, and on some platforms you are limited to just one. Again, getting into the mind of your buyer will help. Where would they look for your products? Try searching for similar products to yours and see where those sellers are listing their products.

Product title You are often limited to certain number of characters in your descriptions. So you need them to be concise, descriptive and contain your product keywords. Get into the mind of the buyer and think what they would type into the search box to find your product.

Product description Make the most of the description to tell people exactly what they are buying. List the dimensions of the product, what it is made from, what inspired you, how it can be used, which of your other products complement it and so on. Let people know if you are happy to customize the item, or make it in different colours/sizes. You can also use your product description for SEO benefits too (see page 186 for more information).

SEO Search engine optimization will help your products come up in more searches on the marketplace itself and also help search engines pick it up. This allows people off the online marketplace you are using to also find your products. Some more help on keywords can be found on page 188.

Social media Rather than depending on search engines or the online marketplace itself to send you customers, build up a following on social media and send people to your shop. Showcase your products, tell them more about you and build up brand recognition and loyalty. Use social media to promote your offers and new products. See pages 112–163 for more information.

Marketing Other ways to get your shop found include online marketing and advertising (see pages 208–213 for more information), handing out business cards with your shop link on at events, getting press coverage and cross-promoting with other businesses. Anything you can do to get your business name, and ideally shop link, out there will help send customers to your shop.

Keep learning Follow the blogs of the selling platforms you are using to keep up to date with any policy changes or tips for selling. If they have a discussion forum, you can often find useful advice there. Use the links sections on pages 220–221 to keep learning about SEO, marketing, photography and social media. As your skills grow so will the reach of your shop, leading to more sales.

> ### FIRST WORDS
> Only the first few words of your product title will show in search results, so make sure the most important words are at the start of your product title.

Setting up a website

Having a website – even if it is just a simple three- or four-page information site – makes you look more professional. Indeed, some businesses trade only on online marketplaces, or on Facebook, without having their own websites.

A website offers you control. If all the information about you and your business is on an external platform, you are at risk: that platform can decide to delete it, or can simply close down.

Domain names can be purchased cheaply, and free software can be used to design your site, so why leave yourself at the mercy of others when you could have a site you control yourself?

SEO FOR BEGINNERS

This advice is by Ruth Burr Reedy, Director of Strategy at Upbuild.io.

Whenever possible, build your website with SEO in mind. Often, businesses will design, build, and launch a website and only then call in someone to 'do SEO' to it. This usually means there is more SEO work to do and that changes will be harder and more expensive than if SEO was a consideration in the first place. Part of building your website to be SEO-friendly from the beginning is making sure you choose a content management system (CMS) or platform that allows you to make back-end changes to the website; it also means having someone on staff or under contract to make continuing changes to your site. Too many companies hire a 'one-and-done' developer to build their sites and end up stuck with a website that they cannot improve.

Think of the processes of getting inbound links to your site and getting social shares and likes of your content as one giant strategy. To that end, make sure it is easy to share your content on social networks, and start building your social followings so that when you have something really cool to share, you have people with which to share it. It is tempting to buy links or to resort to get-links-quick strategies like submitting to many online directories, but the best links are ones that will drive potential customers to your site, not merely links for links' sake. If you are outsourcing link building be wary of companies who promise a set number of links per month; instead, look for vendors that focus on stellar content creation, promotion and relationship building to get the right links.

If there is one area to invest in, it is content. Do not fall into the trap of thinking 'I work in a boring industry.' You have a lot to say. Investing in a long-term content strategy will ensure you have plenty of unique content that earns links (something search engines love) and gives you an opportunity to engage with your customers (something people love). It is the foundation of a good SEO campaign and helps you build your brand online.

Choosing your domain name

The first step of setting up your website is choosing and registering your domain name. Do this as soon as possible when setting up your business in order to make sure no one gets there before you. You do not need to use it straight away, once the domain is registered, you can sort out the hosting and web design at a later date when you are ready.

Your domain name should match your business name, if possible. This helps ensure there is no confusion when people look for you online. For instance I was able to register thesewingdirectory.co.uk for my business site. However it is not always that simple. The availability of a domain name may form an important part of your choice of business name – if your first choice has been registered, you might want to adapt or use a different form of your business name in order to ensure that both match.

When searching online, most people will try the business name and add the most common extensions to it (.com, .co.uk, .au or similar regional variant), but you can try more unusual domain extensions if those are already registered. Consider an extension like .net, .biz, .co, or .org.

You could try a descriptive name if your business name is not available. A business called Lisa's Bakery which specialises in cupcakes might try homemadecupcakes.co.uk or lisascupcakes.co.uk.

Some businesses hyphenate their name – sewing-directory.co.uk, for example. However, people often forget to add the hyphen, so if you take this approach, make sure your web domain is very clear on your marketing materials so people come to remember it has a hyphen in it.

Preventing confusion

If a competitor runs a website with a name similar to yours, there is a chance your customers may think it is you and order from them by mistake – or someone may intentionally register a similar name to benefit from your hard work.

There are a few ways to help prevent confusion for your customers and help protect your investment.

- If you take the option of a more unusual extension, check who owns the more common extension.

- If you choose a hyphenated name, check who has the name without the hyphen.

- Where possible, register any domains similar to your main domain so that no one else can. For instance I own: thesewingdirectory.co.uk, sewingdirectory.co.uk, thesewingdirectory.com, and thesewingdirectory.net.

ADAPTING THE NAME

You could shorten the name of your business for your domain name – I could have registered sewingdirectory.co.uk or even sewdirectory.co.uk if I had not been able to get my preferred choice.

Alternatively you can add to the name. My mum's business was called Make Do and Mend. Unfortunately, both makedoandmend.com and makedoandmend.co.uk were taken, so she added the word 'online' after the name.

If you have a physical shop, you could add the location to your domain, for instance makedoandmendcornwall.co.uk.

Hosting and creating your site

If you are skilled at coding, the best option is to design and build the website yourself. If this is not the case, there are a number of avenues available to you.

Free sites

Hosts such as Wix, Moonfruit and Weebly will provide you with a free website and hosting, usually in exchange for allowing them to place adverts on your site. They have a selection of templates for you to choose from, so you do not need any coding or web design skills. This means you can easily set up a simple site in an afternoon that includes a little bit of information about you and what you do, along with contact details and details of how to buy your products or retain your services.

Some free blogging software, like WordPress and Blogger, can also be used to design your business website. Again, these offer many templates, most of which are designed to look like blogs but there are some that look like websites.

There are a couple of downsides to this approach. Firstly, you may have adverts appear on your site, the content of which you have no control over. Secondly, the hosts tend to offer only a limited selection of templates which either cannot be edited or can have only limited changes made to them. As a result, your site will probably look similar to many others. However, if you have no budget, free sites are better than no website. There is nothing to stop you upgrading your website in the future as your budget grows.

Self-designed paid-for website

Services like Create.net, Mr Site and WordPress allow you to design a website yourself using either templates or easy-to-use software. These have a monthly or annual cost, and are a good compromise between free sites and paying a web designer to make a site for you. These sites are ideal if you do not have a large budget, or prefer to have total control over your website. Websites made with this method cost around £5–£10 ($7–$14) a month plus the cost of registering the domain, which is usually around £10 ($14) per year.

These sites give you much more freedom than free sites when it comes to design and personalization. Several offer free trials so you can play around with the software before committing any money. If you want to get technical, you can write or edit the HTML and CSS, but you can also use the more limited but more user-friendly design software many of these sites provide if you are not familiar with coding. If you do not have a knowledge of HTML you may find yourself limited in how much you can do with the site, so as with free hosting, your site could look very similar to others when using the supplied templates.

Most of these services are supported by users help forums, YouTube video guides and blogs dedicated to designing sites using their software. As a result, it is easy to work out how to get your website to do things like linking to your online shop on certain selling platforms, showcasing your products with scrolling galleries, or showing a stream of your social media updates.

MY EXPERIENCE

The Sewing Directory website uses a custom built CMS system, which required some training to get to grips with. I have also used Create.net, which has many simple to use templates so you can get up and running quickly; and Wordpress, which can be as simple or complicated as you choose to make it. Wordpress have templates readily available which you can customize, plug-ins which allow you to add extra functionality, and you can access the code so you can make changes that way if you prefer.

Instructing web designers

The third option is to pay a web designer to make your site for you. This is the approach I used for The Sewing Directory. I needed a fairly complex website and although I could easily make a template-based simple website I had no idea how to create databases (for the directory part of the site), how to create user accounts, or how to integrate payment systems. I got quotes from a few local web designers and met with my favourites to discuss what I wanted from the site, before deciding on which company to use.

If you will be having a site that will require regular updating, I would recommend asking for a site with a content management system (CMS) which allows you to update the content yourself. This means you do not have to pay the web designers for every little change you want to make, only for bigger structural changes. This usually costs a little more initially but saves you money in the long run if you plan to make regular changes. If you do not plan to make many changes in the future then you can normally get a basic site of three to five webpages (without a shop) made for you for around £100–£200 ($140–$340).

Using a web designer means you do not need to spend time creating the site yourself, and they should produce a high quality site. They will normally do the design for you too, if you have no idea how you want it to look. The downsides are the cost – mine cost several thousand pounds – and the fact that you need to refer back to them for big changes. Often this can mean waiting several days for changes to be made and having to pay quite a lot for the changes to be made instead of being able to do it yourself for free.

If you do not have the time to set up your own site, or you need a very complex site, using web designers is the route to take.

Activity: Plan your site

Think about, and write down, what you plan to have on your site. Will it be just text and some photos, or a full e-commerce shop with user accounts and databases?

Once you have made your decision, read about the website building sites (see the links section on pages 220–221) and look up some local web design companies and decide which option will be best for your website.

GO LOCAL

Using a web design company local to you will allow you to visit and talk face-to-face if there are any problems or you want to make changes to the site in the future. It is easy for someone to ignore your e-mails or telephone calls, not so much so when you are on their doorstep!

COMPLETE COST

When comparing web designers make sure you ask not only the initial cost of the site itself but the cost of hosting (if they will be hosting it). In addition, clarify the cost of updating and how long you should expect to wait for any changes to be made if you should need them in the future.

What should be on your site?

Once you have decided how you are going to go about building your site you need to figure out what will actually be on your site. This will then help when it comes to thinking about the layout of the site. There are a few essential sections that should be included on your site:

About us People love to find out more about who they are buying from. Including a back story and a photograph of yourself in this section of your site helps people to relate to you.

Contact details Not only do you legally have to have your contact details on your website but people are much more trusting of a site that has full contact details (including address and telephone number) than one that just has an e-mail address. It assures them that if there is a problem with their order, they have a number of ways to get hold of you.

Terms & conditions/privacy policy/cookie policy
This is covered in more detail on pages 168–169, under the legal requirements for selling online section, but your customers need to be aware of their rights. They want to know when to expect delivery of orders, how to complain if they have a problem, whether you are tracking them with cookies, and what you intend to do with their data amongst other details. You can either buy standard versions of these terms and conditions that you then customize to your own business, instruct a solicitor to write them for you, or you could write your own. If writing your own look at those on other similar sites to get an idea of what to include.

Newsletter/social media/blog Including highly visible links on your website to these different platforms will encourage people to follow you so that you can engage with them, tell them about your latest products and build a following for your brand.

Shop/how to book Your site should highlight how to buy your products or book your service. Even if you do not host your shop on your website, or your booking system, you need a clear tab on your site which can route them to the site where they can place their order.

Gallery or product details People like to see and read about your products or services. Small or unclear photographs along with poor, short descriptions could lead to a loss of sales, or a lot of enquiries from people wanting more information. If you can include testimonials or customer ratings, that can help people make a decision. Customer photographs are also a good idea, showing potential new customers how previous buyers have used your products or services.

Prices/postage Be up front about prices and postage. Visiting a website that does not show the price or cost of postage will put off a lot of buyers. You may not be able to confirm the price of one-off commissions, or bespoke services without the full details, but providing a guide price gives people an idea of whether they can afford it. It is annoying to fill out a whole quote form, and then wait for a reply when that product/service was always above what you could afford anyway; and even more annoying when the postage turns out to be prohibitively high after the customer has spent time browsing, setting up an account and placing their order. This breeds bad will.

SPAM REDUCTION

Putting your e-mail address as an image rather than text can help reduce spam. Spambots use text recognition software to harvest e-mail addresses to which to send spam mail. However, they cannot read addresses which are contained in images; while people can still read them easily. I wish I had known this a few years ago!

Blog/news section/other content An area where you can regularly add fresh content is very good for SEO (see pages 136–138) and can also bring customers back to your site on a regular basis. Some suggestions include: how-to guides, reference guides, technique guides, interviews, and details of forthcoming events, book or product reviews.

FAQs This stands for 'frequently asked questions'. You can save both yourself and your site visitors a lot of time if you put the answers to commonly-asked questions on your site. It will reduce the number of queries you get and allow the visitors to find out what they want to know quickly. Examples of FAQs you may want to include are: Do you post overseas? Do you offer personalization? Can I get one of your products made in a different colour? Do you make to order? Do you sell wholesale or give discounts on bulk orders? What is your refunds policy?

Activity: Organizing your site

Make a note of the sections you need to include on your website – both main sections and subcategories. This will help you build the skeleton of your site. For example:

Main category:

- Necklaces

Subcategories:

- Silver
- Aluminum
- Bead
- Semi-precious stones

WEB DESIGN TIPS

This advice is from Rebecca Kimber, managing director and CEO of Create.net.

Plan ahead! You would not open your high street shop without careful consideration around how you will be displaying your products, and a customer's journey. The same goes for when you are building your own online store.

Start by mapping the pages you will want to include on your website and how you want them to be linked. If you are not sure about what the pages will be, think about the content you want to display, then work on grouping similar information to be placed together on the website. This process will help you to form your pages and the links between them.

Designing your site

Following the activity on page 173, you should have a list of all the sections and subsections you want on your site. This list can be combined with the branding you want to use for your site and some high quality images to bring this together into your final site. The main thing your site design should consider is the end user. Your company's website should:

- Make it immediately obvious what it is that you do or sell, and how to order.

- Be easy for the end user to navigate and get straight to the bits they want. Most people expect to find the navigation options across the top or down the side of the page. If you put them in different places you risk confusing people who may just leave the site. The main categories from your list should be in the menu on the homepage.

- Present all the information a customer needs about your business, products and services. This should be easily visible on the homepage, able to be found within a few seconds. People do not like to click through several pages to get to what they want, so bear this in mind when designing your layout.

- Be full of good quality images to make your site visually appealing and break up the text.

- Be compatible with mobile phones. Many people now browse and buy on their smartphone or other mobile gadgets, so it is essential to make sure your website works just as well in a mobile browser as on a computer. Not being mobile compatible can also now affect your rankings in Google.

- Make it obvious what you want your customers to do once on your site. Your 'calls to action' (see page 196) need to stand out. If you want people to visit your shop, make sure the shop button is highly visible can be found in a couple of places. If your aim is to get readers to sign up to your newsletter, or follow you on social media, make sure you have a 'come and join us on Facebook/Twitter/Pinterest' message and that the social media icons stand out. Remind people what you want them to do. Do not give them too many options or they can get confused. Similarly, do not distract them with flashing gadgets, lots of moving pictures, or bright adverts which send them off your site.

- Be easy to share with their friends. Throughout your site you want to have social media share buttons, and 'pin it' buttons to encourage people to share your products and promote your site for you.

PRESENTING INFORMATION

Drop-down menus work well for presenting information. Rather than having to click from one section to another, a customer can hover the mouse over the area they want and choose from the drop-down.

FIRST IMPRESSIONS

Bear in mind that the top half of the page – referred to as 'above the fold' – is what people see without having to scroll down. There needs to be enough above the fold to tempt them to look at the rest of the page, or a call to action in the top part of the page.

Usability and site flow

Ensure your site loads quickly. This is useful from both a SEO point of view and to keep your visitors happy. If a page does not load within a couple of seconds most readers will tend to go elsewhere. Google Analytics can measure the speed of your site and make suggestions on how to speed it up.

Ensure your branding remains consistent throughout the site and make sure your logo is prominent on the home page, and ideally throughout the site. Aim to keep the site visually uncluttered: avoid having huge blocks of text, images and gadgets all over the place. It can be tempting to put as much information on a page as possible – especially your home page – but this can be overwhelming, leaving readers unsure where to click or what to do.

The Google homepage is the perfect example of good design. Almost the entire page is blank other than its logo and the search box in the middle. This tells people exactly what Google wants them to focus upon, using the search box.

A good design will direct people through certain pages of your site, so make sure those pages link together and send people to your desired destination. This 'site flow' is best explained through an example, see below.

GOOGLE ANALYTICS

See pages 200–201 for more about optimizing your website using Google Analytics.

SITE FLOW EXAMPLE

Assume you have a popular article on buying watercolour paintings on your site. This article gets a lot of Google traffic and social media referrals. You want readers of the article page to come and look at your paintings, so you need something to attract them to your gallery or shop. A big button saying 'browse my artwork here', or a revolving gallery of your paintings on the side of the page with the article on it will draw the eye and encourage a click through, while a simple link at the bottom of the page saying 'shop here' is much less likely to attract attention.

Once the reader is on the gallery or shop page, you want them to either order an existing painting, or to commission a new painting, so present just two clear options for them – buy or commission.

Once they have ordered you may want to encourage them to sign up to your newsletter, or follow you on social media, so have these options highlighted on your sales confirmation page. This will then give you the chance to sell them something else further down the line.

MAKING YOUR PRODUCTS STAND OUT

Tips from Harriet French, PR Executive at Not On The High Street (notonthehighstreet.com).

Photography The way you present your products is key to catching the customer's eye and encouraging them to make a purchase. Product images are hugely advantageous for improving your sales levels. Include as many images per product page as you can, and research simple but effective ways to brush up on your photography skills.

Product titles It is important to think about how you are positioning your products to customers. Product titles are vital in tempting the shopper to click through and see more – they are often the first things your customer will see. Keep product titles clear and concise but make sure they include vital or enticing words such as 'handmade' or 'personalized'. It is always safer to state the obvious than to choose a fancy product title.

Be savvy In order to stand out small businesses need to be very savvy to the ways of online marketing. At Not On The High Street we ask our businesses to make and source brilliant products that we know our customers want; the rest can be left up to us. If business owners also want to have a say in their own marketing, they should have a clear understanding of SEO, social media and the importance of photography and written copy.

Know your customer The customer may not always be right but they are at the heart of your entire business. In order for your business to succeed you need to know your customers well and to be on as good terms with them as you possibly can. The customer should be at the forefront of everything you do for your business – each and every decision should be made based on them. We have had a great experience with our customers; many seem almost as excited as we are to have discovered Not On The High Street. To this day, one of our favourite pastimes is sharing lovely customer comments around the office.

SECURE YOUR SITE

As of July 2018, Google's Chrome browser marks all non-https sites as 'not secure', so make sure you add a security certificate to your site.

Use of photographs

Your images will do the most to sell your products, so it is incredibly important to use great photographs of your goods in your design. Use a consistent background in your photographs as this will look good when images are displayed together on your site.

The photographs you take can also be used to convey more about your brand, so think carefully about how they should look and do not be afraid to try out different styles until you find what is right for your products.

Include photographs of your items from different angles too, and have these visible in a gallery or lightbox on your product pages. Give your customers the opportunity to see product detailing, close-ups and different angles, this will help them with their purchasing decision.

Space and colour

Sometimes less is more. Do not be afraid of a bit of space. By ensuring that your site is uncluttered and not too busy, you will ensure your photographs draw the eye to reflect the quality and uniqueness of your products. 'White space' is the term for empty space on your page – it does not literally have to be white, but can be your background colour or any other colour. Good use of white space makes your page more inviting and the information easier to read and digest.

Once you have decided on your brand's colour scheme, use it consistently throughout the site. Ask yourself how you want your customers to feel: calm and relaxed or alert and excited? Feed this through to the types of colours you use in your site design. Soft pastels will relax whereas bright colours will excite, for example. See pages 77–78 for more on the use of colour in your brand.

Your shop

If you are selling online, your shop will be a very important part of your website. It has to be very easy to navigate, so people can find what they want in the minimum amount of time. The use of clear categories and subsections will help, as will a text search box so people can type in what they are looking for.

- Consider categorizing your products to help people browse the products that interest them most. Many online fabric shops, for example, allow you to search their range by colour, by fabric type, by designer/manufacturer and by collection. Write a full keyword-rich product description for each item so that people can not only find your product through search engines but also when using the search box on your site.

- To encourage people to order more items, add a 'related products' section under your product image and description – if they are looking at a knitted hat, show them the matching scarf and gloves too. Amazon is the perfect example of a company that does this well with its 'customers who bought this also bought' section under the product details. I know I have certainly ended up ordering a few extra items when I look at them. An alternative or complementary option to this is the option of 'add-ons' at the cart stage.

- Make sure you have a good selection of high quality images of your products, as explained in chapter 3. Allow your customers to see the whole item and perhaps a lifestyle shot showing it in use too. Just remember for website use you do not want to be uploading high-resolution images as it will slow your page loading time. Make sure you compress them first.

- Consider your checkout process. Asking people to fill out several pages of information will probably lead to a high drop-off rate as customers grow impatient or annoyed. Keep it to the essentials: name, contact details, delivery address and payment details. Do not have any distractions which may make them click away from the cart and not complete the payment process.

- Make sure your postage cost is clearly visible before the checkout process, not just at the end. Be clear about where you will post to – I wanted to order from an Irish company a while back but nowhere on its site did it tell me if it shipped to the UK, so after reading through several pages of the site I gave up and went elsewhere. You could have a postage tab at the bottom of the site with these details, along with expected delivery times.

PAYMENT GATEWAYS

Using a well-known brand will help to create a sense of trust in your customers; this is important because many people are wary of internet fraud. I have put a few other payment processing options in the useful links section, but here are the most common.

- Paypal is one of the most recognized and trusted payment services. Easy to integrate into your site, Paypal allows people to pay using a special Paypal account, or using their credit or debit card.

- World Pay are another well known payment merchant, plus many of the banks have their own payments systems you can integrate into your site.

- For regular payments/direct debits Go Cardless is a good alternative to Paypal.

- Braintree is excellent if you are handling multiple currencies. It will allow you to accept over one hundred and thirty different currencies with no extra processing charges. It also has a recurring payment option and handles a lot of mobile transactions.

Payment options

Related to the shop is payment, and there are many different ways of processing payment, the most popular of which are explained in the payment gateways box on the opposite page. As with postage costs, it is useful to indicate before the end of the checkout what payment options you accept. You can do this by showing the logos of the cards or payment systems you accept or communicating these details at the very start of the payment process, not the end.

When weighing up the different payment gateways, consider the following:

- Fees: both monthly and/or per transaction.

- Ease of integration into your site.

- How well the gateway meets your needs. Can they process different currencies, or subscription payments, for example?

- Is there an option to use discount codes or reduce prices across the site when you want to run a promotion?

- If you want to take payments at shows and events, over the phone, or in a physical shop, check the gateway has mobile processing options.

- Support. Can you call someone if you need help? Are there help forums, useful FAQ sections? How quickly will they reply to an e-mail? Are they available out of hours?

If you are unsure of what to go for, ask around and see which payment options other people recommend, and if they have had problems with any of them. You could use market research questions (see pages 18–19) to ask your target market which payment methods they prefer to use; or try looking on craft forums or small business forums for advice.

Be creative!

Once you have figured out what will be on your site, how it will look, and what payment system you will be using, it is time to put it all together into your website design. Given that you run a creative business, be creative with your website too. Add quirky touches, buy illustrated social media buttons or design your own, avoid the standard commercial look website and make yours unique. The little touches are what will make your website stand out from all the others.

BEAUTIFUL BUTTONS

You can buy artist-made graphics, or buttons to add to your website on sites like Etsy or Creative Market.

Activity: Final checks and going live

Once you have made your site, check it in several different browsers to make sure it works properly in all of them. Ask your friends to check it over as they may spot something you have missed.

Once your website is live, submit it to Google using the following link:

google.com/submityourcontent

Search engine optimization

Search engine optimization, or SEO, is the practice of trying to get your site to rank well in search engines so that people can find and visit it.

SEO can seem very daunting when you first start looking into it, and can get really complex if you want. However, it is essentially based on common-sense principles, so you do not need to be technologically gifted to make sense of it.

Bear in mind that the search engines' goal is to make sure that people get the most relevant search results to their query. You will find that most of the factors they consider relate to that goal.

WHY GOOGLE?

This section focuses on Google because it is the number one search engine, with two-thirds of the search engine market. However, the principles are relevant to other search engines such as Bing and Yahoo.

GOOGLE

Google Search, commonly known simply as Google, is the most-used search engine in the world, with more than three billion searches a day. There are millions of websites on most subjects so in order to ensure the most relevant sites appear at the top of people's searches, Google has a system known as the 'Google algorithm'. Google does not reveal exactly how its algorithm calculates how it ranks pages, so the majority of what we know comes from hints and guidelines given by Google and from people finding out what works and what does not work.

Google is constantly adapting its algorithm to attempt to combat spammers, so quick fixes that fool the search engine now may not work in a year's time. The best advice that I can give is to concentrate on delivering what your customers want and not to focus on tricking Google to optimize your results in the short-term. Google measures various factors which tell them how much people like your website, so the more customer focused you are the more Google will see that people like your site and will rank it higher. Some of the main factors that Google and other search engines consider when ranking a page are summarized on the opposite page.

GOOGLE CHANGES

If you want to keep up to date with Google's latest updates and what the changes mean for you then keep an eye on this page: moz.com/google-algorithm-change.

Search engine strategy

SEO is not just one technique. Focusing on just one aspect will not reap the full benefits of SEO, and you risk losing everything if the search engines alter their method of measuring rankings. If you have a strategy that combines all four of the main points below, you should be relatively unaffected by any future changes to Google's algorithm.

Quality content Optimizing content for search engines does not mean ramming it with keywords, as this can compromise the information's usefulness and readability – its quality. Make your content unique and do not use content from elsewhere on the web. The more people like your content the more likely they are to link back to it, or to share it on social media. The content does not have to be written by you. Invite people to guest post on your site, or pay people to write for you if writing is not your strength. Base content around your keywords so that you attract the right kind of traffic with your content (see the Keywords activity on page 189 and content ideas on pages 132 and 156–158 for more on this).

Backlinks If your site is linked to from other well-ranking sites, Google considers your site to be important too. You can check your backlinks in Google Webmaster Tools (see pages 206–207). Offer to guest post or give people a reason to write about you: set competitions and offers or write interesting news and great content that people will want to share. Your backlinks should develop as organically (naturally) as possible, and also to build over time. Google can track when you have had a sudden unnatural increase in backlinks, so concentrate on building over time and not just putting your link everywhere you can find or paying for backlinks.

Social share Google places importance on the amount your content is shared socially. They see this as a sign that your site has quality content. Make it easy for people to share your content by adding share buttons to your site, using good quality images for people to pin to Pinterest and having your own social media accounts so followers can share your updates directly from your social media pages. Having good quality content or something of interest is more likely to lead to social shares, so this also links back to the quality content point above.

Regularity If your site is regularly updated, it shows search engines that the site is still active, kept up to date and worth them directing people to. Having a news section or blog on your site is an easy way to do this, but any section that you can regularly add new content into will help. This might be a projects section, articles section, special offer section, trends section, or a combination of these. Remember to go over your existing content from time to time and update that too. Re-promote older content as well as adding new content to drive a steady stream of traffic to both, indicating to Google that it is still relevant.

ANCHOR TEXT

Anchor text is the visible part of a clickable link to a site. It usually appears blue so you know it is a link. Google used to place importance on those words which contained the link, – if you had lots of sites linking back to you with the link embedded into the words 'quality glass beads', Google would assume that keyword is relevant to your site. Of course, before long people started manipulating this and paying for sites to link to them using specific anchor text. Since realizing this, Google has changed its algorithm; when it sees a site with lots of identical anchor text on its inbound links, it now disregards them.

Keywords

Keywords are the words or phrases that people are most likely to type into search engines when looking for your website, or the products you sell. Keywords are very important when it comes to SEO. They tell the search engines what your website is about and allow them to match your site to specific search queries. Focus on using the right keywords in your online marketplace, your site, your blog and social media too – in fact, anywhere that search engines can scan and index content.

People tend to use different words when looking for the same thing. People looking for sewing classes might type 'sewing workshops', 'sewing lessons', 'sewing tuition', 'sewing school', 'sewing teachers', 'sewing tutors', or 'sewing courses'. If you only use the keyword 'sewing classes' on your site you could miss people who are searching using the other terms.

The more specific your keywords, the less competition there will be on the search engines' results. For instance, if you type in 'sewing classes' to Google you get almost twenty-four million results! The more specific 'sewing classes Cardiff' has under 300,000 results so including the keyword 'Cardiff' in your site already improves the odds of your site being seen. The more specific you are, the fewer results: for 'beginner's dressmaking classes Cardiff' you are down to 24,000 results, 'beginner dressmaking classes Roath' (Roath is a district of Cardiff) gives you just over a thousand results. Geographical location is just one way of breaking down your keywords. Consider the materials you use, the style of your products or how your products are used to get more specific keywords.

LEARN FROM THE COMPETITION

Why not put some of your competitor's websites into the keyword tool to see if it gives any useful keywords for your own?

FURTHER READING

To learn more about keywords I recommend reading the following link: moz.com/blog/how-to-rank

HELP ON KEYWORDS

If you want more help on coming up with keywords for you site, sign up for a Google Adwords account (see page 221). You will then be able to take a look at the Google Keywords tool or one of the many other alternatives.

These tools allow you to generate similar keywords to one you suggest, or you can put in a website and it will generate keywords based upon the content of that site. Not only will it suggest keywords for you but it will tell you how many searches per month those keywords tend to get.

Activity: Identifying your keywords

Grab a notebook and write down the words that you think are important and relevant to your site and the products you sell or service you offer. These words will be your starting point. For example, if you run a sewing school in Cardiff called Stitched Up, write down words and phrases like: sewing, sewing school, learn to sew, sewing classes, Cardiff, Stitched Up and so on.

Refine your list

Go back to your list and think of alternative ways of saying each of the keywords. Write those alternate keywords below the initial keywords. Get other people to suggest refinements, as we all tend to use slightly different language.

Be more specific

Break your list down into more specific keywords. You should now have a long list with lots of keywords phrased in different ways, and broken right down to the specific terms you think your target customers will be using in search engines.

Check your analytics

If you already have Google Analytics or Webmaster Tools installed on your site, they can show you the keywords people are already using to find you site. You will probably want to add some of those to your list, too.

Incorporating keywords into your site

Once you have a list, incorporate these keywords into your site or shop. Your options include:

In the text Fit different keywords into your content, but make sure it sounds natural. Write for people, not search engines.

Page titles Give your page a relevant title, but try to keep it to the point so people can see at a glance what they will get.

Product titles or descriptions Again, use different keywords for each of these. If the product title is 'Bespoke red leather bag', use 'A unique handmade scarlet handbag made from leather, lined with Liberty fabric and closes with a magnetic clasp' for the description to avoid duplication.

Meta descriptions The meta description is a summary of your page that shows in search results and when people share on Facebook. Use these to encourage people to click through. Do not just leave them blank! Try to keep meta descriptions under one hundred and sixty characters, otherwise search engines will cut them down.

Headings and subheadings These are great for breaking up your text and making it more readable but also allow you to emphasise your keywords.

Image titles Never give your images generic names like 'image 1'. Give them relevant titles using your keywords so people find them when doing an image search. If you are using several images on a page, give each a slightly different title: it is the perfect chance to get alternate versions of your keywords in.

Image description Use different keywords or phrasing for the description and title of an image in order to get more alternate keywords in.

Link descriptions When you add a link into your text or to an image, you have to chance to describe that link. This is another chance to squeeze in more relevant keywords.

BE RELEVANT

When I started my site, I was confused to find I was getting lots of traffic for the word 'logo'. Eventually, I discovered the cause – when uploading company logos to my directory I had named the images with the company name followed by the word 'logo'. Having mentioned that word over one hundred times, Google presumed my site had a lot of information about logos!

Using keywords effectively

Meta tags are a way of adding keywords to your site. When adding new content or pages to your site, many sites will generate a keywords box. Keywords typed into that box show as meta tags on your site. You can also add keywords directly in your html. Due to people using adding large numbers of often unrelated keywords which they thought would help them rank well, Google declared in 2009 that meta tags would no longer make any difference to their ranking. As a result, do not waste time planning the perfect list of meta tags for your page. Instead, concentrate on having an enticing meta description which will encourage people to click through to your page when they spot you in search results.

On blogs this is slightly different; you have the option to add keywords to your blog post which can allow you to divide your posts into categories. This can be useful for helping people navigate your blog content when you have a lot of posts so I would continue to use these for that purpose even if it has no SEO benefit.

Focus on a few related keywords at a time and plan your content around them. Work through existing pages on your site to see if you can fit the keywords in anywhere. With that done, track how well you are ranking for the keywords using Google's Webmaster Tools (see pages 206–207). After a few months, pick another few keywords and repeat. This focused approach is much less overwhelming than trying to work with all your keywords at once. Remember: SEO is a long-term strategy. You do not have to do everything at in one go.

> ### LISTS
>
> Keep your list of keywords by your computer so you can refer to it when adding products to your shop, or content to your site. With the list in easy reach, you will likely be able to sneak a few keywords in to any addition to your site.

SOME INTERESTING SEO FACTS

A 2011 study by content promotion agency Slingshot SEO (slingshotseo.com) found that:

- 1st place in Google gets you 18.2 per cent of all click-through traffic.
- 2nd place gets you 10.1 per cent.
- 3rd Place gets you 7.2 per cent.
- 4th Place gets you 4.8 per cent.
- 5th place or lower gets you under 2 per cent.

The Search Engine Journal (searchenginejournal.com) found that:

- 75 per cent of users never go past the first page of search results.
- 70–80 per cent of users focus on the organic results, and ignore paid results completely.
- 65–70 per cent of internet searches are done through Google.
- Search engines are the number one source of traffic to content sites, sending more traffic than social media.

Content and SEO strategy

The main focus of your SEO strategy should be relevant content; if you have good content, people will find, share and link to it. If you use social media, guest posts, work with other sites or blogs to get the word out there, your content will be discovered more often and more quickly.

Content is the core of a long-term strategy. It takes time to build up and to be picked up by search engines and other people, but it does pay off. Once search engines recognize that you have good content on your site, any new content you add jumps up the rankings a lot more quickly.

Types of key content

The following types of content should help you attract plenty of visitors to your site or blog.

Evergreen posts These are posts that will always be popular and get lots of traffic. They are normally problem-solving posts or questions: How can I do X? Where can I find Y? How can I use Z? Evergreen posts can also be the kind that save people time. If you sell cloth and create a post with links to fifty great projects using linen, followers can go to your site and choose the project that sounds most like what they were searching for rather than trawling through hundreds of blogs or search engine results.

Evergreen posts are the sort most likely to be bookmarked or shared on social media. They save visitors time and make things easier for them, and you benefit by including keywords relevant to your business in those posts. Identify relevant subjects that people search for time and time again (use keyword tools to help with this). Do not think only in terms of current trends; what will people still be searching for in three, five or ten years' time?

Linkable assets Similar to evergreen posts, linkable assets are content that people want to link to. They will generate you a lot of natural back links over time. Unlike evergreen posts, they are not limited to being articles; they could be a video, a free download, a software program, or a free tool or e-course.

On-trend content This kind of content may not have long-term benefits but can be give short-term results. It can be related to a season or date: Christmas, or St. Valentine's day for example. While there is only a limited amount of time that these will be relevant, they can attract a lot of traffic in that time. Updating and re-promoting such posts the following year will pay dividends.

On-trend content can also be based upon current events, industry shows, a hot new product, or even a new television series.

Benefiting from your content

There is no point driving lots of traffic to your site and not informing or reminding visitors people what you actually do, sell or offer. It is important to link from your content to your end goal – to your shop if you are selling products, or to your workshop timetable if you teach. Add a sentence at the end saying 'if you liked this, try this product' or 'if you want to learn more about this, book onto one of our classes'. You may be able to squeeze this link into the article itself, or add a box or banner on the side or top of the page.

When writing content or creating something for your site, it may not be immediately apparent that it will become an evergreen post or linkable asset. Keep an eye on your analytics to see if anything is attracting a large amount of traffic, then make sure you keep it updated and promoted.

The key to event-led content is speed. Be ahead of everyone else. Get as much information as you can and post as soon as possible after the event. This gives you something to promote that people to look at immediately, but which can be clarified and updated when you have more time.

Be fast when writing about trends. If you know someone is bringing out an innovative product in your area, find out as much as possible and get a post live before it hits the shops. When people hear about the product and start searching for details, your post will be ready for them to find, and at that early stage it is likely to be one of the few posts from which to choose. A few months later you will probably find that others have written about the subject and you will have more competition for the front page of Google and other search engines, but you will have already benefitted from your prompt action.

When writing about trends, remember that you do not need to know everything. Even some basic details and some (properly flagged) speculation can form a good post. Let people know there is only limited information available but that you will update the post when more emerges. Follow manufacturers, wholesalers and distributors to keep on top of upcoming products and trends. Industry trade shows are also very good for this.

Activity: Generate ideas

Brainstorm and note down content ideas for your site. What customer queries could you resolve? What news could you tell everyone about? What ideas can you share? If you are at a loss for ideas, ask your customers what they want on your site.

Taking it further

Draw up an editorial calendar of content for the next year. Where possible, tie it in with seasonal or industry events.

Other factors to consider in your content

Site speed People like things to be fast when browsing the internet. When they click on a page they expect it to load quickly, so site speed is one of the factors Google take into account when ranking. In Webmaster Tools they will tell you how your site speed is doing and what you can do to speed it up. Images and gadgets can slow a site, so make sure you compress your images and that you do not overload your site with widgets/gadgets. If possible check your site loading speed before adding them, and again afterwards to see if it adversely affects your speed. Some types of adverts can slow or even crash sites so be careful with what you add to your site.

Bounce rate People can bounce – that is, leave your site after a few seconds without clicking to any other pages – for a variety of reasons. One can be because the content was not what they were looking for. If this is the case you may want to check you are using relevant keywords. Google can take a high bounce rate from traffic they have sent to you as an indicator that your site is not resolving the search query and push you down the rankings for those particular keywords. Google Webmaster Tools will show you how you rank for various keywords, so make sure they are relevant.

People may also bounce because they cannot make sense of your content or find it to be low quality. They can be put off by poor web design or slow loading speed. Check your bounce rate in Google Analytics and if it is high, assess your site with a critical eye. If you cannot work out why the rate is high, ask a few friends or other business people to take a look over it for you.

Internal linking Having lots of links between the various sections of your site helps search engines to index your content to ensure they discover all the content on there and not just some of it. A good way to do this is to include references and links to other articles on your site in the article you are currently writing; or, at the end of the post have something directing people to another part of your site, such as 'if you liked this why not look at our projects section' or 'find our latest news and offers here'. This also helps your site visitors to discover other parts of your site too.

The copywriting site Copyblogger is a great example of good internal linking. If you read any of its articles, you will find embedded links to many of their other articles, products or services. It is hard to just read one page of the Copyblogger site as you find yourself clicking through to many others.

HOW TO USE CONTENT STRATEGY TO YOUR BUSINESS ADVANTAGE

Shae Baxter (shaebaxter. com) provides entrepreneurs and bloggers with proven practical strategies to generate more search engine traffic so they can grow their business.

Great content is created for a specific purpose. You need to define what this purpose is. Do you want to create content to boost brand awareness, get more e-mail subscribers, generate leads, attract new and past customers, or improve your search ranking? Or is it something else altogether? I work with clients to create a content strategy that achieves one main purpose: To position you as an expert and an authority.

When you have positioning in your market, you can virtually do anything. Therefore, the primary goal of your content strategy should be centred on positioning you as the expert authority in your niche. Once you have defined your goal and purpose, build your content strategy around the three main stages of the buyer's journey to create a deeper and more meaningful relationship with your market.

Stage one: Awareness

The stage is also known as the 'top-of-funnel' stage. This is your cold market and content at the top of the 'funnel' is used to educate prospects and build and spread awareness. People at this stage have little-to-no intent to buy or purchase – they may not even be aware they have a problem or need. It is your job to make them aware that there is a problem and that you or your business has a solution. For example, people might search for 'knitting ribbing tips', 'how to knit', or 'how do you knit a garner stitch'.

Stage two: Information

Also known as the evaluation stage, or middle-of-funnel. This is the stage where people evaluate potential solutions to a problem. Purchase intent is clear, but not imminent and the person is often still in research mode. This means that people are evaluating the choices or options available to them and trying to determine what course of action to take to solve their particular problem. For example, 'top rated knitting needles', 'best knitting needles' or 'interchangeable knitting needles comparison'.

Stage three: Action

The action stage, also called the bottom-of-funnel. When people progress to this stage, they are ready to act and the goal here is to convert those leads into buyers. In other words, people here have often have immediate buying intent. People may search for 'buy knitting needles online', 'knitting needles for sale', or 'what size knitting needles for a baby blanket.'

You cannot move a prospect into the action phase until after they have become aware of the problem and evaluate potential solutions and possible courses of action.

In his book, *The Ultimate Sales Machine*, Chet Holmes reveals that his research has shown him that only three per cent of people are actively buying now; and seven per cent of the population are open to the idea of buying. The remaining ninety per cent fall into one of three equal categories:

- One third are not thinking about it
- One third do not think they are interested
- One third know they are not interested

This means that about ninety per cent of your market is in the Awareness or top of funnel stage. In other words, most people do not know you exist or that they have a problem.

Despite this, most content and marketing material is created only for the buyers (three per cent). This means you are only appealing to a tiny sliver of your market that already know you exist or are aware of your products or services. If you only market to those that are already looking for, you miss out on opportunities to reach those early in the buyer's journey. A solid content strategy will produce content that appeals to your entire market across all stages of the buyer's journey.

GUEST POSTING

Matt Cutts, head of Google web spam, confirmed in January 2014 that guest blogging as a strategy to get more backlinks and help improve your rankings will not work (source: mattcutts.com/blog/guest-blogging). Once again, it is an area that has been abused by spammers to the point that Google is now having to stop using it in its ranking algorithm.

However, that is not to say that you should not guest post. Guest posting is a great marketing strategy because it can help introduce you and your brand to a whole new range of potential customers or followers. So keep it in your marketing plan but do not expect any SEO benefits from it.

Concentrate on making your content as good as you can. As Matt Cutts put it: 'Try and make a site so that is so fantastic that you become an authority in your niche'.

A CALL TO ACTION

A call to action is a prompt towards the action you want your site visitors or social media followers to take. It is a way of reminding people what you want them to do – whether that is placing an order, attending an event, or joining your newsletter.

The example below shows a call to action on my website – the grey button with a link to sign up to my newsletter (highlighted).

TIPS ON REPURPOSING CONTENT FROM BRITNEY MULLER

Britney Muller is SEO & Content Architect at Moz. A graduate from the University of Minnesota, Britney taught herself how to program and manipulate search results in her spare time and founded Pryde Marketing in 2012.

Repurposing content is key for Craft Business SEO! Someone who makes custom necklaces can record video on how they create them, and host that video on their website for around three months, using services like Wistia (wistea.com) or Vimeo (vimeo.com).

Avoid the temptation to put your video on YouTube immediately, because that would be giving YouTube.com the authority without owning it on your own website first. After three months of the video being up on your site, put it on YouTube to get the extra visibility.

Make sure to put plenty of thought into the title and thumbnail image: research which DIY necklace video titles and thumbnails currently rank highly. You can save screenshots of your video for images, though make sure to compress them before uploading them to your website to help keep your website fast. You can use services like Optimizilla (optimizilla.com) to compress images.

Taking screenshots of important stages of the video will also allow you to write a 'How To' blog post complete with step-by-step images. Your 'How-To' post can then be refurbished for other websites like; instructables.com, eHow. com, craftsy.com, hometalk.com, and pinterest.com. Make sure to include a link back to your original post.

These external links will not only help send traffic to your website, but they also tell search engines that you are indeed a credible, trusted resource on the internet and when done properly, you will see an increase in organic traffic.

Analysing your site

This section explains how to use Google Analytics and Webmaster Tools to help measure the performance of your site, your online advertising, social media campaigns and SEO efforts. It is important to keep track of whether these efforts are paying off – if not you need to re-think your strategy or focus elsewhere.

Google provides free and very useful tools that help measure traffic to your site and how you are doing in terms of SEO. There are of course other analytics providers (see the links section for more) but the two I cover here are widely used and free, which is always good for a small business. Just to warn you, checking your site's stats can be addictive!

You need a free Google account to register Analytics and Webmaster Tools, but both are fairly simple to set up. Both tools generate a line of code which you need to insert into your website to prove you own the site. Once inserted, the program will start to track traffic to your site. You can register multiple websites at no charge. You can also add other team members or your web company to the account so they can also view your stats.

The fastest way to learn how to use these programs is to click through the different links and see what information it brings up. Do not be afraid to explore the different options and experiment – you will find useful new information all the time.

Google frequently change the layout and labelling of the data in Analytics and Webmaster Tools. Therefore, you may not find things in the exact places I have indicated, as it might have moved or been relabelled by time of publication. Currently, however, you will find the various navigation options on the left hand side of your page. Do not be scared to explore them even if you are not sure what they mean at first – constant exploration and experimentation while help you to discover new things – I do all the time from doing this.

Google do provide free online training for using their analytics software, visit analytics.google.com/analytics/academy to sign up to one of their courses.

OTHER ANALYTICS

Sites like Facebook and Pinterest have their own analytics that give more precise stats for interactions with your accounts. To access the Pinterest analytics you need a business account. You can convert a personal account into a business account in the account settings.

USEFUL TERMS

Bounce rate The number of people that visit just one page of your site, then leave.

Conversion rate The number of people that complete a goal you specify, such as purchasing from your site, viewing certain pages or signing up to your newsletter.

CTR This stands for 'click through ratio', which is the percentage of people seeing your site in search results (or viewing your adverts) that go on to visit your site.

Direct traffic Visitors who typed your web address (URL) into their browser taskbar and went straight to your website – i.e. people who already knew your web address.

Impressions Impressions are the number of times something (such as a webpage or advert) is seen by viewers. For example, an advert may have one hundred impressions and eighteen click-throughs; which means that only eighteen of the one hundred people that saw it clicked on it (an eighteen per cent CTR).

Landing page The first page people see when they visit your site – the page they 'land' on. Note that this is not always your homepage.

Referral traffic Traffic sent to you from other websites. This could be due to online adverts, guest posting or someone writing about you on their site or blog.

Organic search The number of people finding your site through search engines such as Google or Bing.

Social referrals People who come to your site from social media platforms like Facebook, Twitter and Pinterest. These visitors include those referred from your own social media accounts along with those referred by others who have posted links to your site on these platforms.

Traffic sources Where the visitors to your site are coming from.

Unique visitors or page views Some people will visit your website more than once, or view a page more than once on your site. The 'unique' figure counts visitors to the site only once, not once per visit or view.

Sessions The number of visits to your site in a set period. However, this is not the same as unique visitors, as a single person may visit your site several times. This would create multiple sessions in your stats, but count as only one unique visitor.

Google Analytics

To set up Google Analytics, visit google.co.uk/analytics and follow the instructions to set up your account. This service can tell you many useful things, including the following:

- Exactly how many sessions you have had per day.

- Where the visits came from, including how many from search engines and how many from referring sites.

- What content is most and least popular on your site.

- Which search engines people used to find your site, along with what keywords those people used.

- What browsers your visitors are using so you can ensure your site is compatible with those browsers.

- Your bounce rate: how many visitors look at only one page of your site, then leave.

- What percentage of visitors convert, i.e. complete an action you specify, such as purchasing a product.

Keeping a close eye on Google Analytics' statistics for your site will make you aware of any potential problems as soon as they start, and help you measure any successes accurately. If you do something that leads to a huge surge in traffic, you want to know as soon as possible so you can quantify and replicate that success. Equally, if you do something that causes your traffic to plummet, the sooner you know, the sooner you can resolve it to get your traffic back to normal levels.

Google Analytics is a powerful tool that can help you with many aspects of your business, including helping you identify and track which areas of your business are best for you to invest your time and money. If you are spending hundreds of pounds in advertising, for example, you want to be able to track the response you are getting in order to check it is a worthwhile investment. If you are spending large blocks of time writing content for your site, the statistics can show you the traffic the content is attracting, and the results of the visits. If you are considering investing in a mobile site, it will allow you check that your site visitors do actually view it on mobile devices.

SAVE AND EXPORT

You can save and export any of the reports in Google Analytics by using either the share or export options on the top right.

MY EXPERIENCE

I use Google Analytics to make sure I am advertising in the right places online, and getting my money's worth. I also use it to make sure my social media, SEO and content marketing strategies are paying off. From looking at the statistics for my site I can see what is and what is not working, and where to concentrate my efforts to increase my levels of traffic.

SHORTCUTS

If there are data sets you find yourself checking regularly in Google Analytics, you can create a shortcut to go straight to them. When viewing the report click on the 'save' button on the top right and give it a name. The shortcuts can be found under the customization tab on the menu to the left.

Site traffic

When you view your Google Analytics data, you are presented with a dashboard of the information that Google thinks is most useful to you. This varies between updates, but at the time of writing, the dashboard includes number of sessions, number of unique visitors, how you acquired your site visitors, the time of day they tend to visit, what pages they look at, where in the world they are located and what device they are using.

On the bottom left of each box of data, it tells you the time period the data covers (eg. '7 days', '1 month'). You can click on that to change the data period. To the bottom right is the option to view the full data. When viewing a full data report you will notice there is a date box in the top right which allows you to change the date period.

Under the date box there is a tick box to compare the dates with another date period. You can use this to see how your traffic is improving over time. Keeping an eye on the amount of traffic you get to your site can be useful to help see the following:

- Whether your SEO efforts are improving your traffic.

- Whether adverts you have are generating traffic.

- What social media activity increases your traffic.

- Which content you have added is bringing new visitors.

- Peaks and troughs in your traffic.

Activity: Looking for patterns

Look at your website stats for the last year (or the last few weeks if you have not had Analytics running for long) and look for any pattern in your peaks and troughs. Write down the day of the week that tends gets the most traffic, and the day of the week that gets the least traffic in your notebook.

Try to identify any reasons that these days are busy or quiet. If the reasons are something within your control – for instance, if Monday is always busy because you add new products that day, or weekends are always quiet because you do not do any social media updates at weekends – plan to try to increase your traffic on the lower-traffic days. Some examples for achieving this are below:

- If you do not update at weekends because you are not working, consider prescheduling your weekend updates.
- Space out adding new content over a few days, rather than in one big update.
- Run a special offer on the quieter days to increase traffic.

It is important to realize that some things are out of our control. If your traffic drops at weekends because people are not at their computers, there is not much you can do about that. Rather than trying to increase your traffic on those days, save your content for the weekdays when more people will spot it.

Acquisition

The 'acquisition' tab on the Google Analytics menu (on the left of the site) contains information on how people found your site. The 'overview' option in the submenu will bring up a summary and tell you about visitors' behaviour and conversion rate. This is split by traffic source, so you can find how long visitors from a particular source stayed on the site, how many pages they looked at, and the bounce rate.

This lets you see if certain sources attract better quality traffic than others. Site visitors who spend time or purchase something from your site are good quality traffic; those that just read one page and then leave are not. This information can help you prioritize. For example, If you spot that visitors who come via your newsletter tend to place double the number of orders than visitors from other sources, focus your efforts on getting more newsletter sign-ups. If visitors from Pinterest have a very high bounce rate and low order rate, you need to either re-think your Pinterest strategy or spend less time on there.

Clicking on 'organic search' where it shows you the list of traffic referrers to your site will reveal a list of the top ten keywords used in searches to find your site. Click on the arrows in the bottom right corner to see other keywords that people used to find you, then compare the results to your keyword list that you generated earlier (see page 189) to see which keywords are proving effective.

To get more information on the keywords that bring traffic to your site, log into Google Webmaster tools where you will be able to see:

- **Impressions** How many times your site appeared in search results viewed by a user.

- **Clicks** How many people using that keyword in a search clicked through to your website.

- **Average position** Where you ranked in Google for a particular keyword.

- **CTR** This is the click-through rate – the number of people who saw your site link in their search results and clicked through to visit.

Selecting any of these headers allows you to sort the results based upon that metric. Clicking on 'average position' will allow you to see your rank in Google for those keywords, for example.

In Google Analytics, you can click on 'Referrals' to see which websites are sending traffic through to you; and thus at your traffic sources. This will not show social media referrals, as those are counted separately. Referrals can help you assess the effectiveness of online advertising you are running, guest posts you have written, and which sites – some you may not have heard about – have written about you. Click on the site name to see a breakdown of the specific pages they have linked to you from. If you click the double grey rectangle symbol next to the page link, it will open that page in a new screen so you can read what has

PROTECTED KEYWORDS

The phrase 'keyword not provided' is common. Search keywords are protected while logged into a Google account, so data from people using one is not provided in the stats.

been said about your business/site. It is nice to leave a comment thanking people for featuring your site in their content. Another good section worth looking at in the referral traffic data is the social media one. Click on the words 'social' and you will find details of which social media platforms are sending you traffic, how much traffic, how long they stayed on site and how many pages they looked at. This can help you plan your social media strategy.

Activity: Checking sources

Check through the top thirty referral sources in the last month. If there are any sources you were not expecting, visit those sites and blogs to see how people got from their site to yours. You may find people have written a nice blog post about you, or recommended you in their links section. If so, leave a comment or drop them an e-mail to thank them for it.

Behaviour

The 'behaviour' tab shows you how people act once they are on your site. Click on the overview tab to get the summary of this information including page views, average time spent per page and bounce rate. You also get a list of the top ten most popular pages on your site in that period. You will normally find one that just says '/'. This signifies your home page.

On the bottom right of the page you can click 'view full report' to see the full list of content viewed on your site in order of popularity. Clicking any of the content page names will show you a breakdown of how many clicks it got per day. You can also find out which sources sent traffic to that page. If you want to see how many people have looked at a particular page of your site, use the search box to the top right of the list to type in the page name to bring it up.

Just under the graph to the left, there is an option that says 'secondary dimension'. This allows you to break the data down further. Selecting 'acquisition' and then 'source' in that menu will show you where the traffic to that particular page originated. There are plenty of other options there to play round with too to get even more detailed data. Getting as much information as possible about your site visitors will help you attract more.

If you click the 'Landing Pages' or 'Exit Pages' options on the left-hand side, under the behaviour heading, you will be able to see where people enter your website and where they leave. Where they are coming from helps to show you which parts of your content is popular and attracting site visitors. Pay close attention to the exit pages and think about whether you could change them to keep people on your site for longer rather than making them leave.

SITE SPEED

The 'behaviour' tab also gives information about site speed and help to identify ways to improve your site speed.

Audience

The 'audience' tab tells you more about your visitors – which countries they are from, what age and gender they are, what browsers they are using, and more. A few things worth looking at under this tab are:

Browsers Seeing which are the audience's most popular browsers will allow you to make sure your website works as it should in them. You can find this under the 'technology' subheading.

Mobile If many of your visitors use smartphones or tablets to view your site, be sure that your site works well on these devices.

Demographics This details the age and gender of your visitors. Aim your content appropriately and appeal to your target audience.

Geo Use this to see where your visitors are based geographically. Click on a country to break it down further by region or city.

The information in this tab can help you ensure you are reaching the correct audience with your marketing and SEO efforts. It is worth cross-referencing this with the notes you made on your ideal customer (see page 16) to see if your customer base is what you expected it to be. The results may surprise you.

Conversions

The 'conversions' tab helps you set goals. Using the goal setting function in Google Analytics allows you to check if visitors to your site are doing what you want them to do, which shows you whether your site is fulfilling its purpose.

For instance if you want to track how many people spend money on your site you can create a goal to measure that. If you want your visitors to sign up to your newsletter, or visit a particular page of your website you can set goals to record how many people do so.

GEO

The Geo information is particularly useful if you have just done an event or advertising in a particular location and want to see if people are looking you up there as a result.

USING YOUR EVERGREENS

Most websites have a few 'evergreen' pages – those that, like evergreen content (see page 192), continually attracts steady amounts of traffic. When you identify your evergreen posts, make sure you update them every now and then. Keep building on them and putting more information in them and they will keep attracting good amounts of traffic.

Make sure your call to action (see page 196) is included on each of these reliable pages to remind people what you want them to do while on your site. You do not want them to simply read one post and then leave your site again.

The four types of goals you can set are as follows:

Destination goals Getting people to visit a particular part of your site, such as the 'transaction complete' screen which would show they have placed an order.

Duration goals Measuring visits which last for or exceed a particular period of time. Visitors staying on your site for more than five minutes, for example.

Pages/screen goals Tracking how many visitors look at a particular number of pages or screens. For example, if a visitor views eight pages (or the number you choose) on your site, this type of goal is recorded as completed.

Event goals This is completed when a visitor performs a specific action such as clicking on an advert or a social share button.

Bear in mind that you do not have to have a shop on your site to set goals. Even if you do not sell any products on your site, you can track particular content on the site that you want people to view.

Using this tab, you can specify the web address (URL) that you want to track and you can see not only how many people visited that page, but what their route through the site was, which pages fed traffic into your goal page, and where the visitors went after that. You can use this information to try to refine your site flow, as described on page 181.

USING GOOGLE ANALYTICS

The best place to get information on how to set goals and track e-commerce is in the Google Analytics help section (support. google.com/analytics), which walks you through the practical side step by step, so I will not repeat it here.

Activity: Increasing traffic

Scroll to the end of your popular content list in Google Analytics and find your site's least popular pages. Ignoring pages which concern a particular event in the past (it is obvious why these are no longer popular!), write down a list of the ten least popular pages in your notebook, along with the number of hits they had last month. Identify why these pages do not get much traffic. Are they old articles you have not re-promoted since writing? Are they for products you no longer sell? Are they not properly linked into the rest of your site?

Next to each of those pages, make notes about ways you can increase the traffic to those pages. Can you post a link on Facebook or Twitter? Could you pin some of the images from those pages onto Pinterest? Could you update them so they are more relevant, then re-promote them? Could you link to those pages from other pages on your site?

Over the next few weeks, work your way through the ten pages and do what you can to increase traffic to each. Repeat this activity on a regular cycle to help drive traffic to the less popular parts of your site.

Google Webmaster Tools

Google Webmaster Tools helps you understand how Google views your site. To set up Webmaster Tools, visit google.com/webmasters. These tools can tell you:

- The number of clicks you are getting for certain search queries.

- If you are violating Google's policies on spam.

- If there are broken links on your site or pages that do not load.

- The number of impressions and what your average position is in Google for those keywords.

- Incoming site links – i.e. who is linking to your site.

- You can also use the Webmaster Academy, which gives lots of useful SEO information.

In contrast to the data from Google Analytics, which are focused on who is coming to your website, how they found it and what they are looking at, Webmaster Tools is more focused on how your site is perceived by Google, from the point of view of a search engine.

A lot of the data from Webmaster Tools can also be found in Analytics but personally I still prefer to keep both running as there is a lot of useful information you get from them separately. Do not be scared to take a good look through these free resources and learn where to find the information you need to help improve your website.

Main tabs

In Google Webmaster Tools, the navigation bar is on the left-hand side. The main menu tabs give you the following information:

Messages This is where Google will notify you of any problems with your site such as it being down when they tried to crawl it, your site suffering a spam penalty or being hacked. Keep an eye on these messages!

Search appearance How your site appears in the search engine. This section includes alerts about things like duplicated meta tags or titles, or content that cannot be indexed.

FETCH AS GOOGLE

'Fetch as Google' is a very useful tool in the Google index section of Webmaster Tools. The tool allows you to give Google a link and ask it to crawl that page. Once it has successfully done that, it will ask if you want to submit it to Google's index, which makes it far more likely to appear in search results.

This is a huge bonus for time-sensitive content, which you want Google to find as soon as possible. This tool will get it indexed straight away so people can find it. It can also be very useful when you first launch your new website and want to make sure it starts appearing in Google straight away.

TIMELY POSTS

I used Fetch as Google for all of my 'Supplies from The Sewing Bee' posts that I put live straight after the show (see page 192). It is the kind of thing people would be searching immediately and not so much a few weeks or months down the line.

Google index This shows the total number of pages indexed from your site. This number should correspond with the number of pages on your site. If it does not, it may mean you have not linked your content into the rest of the site so Google can find it, or you may have recently added pages which have not yet been indexed. If you want them to be indexed quicker use the 'Fetch as Google' tool (see the box on the opposite page).

Search traffic This tab has useful statistics including 'search queries', which shows where you rank for various keywords, how many impressions you get in search engines for those terms, and what CTR you get. This section also shows you all the links to your site, where they come from and who links to you the most, as well as your most linked-to content. The 'manual actions' tab in this section is where Google will let you know of any spam actions taken against your site, why they were taken and what you can do about it.

Crawl The crawl section will let you know if Google is having any problems crawling your site, if there are any pages which are no longer found or pages that cannot be accessed. This can be useful to see if you have accidentally taken a page offline or password protected something unintentionally.

INTERCONNECTING YOUR SITE

Associated articles and pages strengthen the authority of an already-popular page as Google identifies your site as having more than one page using those keywords.

As a result, your site as a whole will be considered more of an authority on the subject – in the example below, birthstones.

Activity: Increasing your popular content

Identify and analyse your most popular pages using Google's tools. Do you spot a trend? Are projects very popular? Is it a particular type of product? Once you know what is popular you can produce more related content elsewhere on your site to increase good quality traffic. You can also make sure you use those pages to link through to the areas where you want to direct more traffic.

If the popular content is a product, consider:

- Producing variations on that product.
- Writing an informational guide about that product.

Assume you sell jewellery, and you identify that birthstone necklaces are very popular on your site. You could add a guide to birthstones; telling people which stones are for which months, explaining the history of the tradition of birthstones in jewellery, and detailing how different counties use different birthstones for different months. When writing the article, include the word 'birthstones' and associated keywords where possible without making the text seem unnatural.

If you also sell birthstone rings then make sure you include a mention and link to them on that popular page to help direct traffic through to other parts of your site which will hopefully lead to sales.

Online advertising

Social media, which we looked at in more detail in chapter four, is an important way of promoting yourself online, but there are many other ways. Some are paid for – such as Google Adwords or Facebook adverts – and others are free, such as getting press coverage on a website for local or industry news.

However, it is important to track the results of any advertising and promotion that you do, whether you are paying or not. If you are giving out free products in exchange for a mention on a website, for instance, you want to be able to see you are getting results from it, otherwise you are giving something away for nothing. Even if all your are investing is time, you still want to know that it is worthwhile.

You may want to sell advertising space on your site to generate some extra income. There is information on this in this section as well.

ADVERTISING AND PROMOTION

Advertising and promotion both have the same goal, increasing the awareness of your business and ultimately bringing you more sales. However, they are different concepts, and an understanding of this is necessary to get the most from both.

Advertising

Advertising usually takes the form of a set format which will appear in a specified place for a fixed period. You tend to pay a fixed price up front and know that your advert will run for a certain period of time. Advertising includes press adverts, television/radio adverts, online adverts on blogs and websites, and advertorials in magazines.

Promotion

Promotion is a more fluid concept; it is a variety of methods for making people aware of your business. Promotion includes articles in magazines or newspapers, online blog or news posts about your business, giveaways, listings with online directories, social media business pages/accounts, flyers, product demonstrations and samples. It encompasses any way you can think of that gets your business name out there.

Where to advertise?

Advertising – of any kind – can be expensive, so you want to make sure you are putting your money where it will give you the best results. Unfortunately there is no set list of places that guarantee you will get brilliant results; this depends upon the nature of your business, where your customers spend time and the actual adverts you use.

Google Adwords

Google Adwords is a paid-for service that places advertising copy above or to the side of the organic search results. Many online shops do well with Google Adwords, as they can target the precise names of the products they stock, so that when people are looking for those terms they will see their shop.

However there can be a lot of competition for popular terms and it can be expensive, so using this service tends to work best if you have something unusual or hard to find, such as a fabric by a designer not many retailers stock, or a product that not many people make. In addition, bear in mind that seventy to eighty per cent of users ignore paid-for results in search results.

Blogs and networks

If your target customers spend a lot of time browsing blogs for inspiration, then you need to find out which blogs and look into whether you can advertise with them. Not all bloggers accept adverts, so if you cannot advertise, ask if you could work with them in another way, providing supplies for their tutorials, or supplying products for them to give away.

You may identify particular networks where your target customers spend a lot of time. Most social networks now sell advertising so it could be worth experimenting with them. Facebook not only has sidebar adverts but also lets you pay to promote a particular post from your Facebook page, either to just your current fans or to friends of fans too. Facebook adverts can be targeted to a very set demographic and to people with particular niche hobbies. Twitter, Instagram and Pinterest are all going down the sponsored post route now too so take a look on their sites to find out how they work.

Some bloggers use advertising networks like BlogHer, where you can bid to place adverts on certain blogs. These are usually done at a daily or monthly rate. You can also search their database for relevant blogs on which to advertise.

Magazine websites

Many magazines have websites as well as their print publication. It may be cheaper or more measurable to advertise on the site rather than in the magazine itself. You may be able to negotiate a discount if you do both.

GOOGLE'S VOUCHERS

I have found that if you sign up for a Google Adwords account but do not purchase any Adwords they send you a free voucher after a few weeks. If you do not use that voucher they then send a larger voucher a month or so later to tempt you to try their service.

I cannot guarantee they will continue to do this forever, but it is worth trying.

FINDING OUT

A customer survey is an excellent way to find out which blogs your customers follow.

Budgeting for advertising

Using the funds allocated to marketing at the business planning stage (see page 44), draw up a monthly budget for advertising and each month look at the different places you could advertise. Try a different place every few months and by the end of the first year you will have a much better idea of where to advertise and where not to. Remember to stick to your budget!

Activity: Advertising your business

Make a list of ten popular websites, magazines and blogs in your industry which you think have a similar target audience to you. Make a point of engaging with them on social media or through their sites/blogs over the next month. Once you have established a connection, look into their advertising costs, and whether they accept guest posts or competition prizes. If they do, approach one at a time with an offer.

Space out the approaches so you are not suddenly appearing in several places at once. People get bored of reading a similar thing over and over, and after that sudden rush the response will die down. It is better to space them out and have one feature per month driving a steady stream of traffic – and customers – to you. This will help to spread the cost, too.

KEY ADVERTISING LESSONS

Advertising your business on other sites

The key to advertising your own business online is identifying where your target customers are and then advertise to them there. There is no point advertising to people who are never likely to purchase from you.

Use your website stats to measure the effectiveness of your adverts and make sure you are still getting value for money. Consider changing your adverts around every few months so that they reach people in different places. This is a good option if you cannot afford to advertise in several different places at once.

Advertising other businesses on your site

People do not want to be one of many, so limit the adverts you sell on your sites. The more advertisers you have the less response they will each see. As your traffic goes up you can add more advertisers, but do not just take as many as possible because you will probably find they will drop of the site after a few months when they do not get much traffic.

Think about how much traffic you would expect to get for the price you charge and ensure your advertisers get the same. If they start to drop under that level, this is a sign you have too many advertisers. If they go well above that, there is space for a new advertiser.

Selling adverts on your site

Of course, rather than buying advertising, you may have a business model that revolves around make money by selling adverts on your own site or blog. If you have a popular site and want to start making money from it, this is a great place to start. To do this you need to have:

- The facility to add adverts to your site or blog (preferably ones you can track).

- Provable statistics for your website. Google Analytics is the best thing for this, as it allows you to extract reports that show how many visitors you get per month. If you run a blog, the number of followers you have is also something advertisers like to know. Find out your page rank too, as some people will ask for that. This helps you to show them how important Google thinks your website is.

- A target list of businesses with which you want to work. Promote products and companies you believe in. If you seem to be promoting anything and everything just for the money, your followers will lose faith in you. In addition, you will not be happy if you feel obliged to promote something you do not really like, and that will show.

- Details of any extras you will offer advertisers. Will they get a mention in your content? An annual feature in the newsletter? The option to run giveaways through your site or blog?

- An idea of how much you want to charge. This part is difficult. It is best to look at other similar sites and blogs to see what they charge to help you decide on the right price for you. Where possible, fix people in for three to six months or longer to reduce the amount of administration you have to do. Offering discounts for longer terms helps to sell a few months at a time.

Once you have your statistics to hand, an idea of what you can offer advertisers and your pricing, contact the businesses on your list and offer them an advert on your site. Explain that you have handpicked them and only want to work with businesses you love. Tell them how it will benefit their business to be working with you and if you have time design a press pack and send it over to them. See the links section on page 220–221 for more on this.

MY INCENTIVES

I give my advertisers priority when it comes to editorial content or giveaways. This is a simple but effective incentive that encourages them to advertise with me.

NETWORKS OR NOT

You can sign up to networks like Passionfruit or Google ads but you will have less control over the adverts. I prefer to work directly with my advertisers to make sure I am advertising companies I like and with which I want to work.

The personal relationships you develop with these direct links can also help lead to you working with them in other ways.

Online promotion

Getting your business featured on blogs or websites is another way to get coverage online. There are a few ways to go about this:

Press releases If you have something newsworthy that you think certain website would like to write about, send them a press release and a couple of web size images. Press releases should be reserved for important news: do not send them all the time for every little thing you do with your business. Target only relevant sites who accept press releases – do not annoy people by sending them to anyone and everyone! One of those people you annoy may be someone you want to work with in the future.

Giveaways Most websites and blogs love the offer of a prize for them to give away. It is usually win–win for both parties: the website owner or blogger gets more traffic to their site and gives something back to their readers, while you get promotion and traffic. Where possible, ask them to make the competition question something about your website, so that they direct traffic to you.

Guest posts Many website owners are always on the lookout for good quality content to share with their followers. If you can offer that to them it saves them having to write it themselves. Remember that by guest posting you are asking to use someone else's platform that they have spent time, energy and effort building, so you need to convince them to allow you to use that platform by providing good quality material.

Target your offer appropriately and show how it is relevant to them. The website owner will want to know it is something you are specifically offering to them and not anyone who will reply to your group e-mail. Most website owners that accept your guest post will credit and link back to the writer, and if people like your content they will visit your site to look for more.

Give freebies If you offer a review product or supplies for people to use in their projects that will normally lead to exposure on their site or blog and sometimes social media too. Track the response to the promotion and make sure that is is worth the cost of what you are giving away.

Promote someone else Whether you feature their products, interview them, or ask for their tips on something, if you promote someone else on your site they will often promote you back. If nothing else they will usually share with their followers and send them to the post on your site. Sometimes they will offer to return the favour and feature you on their site or blog.

> ### FINDING THE RIGHT BLOGS
>
> If you need help finding craft blogs in your niche, visit: craftyblogs.co.uk for a list of UK craft blogs.

Building relationships

Wherever possible, try and build a relationship with people before approaching them for promotion. If you have commented on their blog a few times, had a chat with them on Twitter or met them at a show they are more likely to remember you and want to work with you. Make sure you emphasise the benefits for them. They have no obligation to promote you and need to get something out of it too.

Always take the time to find out the name of the person you are approaching and tailor the e-mail to them, not just a 'Dear blogger' type e-mail which will go straight into their trash folder. When an offer of content looks like a form e-mail, most recipients will simply delete it. Taking time to address an e-mail personally and tailor it to the recipient is much more likely to get a response.

If the business you approach does refuse the offer, take it in your professional stride, but do persevere. You could respond by asking if they have any suggestions of how you could work together, or let them know that they can contact you in the future if they need anything. The company might have turned down your offer of a prize because they have their next few months' worth of competitions booked. If they know the offer of your giveaway is still open, they may contact you when planning their next block of contests.

IS IT WORKING?

The good thing about online advertising and promotion is that it is very easy to measure the results. Using Google Analytics's goal tracking you can see exactly how many site visitors you have received as a result of a particular campaign, how many signed up to your newsletter and even how many of them purchased from you.

Newsletters

Creating a newsletter allows you to build a customer database, which can be more valuable than simply accruing social media followers. Social media is out of your control: if Facebook or Twitter closed down for some reason, or your account got hacked, you could lose all your followers and have no way to contact them. Having a newsletter mailing list means you always have the details of people who are interested enough in what you offer that they have given you their e-mail addresses.

If you sell anything through your site, add a 'join our newsletter' tick box at the end of the checkout process to encourage customers to join. Take a newsletter sign-up sheet to shows and events that you attend, and have a newsletter sign-up option highly visible on your homepage.

Attracting subscribers

The important things with newsletters is that customers have to 'opt in'. You cannot just add people's details to a database and e-mail them whenever you feel like it – this is spam and will not get good returns. Encourage people to sign up by offering something of interest to them, whether that is a regular delivery of great content, a free download, a discount code, a competition entry or something else.

Once signed up, let subscribers know what to expect from you, and when. Will you be e-mailing daily, weekly or monthly? Will the e-mail have special offers, freebies, great content, useful tips or just sales messages? If subscribers do not get what they expect they will unsubscribe or even worse mark your e-mail as junk. Be realistic, and up front from the outset, as to what people can expect from your newsletter.

The goal of a newsletter

Use newsletters in conjunction with your site and social media to give value to your customers/potential customers. 'Value' means something that viewers will find useful and which will keep them coming back to you. Many newsletters contain free advice or content such as downloadable patterns, technique guides, or free webinars, podcasts and projects. The aim of this is to lead them to your website and to buy from you.

Use your newsletter to support your business. Let people know about any news, things that have recently been added to your website, customer or sponsor's news and any events you are holding. People do expect that there will be a certain amount of promotion in your newsletter but when it is all promotion, it tends to switch people off. People do not like being 'marketed at', but when you mix it with something attractive to them, they mind it less.

NEWSLETTERS AND YOUR BUSINESS

Your newsletter should be an extension of your business, using the same branding and ethos. The tag line of my business is 'making it easier to find great sewing resouces' so my newsletter continues that theme.

In each newsletter we highlight special offers, new fabric collections and new products that might interest our readers. We let them know the latest news from our customers, including new sewing pattern releases, new shops opening, big sales etc. We also share new projects, tutorials and giveaways. It is essentially a condensed version of what we share on our site and social media.

One of my favourite newsletters is Abby Glassenberg's newsletter. Abby, who co-wrote the foreword to this book, is well known for sharing craft industry news on her site, and her newsletter is also jam-packed with news of what has happened in the industry over the previous week. She saves you having to read loads of blogs and sites to get the news, by collecting the highlights and putting them in her newsletter.

Both of us are giving something useful to our newsletter subscribers; saving them time by bringing lots of useful information on a topic they are interested in all into one place.

BACK UP

Make sure you download your mailing list a couple of times a year to keep it backed up.

The benefits of a newsletter

Apart from being in direct contact with people interested in your business, a mailing list will tend to generate a better response than social media when asking for something like a feedback survey to be completed.

You also tend to reach a higher percentage of people through your newsletter than you do through social media.

Newsletter providers

You can create your own newsletter using whatever e-mail program you prefer, by you do not have to. There are a number of services, like MailChimp or AWeber, that make creating and sending newsletters easy. Most have design templates for you to use, simple subscriber option processes and detailed statistics. The statistics tell you who has opened your newsletter, what links they clicked within the newsletter, if any newsletters failed to deliver and if so why.

Activity: Planning your newsletter

How can you continue the ethos of your company into a newsletter? What can you offer readers to make sure they open your newsletter and stay subscribed? Make a note of some ideas.

You might consider using your newsletter to send exclusive discount codes, access to new products or sales before non-subscribers; or send subscribers useful tips and advice.

Think about some of the newsletters to which you subscribe, and work out why you signed up, why you want to receive them, and what makes you want to read them when they arrive. This might suggest valuable leads on generating your own ideas.

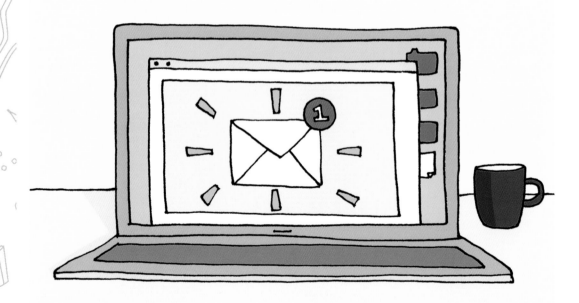

TIPS ON E-MAIL MARKETING FROM ABBY GLASSENBERG

The co-founder of the Craft Industry Alliance, Abby Glassenberg is also a sewing pattern designer, teacher, and the author of three sewing books. On her blog, WhileSheNaps.com, Abby writes about the sewing industry, running a creative business, and the online culture of craft.

E-mail is the most direct and effective way to bring customers to your shop and blog and to keep them coming back. Think of your e-mail newsletter as a special gift you are delivering each week, or twice a month, to your favourite fans and most supportive followers.

Ideas for content include behind-the-scenes glimpses into your process, a round up of relevant links, reviews of your favourite tools, and excerpt from your recent or archives blog posts. When your newsletter is providing value you will not feel afraid that you are annoying your followers. Instead you will feel confident that you are sending them something they look forward to opening.

Be sure to include a call to action in every newsletter. Make it crystal clear what you expect your readers to do. Phrases like 'shop now', 'read more', and 'get the rest' are examples of strong calls to action.

To grow your list mention it everywhere including in your bio, at shows, on your business cards, at workshops, on your website, and in your e-mail signature. You may also want to offer a freebie, known as a lead magnet, in exchange for people's e-mail addresses. A simple tutorial, short e-book, quick video, checklist, or template all make great lead magnets – and do not be afraid of installing a pop-up on your site. Pop-ups are incredibly effective list-building tools.

When it comes to e-mail marketing, consistency is key. Set a date on your calendar when you will send your newsletter (two to four times a month is ideal) and stick to it! Building a large, engaged list takes time and effort, but it is well worth it when the clicks and sales flood in!

WHILE THEY WAIT

Consider setting up an auto responder, which automatically sends an e-mail to new newsletter subscribers a set time after they join. You can use this to direct them to the most popular content or products on your site, or to offer them an exclusive discount whilst they wait to receive your newsletter.

How often to send a newsletter

Many people are unsure of how often they should be send out a newsletter. Ultimately, the answer comes down to what works best for you and your subscribers. If you have new things to promote every week, along with other useful content or benefits to share that frequently, a weekly newsletter is suitable. Unless you are giving something really valuable that people will take the time to read every day, a daily newsletter is likely to be unwelcome.

As with social media, consistency is important, do not over-promise and then fail to keep up with what you said you would deliver. If your newsletter is in-depth and takes several hours to draft, a monthly rate is more sensible to ensure you can keep up a regular schedule.

BUILDING AND RETAINING YOUR READERSHIP

Make sure your newsletter sign-up link is obvious and easy to find on your website to help build your subscriber list. I had mine moved from my menu bar to a box at the top right of the site and my subscription rate tripled! It was so easy to find and one of the first things people saw, so I got a huge number of sign-ups.

Do not panic if you notice you get people unsubscribing after you send an e-mail. It is normal for a few people to unsubscribe each time. Sometimes they find the content is not what they expected, or they forgot they had signed up, or they may be no longer interested in your business. If you are getting over a five per cent unsubscribe rate then look into the causes.

- Are you not delivering something interesting?
- Are you e-mailing too frequently or not frequently enough?
- Is the newsletter too focused on sales?

Once you identify the problem, you can start to fix it.

TOP TIPS FOR NEWSLETTERS

- Think about the timing. When will your target customers be free to read the newsletter? If it is going to work e-mail addresses, then during working hours is best; while sending to personal e-mail addresses will likely get more readers out of hours. First thing on Monday and last thing on Friday are normally not good times. People tend to come into lots of e-mails on the Monday so will skip non-urgent ones, and by late on Friday most people are thinking of the weekend. Of course, if your product or service is more relevant to the weekend that could be an ideal time for you.

- The subject line is important. It needs to tempt the recipients to open it and to be able to see what it is straight away, but it also needs to pass through people's spam filters. Most people are wary of opening e-mails if they are not sure what they are or who they are from.

- Ensure your company branding is on the newsletter so people can see it is a genuine newsletter from you. Also do not forget to include your social media links as this may lead to an increase in your follower numbers.

- Use images! Text-only e-mails are boring. They do not tempt people to click to your site and after the first few, most readers will probably stop even opening them. Make sure the images you use are clickable too.

- Double check all your links. You do not want to have to re-send an e-mail and risk annoying people because your links did not work. If they do not work most people will just give up and not bother trying to figure out what the link is or find it another way. Send yourself a test e-mail and check that the links work before you send it to your mailing list.

USEFUL LINKS AND FURTHER READING

General online selling advice

Tips for choosing a domain name:
godaddy.com/garage/smallbusiness/launch/10-tips-for-choosing-the-perfect-domain-name

Checking domain availability or ownership:
whois.com

Free websites:
wix.com; moonfruit.com; weebly.com; yola.com; wordpress.com; blogger.com; tumblr.com

Paid-for websites:
create.net; mrsite.com; wordpress.org; fasthosts.co.uk; 123-reg.co.uk/make-a-website

Legislation for selling online: See links on pages 72–73.

Useful articles for your web design

Call to action buttons:
copyblogger.com/call-to-action-buttons

Using white space:
bigbrandsystem.com/use-white-space

Checkout page optimization:
moz.com/blog/checkout-page-optimization-just-follow-the-facts

Web design tips: create.net/blog

The Paypal blog: paypal.co.uk/blog

Things to get right on your website:
enterprisenation.com/blog/make-sure-you-get-these-5-things-right-on-your-website

Ten critical home page elements:
marketingtechblog.com/critical-homepage-elements

Payment systems

Paypal: paypal.com

World Pay: worldpay.com

Streamline: streamline.com

Go Cardless: gocardless.com

Braintree: braintreepayments.com

Pay360: pay360.com

Stripe: stripe.com

Card save: cardsave.net

Graphics to add to your site

etsy.com or creativemarket.com

Online marketplaces

Information about selling on Etsy:
handmadeology.com/10-real-tips-for-successfully-selling-on-etsy; everythingetsy.com; etsy.com/uk/seller-handbook ; youtube.com (search 'selling on Etsy')

Dummies guide to starting an Etsy Business:
bit.ly/2dnP5ND

Information and advice about selling on other online marketplaces:

Folksy:
folksy.uservoice.com/knowledgebase; blog.folksy.com/category/seller-tips; sayitsays.blogspot.co.uk/2013/08/top-tips-for-selling-on-folksy.html

Not On The High Street:
notonthehighstreet.com/email/10goldenguidelines/guideline-1.html

Amazon's section for selling handmade products:
services.amazon.com/handmade/handmade.html

DaWanda:
en.dawanda.com/cms/c/en/Seller-Portal

Comparison of several platforms:
thecraftynetwork.wordpress.com/where-to-sell/where-to-sell-your-crafts

Selling on Artfire: theonlineseller.com/2012/09/17/marketplace-focus-artfire/

Where to sell art online: theabundantartist.com/15-ways-to-sell-your-art-online; moma.co.uk/10-ways-to-sell-art-online

Selling handmade products online: smallbiztrends.com/2011/10/29-places-sell-handmade-creations.html

SEO

Google Keyword Tool: adwords.google.com/home/tools/keyword-planner (You will need an Adwords account to access this, but it is free to sign up and you do not have to run any ads.)

Google trends: google.co.uk/trends

Keyword generator: ubersuggest.io

Moz's whiteboard videos can be very useful and their free beginner's guide to SEO is worth downloading: moz.com/blog

Information on linkable assets: moz.com/blog/9-tangible-linkable-asset-ideas-and-how-to-build-links-to-them

Information on meta descriptions: moz.com/learn/seo/meta-description

For an alternative view on SEO (sign up to the newsletter for bonus content): viperchill.com

Content marketing advice: copyblogger.com

Useful tips for blogging, content creation and a little SEO relevant to the craft industry: ukcraftblog.com

7 Simple seo hacks for non techie bloggers: blogher.com/7-simple-seo-hacks-non-techie-bloggers

Information about evergreen posts: ukcraftblog.com/2011/09/evergreen-blog-posts.html

Advice on using Google Analytics, including setting up goals and conversion tracking: support.google.com/analytics

Beginners guide to Google Webmaster Tools: blog.kissmetrics.com/beginners-guide-to-google-webmaster-tools

Google Adverts: google.co.uk/ads

Google Adwords: google.co.uk/adwords

BlogHer Publishing Network Momentum: blogher.com/marketplace/opportunities/publishing-network

A site to check for broken links on your site: brokenlinkcheck.com

How to make a media kit for your site: theblogmaven.com/make-a-media-kit-that-rocks

Page rank checker: prchecker.info

Newsletters

Mail Chimp: mailchimp.com

AWeber: aweber.com

Advice on e-mail marketing: moz.com/blog/category/email-marketing

Avoiding words that can get your newsletters marked as spam: blog.automational.com/2016/03/08/spam-trigger-words-to-avoid/

YOUR LINKS AND NOTES

You can use this space to keep a list of links to websites and services you find helpful.

SELLING

OFFLINE

THE OFFLINE MARKETPLACE

In addition to – or instead of – selling online you may want to also sell your products 'offline' at craft shows, in galleries or at retail outlets. This chapter will explain how you go about getting other people to stock your products, and looking into the best way to set up your own shop or stall.

It is also worth complementing any online marketing you do with offline marketing such as features in the press. This section of the book will help you get started with both selling and promoting your business offline.

Why sell offline?

It makes good business sense to have several streams of income rather than being solely dependent on one source. That way if something goes wrong with one of your sources of income you still have money coming in from other areas. Offline selling can be the perfect complement to selling online, and it gives you the chance to get out and meet your customers or the people selling your products in person rather than just dealing with them by e-mail.

Offline selling also ties in to online sales. Including your web address on your product packaging, and business cards or flyers handed out at events, may lead to future business being driven to your online shop or service.

If offline selling is not for you, it is still worth looking through this section for information and tips on promoting your business offline through advertising, and through the press and broadcast media, all of which will help you to direct people to your website or online shop. It also includes guidance and suggestions for networking at events to make contacts, build your brand and strengthen your business.

Selling at craft fairs

You can do craft fairs for publicity, to get feedback from potential customers, or simply to make money by selling your products. Whatever your focus, you need to decide in advance what you want to get from the event, and how much you are prepared to spend.

The first practical step of selling at craft fairs is to conduct research. Find out what events are going on around you, and you can then decide which are worth the investment of a stand and, if appropriate, which products to sell on that stand.

It is easy to be tempted by fairs with cheap stall prices, but although you may not be spending a lot of money you are still spending time, so you want to make sure you are getting something back for that time – whether this is cash, publicity or customer interaction. Remember to check back on whether you achieved your goals after the event.

Choosing an event

When looking for events at which you could sell, good places to start are your local newspapers or magazines; websites like ukcraftfairs.com or stallfinder.com; local 'what's on' websites; discussion forums such as Crafts Forum (craftsforum. co.uk); or you could ask other crafters which events they recommend in your part of the world.

As part of your research, once you have identified a few potential events, attend them as a visitor before investing any money. Look at how many people are attending, who else is exhibiting, what kind of prices they are charging and whether they are successfully selling their products at that price. Take a look at both the layout and the visitor flow – you want to be situated somewhere where you get a good number of visitors and not hidden in a corner. Take a look at the vendors' stall displays for inspiration: which ones are attracting the most visitors, and why?

See how well the event was advertised, and whether it attracted a large number of visitors. Will those visitors be interested in your products at the price you need to sell, or are they just looking for bargains?

If you do not have a chance to attend the show beforehand, you can still contact the event organizer to ask for information about the advertising, expected visitor numbers, other sellers and similar information. If you look on the event organizer's social media accounts, you may find photographs of the event and feedback from both visitors and exhibitors.

THE MODERN CRAFT FAIR

In recent years craft fairs have shaken off the image of old-fashioned items sold in musty church halls. Modern makers have embraced the craft fair, turning them into popular events in big demand by both stall holders and visitors.

Several crafters who found themselves disappointed with the more traditional craft fairs have started up their own fairs. Susie Daly founded the internationally successful Renegade Craft Fairs; Sean Mort and Carley Batley launched Northern Craft and Rosie Drake Knight runs Native Makers craft fairs in Devon. These modern craft fairs understand the benefits of online marketing and social media as well as local advertising to help attract visitors and stall holders.

Preparing for the show

Once you have chosen which events at which you want to exhibit and have booked your stand, the next stage is planning. Think about what stock to take – and how much. Think also about how you will transport it to the show, lay it out, and what to charge.

Tips to help with planning

- A tablecloth on your table allows you to store things out of sight. Take one that reaches the ground, and keep it fairly plain so that it does not draw attention from your products.

- Do not clutter your stand. Giving people too much choice can lead to them buying nothing at all.

- Making sure everything is clearly priced will leave you free to serve your customers rather than having to answer constant price queries. In addition, some people may be afraid to ask and may just leave if they cannot see a price.

- Pricing in round figures (to the nearest pound for instance) means you do not have to have lots of different change on you.

- A supply of easily-accessible leaflets or business cards allows people to look you up later. If they do not have time to stop, they can grab a card on their way past. Take lots – it is better to have too many than not enough.

- Bring food and drinks with you so you do not need to leave your stand unattended.

- A money apron will allow you to keep your cash safe and to hand.

- If it is a long or busy event, bring a friend with you to allow you to take breaks and to help serve when it gets busy.

- Take something to sit on if you have space; your feet will thank you by the end of the day!

- Keep pen, paper and calculator to hand. You never know when they will come in useful.

- Talk to the other stall holders when you get the chance. You can use down-time for networking or getting useful advice.

WHEN TO STOP NETWORKING

Stop when you have a customer at your stand: some will be reluctant to interrupt and you could lose a sale.

- If another seller seems to be very popular and getting lots of sales, try to identify why and think about whether there is anything you can learn from them.

- Make sure your products can be seen from a distance, and that your signage tells people what you do. This allows customers to see if your products are of interest to them.

- Do not be afraid to use props, but make sure they enhance rather than overshadow your products.

- Do not be too pushy and sales-focused. Smile and greet people, and then let them browse. Engage them if they want to chat to you.

- Craft in the quiet times if you can; this could lead to people taking an interest in what you are doing which could then generate a sale. It also demonstrates that the products are handmade by you.

- It is good to have things at a range of prices to suit all budgets.

- Put a card or flyer in with everything you sell, in case the buyer wants to buy more in the future.

- Look happy, no matter how bored or exhausted you are. If you look like you do not want to be there, it will put off potential customers.

After the show

The first thing to do after a show is to reflect on how the show went. Did you sell what you expected? Was there anything you could have done differently? Did you get any useful feedback from the customers? Did any of your products prove unexpectedly popular or surprisingly disappointing in terms of sales? Note down in your notebook anything you learnt and want to do differently at the next event.

A report on the show makes a good blog post or social media post. Let people know how it went and what you thought of the event. If nothing else, it may help send you some search engine traffic from people looking for information about the event. If you took photographs, include these. As discussed earlier, images help generate interaction. Make sure that some of the photographs are of your stall and products, as that is another way for you to showcase them online too.

If you had the chance for any networking (see pages 242–244), leave it couple of days after the show for people to catch up and then send them an e-mail or get in touch on social media. It will start building a relationship that could in time turn into a good business relationship or a friendship.

ONGOING EFFECTS

Remember that you may not see all the effects of the craft fair while at the fair itself. If you have handed out lots of business cards, for example, you may find you get orders in after the show too. One way to track this is to hand out a unique discount code at the show.

Craft fair displays

When exhibiting at a craft fair, find good ways of displaying your items so that people can see them properly, can touch them and can look through your selection at a glance. Your products should face outwards, towards your customers, not up at the ceiling.

You can use boxes or shelving to raise your display and place some products at eye level. Do not limit yourself just to the table itself: you could have things attached to the walls of your stand, hanging from the top of it or standing beside the table if you have space.

There is no need to display all of your stock at once. If appropriate, put a few samples out with a sign to explain that different colours and sizes are available on request. You can rotate your stock throughout the day to get an idea of what sells best at that particular event.

Think about the layout of your products, you may want to keep more valuable products towards the back of the table so they do not get taken. Remember that children may be able to reach the items you put at the front of the table, or they could get knocked off as people brush past. You will want bestsellers within easy reach of both the customers and you for quick restocking as they sell.

Your stall and you

Ideally you want your stall to stand out from the others, to catch potential customers' attention and draw them in. If you have electricity, use it to your advantage. Light up your products so that they stand out. You can use spotlights to highlight your bestsellers or major pieces. If not, you can still use signage to tell people why they should buy your products: explain what is unique about them, how they are made, what materials or techniques you use, and suggest how they could be used.

If possible, have a banner or poster with your branding on to help build brand recognition, and to help people remember your business name, which will make it easier for them to search for you after the show.

Finally, remember that you will also form part of your display. Think about what you are going to wear and whether it fits in with the image you are portraying with the rest of your stall.

PINSPIRATION

I would highly recommend looking at Pinterest for craft fair display ideas. You will find a huge amount of inspiration there.

BE ORGANIZED

Having to rummage through your products like they are at a second-hand sale may lead to customers expecting to pay second-hand prices.

WHAT TO DO AT CRAFT FAIRS

These tips are from Wendy Massey from Handmade Harbour (handmadeharbour.co.uk).

Before the fair

Do your research! Attend fairs as a customer, speak to stallholders and organizers and read what people are saying online. Look for more than just dedicated craft fairs: carnivals, car shows, county shows, green events, winter markets, wedding fairs and even local school events might be good choices.

Make sure you have a web presence in place: a blog or Facebook page gives people something to look at and a way to contact you – a phone number is not enough to generate repeat sales. Being able to see your products online makes it easier for people to spread the word as well as return and buy from you themselves. Tell your online followers about the fair – they may want to attend and see you in person.

During the fair

Be friendly but not pushy. Hand out business cards like they are sweets. Do not take it personally if people stroll by without a glance – you cannot appeal to everyone. Chat to customers, listen to feedback and write down any comments so that you do not forget them. If you offer a bespoke service, you may find that customers come up with ideas that could become bestselling items. Have an order book or print out your own order sheets to use with a clipboard and carbon paper (give the customer the top copy).

After the fair

Analyse what went well and what you could do better next time. Look at the comments you noted down – is there anything useful you could use? A slight change to a product might increase sales, someone might like to sell for you (have you considered wholesale or drop shipping?) or you may have a new product idea. If you sell online, alter your PayPal settings to automatically ask where people found you – this is a great way to discover if fairs are working to promote online sales.

Remember that fairs are much more than just a selling platform. They work really well for face-to-face market research, promoting your online presence and showing off your range to independent shop owners who may want to stock your products. Other stallholders may also become friends – you can learn a lot from each other, too, so try not to be shy!

Selling through art galleries

Selling your art through galleries gets them in front of the relevant audience without you having to sell directly. It can free you up to spend more time creating your art rather than selling it.

Approaching galleries

The first step towards getting your artwork stocked in art galleries is to research the galleries, as they all have their own niche. Make sure your work fits their style before approaching them.

The next step is to check out their website, as many art galleries now handle applications online rather than in person. Make sure you submit good quality images of your work, both for the best results, and for future licensing.

Payment

A few galleries will buy your work outright and pay you within thirty days. Most will take it on a sale or return deal: you only get paid if the artwork sells, and if it does not sell it will be returned to you at the end of the agreed period. Sale or return is less risky for the gallery, so it tends to be the most common option. Galleries will take a commission from any art they sell on your behalf. There is no fixed rate, but your should typically expect them to take a cut of one third to one half of the price.

Some galleries may try to make you pay to exhibit with them, or to pay for the opening event. You should not have to do this. If a gallery likes your work and is confident that it can be sold, they will not need to charge you upfront. Be sceptical if the gallery asks you to pay to exhibit.

It is important to build up a good relationship with the galleries with which you work so that they will continue to stock your work in the long term. If your art is in the same gallery a lot you will start to build a customer base in that area. It is better to do that than to distribute your work all over the place and not have the time to form proper relationships with the galleries.

OTHER WAYS OF SELLING

In addition to selling through galleries, Nel Whatmore (see box, above right) also sells her artwork directly, through her website and at local shows and events. This has allowed her to build a mailing list so she is not solely dependent on galleries to sell her work. It has also allowed her to build a personal relationship with her customers.

However, she does find it cuts into her painting time: you need to be happy to be on stalls all day, chatting to the public. It is not suited to everyone: if you would rather be in the studio painting all day, then galleries are probably the better option for you.

TIPS ON SELLING YOUR ARTWORK

These tips come from award-winning artist Kerry Darlington (kerrydarlington.co.uk).

Before approaching a gallery with your work, it is important that you have at least the beginning of a strong definite style. You can have a mixture of subject matter but if the same style of painting runs through them all, the galleries will have a strong image to promote and your work will stick in people's minds more. As a result, you will be remembered and requested, and you will be commissioned to paint more as the first ones sell.

Artists that have not formed their own style often look to popular current work and are tempted to bend their work to try and 'fit in'. This is all very well if you can give a current trend a complete twist, but being heavily inspired by someone else means it may be hard to be taken seriously and it could affect your reputation long term. It is always better to create a trend than to buck a trend.

Before approaching a gallery, do a bit of research first. There are several streams of galleries, from independent highly priced art shops representing a handful of artists, to small framing shops using a wall or two to sell very affordable art to their customers. See what type your art would fit into first. All are open to new artists, they too are looking for the next big thing, so never be frightened of approaching them.

Some artists use publishers or agents to get their work into galleries. This can be great for some artists but terrible for others. Publishers usually take over all of the framing and distribution, which means more promotion but much less of the retail price. It is a good idea to contact other artists who are currently with an agent or publisher you are looking at, and also artists who used to be with that same agent/publishers to see how it worked for them.

Most importantly, create work of which you are proud and are happy to represent. I believe that the viewer can often feel the passion that has gone into creating something, and that alone can sell the work.

Getting your craft products into stores

Getting your products stocked in stores can give you more time making and less time selling directly at events and shows. If your products sell well, being stocked in stores means you are likely to have a steady stream of orders which can help with your cash flow.

Independent stores

As with selling anywhere else your first step should to be research. Make sure that your product fits with the range in the store before approaching them, and check that they do not already have something too similar to your product.

Contact the store to make an appointment, and using your research, tell them why your product is perfect for their store. Explain why and how it is better than, or different from, items they already sell; and lay out the benefits to them of stocking your product. Let them know what your USP is. Make sure you have the answers ready to all the questions they may ask. Be ready to let them know:

- What variations (size/colour, etc.) you can offer on your products.

- How many you can produce for them and by what date.

- How your product will be packaged or presented.

- What your wholesale price is.

- What your payment terms are.

- Whether you are happy for them to take them on a sale or return basis.

- What the postage costs are.

- What your returns policy is.

- Whether you are prepared to offer any discounts.

Prepare samples of your products ready to show buyers, as well as samples of packaging and any display or promotional materials you may have. Also, remember to take your order form in case they want to place an order.

Big retailers

The ultimate dream of most makers is to get stocked in one of the big retailers; to bag the kind of order that will keep your company afloat for the next year, regardless of whether you get any other orders or not.

Benefits

There are of course many benefits to getting a large retailer to stock your products. As well as increasing sales numbers, the presence of your products in a big store will help build your brand recognition by getting your products in front of thousands of people who would never otherwise have seen them. It also gives your business kudos. One big company paying you attention and wanting to work with you could lead to others.

Potential problems

Before you think about approaching big retailers make sure you have the capacity to make large quantities of your products in a short time scale. Taking on a large order can badly affect your business: if you will not be able to deliver in the time scale promised it will affect your chances of ever working with a big retailer in the future.

You will need to ensure you have the systems in place to cope with large orders before you start to seek them. If you will have to close your online stores for a month while you work on the order, your other customers may end up going elsewhere. If you do not have anyone who can help you and you fall ill, you may end up unable to complete the order. If you do not have enough packaging available the retailer will not accept your product.

Larger companies can have complicated accounting systems which may result in you having to wait for months before you get paid. Clarify when you can expect to receive payment; and make sure you have sufficient cash flow to survive at least another two months without that payment in case of problems.

Getting noticed

The advice opposite for selling to smaller independent stores applies equally to larger retailers and chains, but the following additional steps can help to get large retailers to notice your products and want to stock them:

Be unique Make sure your product is different from the retailer's current range.

Have a clear aim Be clear who your product is aimed at and communicate that to the retailer.

Be prepared Make sure you have wholesale pricing and details ready to send to anyone who inquires.

Research Take the time to look into who you should contact and personalize your approach. Address them personally and by name, not just 'dear head buyer'.

Send samples It is much more convenient for buyers to see the quality of your products through samples than descriptions and photographs.

Minimize risk The retailer is more likely to take a chance with your products if you can minimize the risk to them. Examples of this include offering sale or return, or smaller pack sizes.

Events Some big brands run events where they invite people to pitch products to them. Keep an eye on likely sites or social media for details.

Attend trade shows Ask around and find out which trade shows are worth exhibiting at, and which shows are attended by the buyers from the shops in which you want to be stocked. You can always contact the buyers before the show and ask them to visit your stand or arrange a meeting.

TIPS ON GETTING YOUR PRODUCTS STOCKED BY A LARGE RETAILER

Ian Ellis is Haberdashery and Crafting buyer for John Lewis (johnlewis.com).

As the haberdashery buyer, I see a lot of new product ideas, and brands who are launching into the market. We have to review these on the merits of what we receive, as often the first contact is a parcel or presentation sent in the post.

I can only stress the importance of that package. The best and most well-received give a comprehensive overview of the product along with strong visuals. You must make sure the product is brought to life. If we receive a box with a set of parts, it does not inspire nor give the product the impact it needs. If we get a finished sample, we can see what the creators will achieve with the raw product or kit. This is the most important consideration for us: our customer's satisfaction.

In addition, make sure that we understand that you have thought through the realities of retail, pack design, photography and price positioning. The realities of commercial success are not just based on great product design.

Getting featured offline

In the previous chapter we covered getting featured online to help increase your brand awareness and drive traffic to your site – and custom to your business. Although it seems like most people are online nowadays, it would be foolish to neglect offline promotion too. Look for coverage in local newspapers, trade magazines, industry relevant magazines, and on radio and television.

Press releases

A press release is a communication that you send to the media to tell them about your business, which you hope they will use. News about new premises or product ranges, or about events you are attending are good examples. The press are often looking for stories, and if you can send them something that is ready to use it saves them time and effort. Do not wait for them to approach you. Be proactive and send out targeted press releases – that is, to the right people at the right publication. Do your research to see how your business can fit into the publication, what angle is best to take in your press release, and to whom you should send it.

Contacts come in very useful. If you build a good relationship with staff at magazines and newspapers they are much more likely to feature you, and to let you know if they have anything coming up which they could include you in. If you get the chance to meet journalists at local events or industry shows, introduce yourself and establish that contact. Build on the relationship by thanking them when they feature you, and let them know that if they have some space to fill, they can get in touch with you.

Unfortunately some publications will only feature you if you advertise with them. If that is the case with the publication you are approaching, you need to weigh the cost of advertising against the benefits of the promotion, especially if there are others that will feature you for free.

Writing a press release

Editorial space is often at a premium, so keep your press releases succinct. You can include further information at the bottom for the journalist to use, but the core of the piece should be concise. Try to include a few quotes with your press release so that the publication can make it sound as if they have interviewed you, should they choose to do so.

Because the piece may need expanding upon, always include details of whomever they can contact from your business for more information. You should always send over relevant, high-resolution images (see page 88 for more details on supplying images) to go with your news story. It helps if you can send a selection so that they have a choice of which to use. Do not forget to include your web address along with your business name and premises address (if you have a bricks and mortar shop).

The more effort the publication has to make to use your press release, the less likely it is to use it. Send all the images, the text ready to be cut and pasted plus full contact details, so they should not need to get back to you for anything. When writing your press release, you can make the journalists' life easier by writing it in the third person, as the story would appear in a magazine. Do not say 'me' and 'I' but rather 'the business' or 'they'. This means it will not have to be entirely reworded, and press releases that require little editing are more likely to be accepted.

JULIE BONNAR'S TIPS ON APPROACHING MAGAZINES

Julie Bonnar is the former editor of both **Craft Focus** *and* **Sewing World** *magazines, and has over fourteen years experience in the craft industry. She trained as an interior designer but found she liked making her own clothes. Julie also runs her own dressmaking website and e-zine called* **The Pattern Pages**.

As a craft business, your aim is to get your products in plain view of your customer, and ultimately make sales. For many small businesses, dealing with editors can be quite a daunting prospect, but magazines can help you reach a large circulation of people who will be interested in buying your products. Here are six tips on how to approach a magazine and persuade the editor to pick your products:

- **Do your homework** Find out what the magazine's target audience is, and is it the same as yours? Relevance is important – it is pointless and a waste of your time and theirs to contact the wrong magazines. Try engaging with them on social media to plant the seed that you are interested in their magazine.

- **Contact and style** Find the name of the right person to e-mail. Larger magazines may have feature editors that look after certain topics. Check out the magazine's website to get a feel for the writing style of the publication, and perhaps give the magazine a quick call to ask what the features are for the next issue. You may be able to get hold of a feature schedule that has the features planned for the next twelve months.

- **Content** Essentially it is an editor's job to fill the magazines pages with quality content, compelling and stories so they are always on the look out for new products. Make sure you do not miss the boat, some magazines work as far as four months in advance so Christmas is a topic for August and September. Editor's will be looking at websites to check facts about your business so make sure what you are telling them is correct.

- **Pitch** Magazines receive hundreds of e-mails every day so you need to make yours stand out from the crowd and keep it out of the spam folder. Come up with a creative subject line and keep your pitch short and sweet. Avoid waffle and make sure they can spot the dazzle from the drivel. Make sure there are no typos and that all links work, and read it again before sending to make sure it makes sense!

- **Picture perfect** Make sure your images look professional. Use low resolution images to start with and offer high resolution images on request, this way they will come back to you if they are interested. Send images on a white background, there are more opportunities to use this sort of image and can easily be cut out.

- **Follow up** Many businesses get despondent when they do not hear back so take it upon yourself to follow up but make sure you leave a respectable time before contacting gain. Sometime editors just have not got around to replying. Remember to offer a special discount, prize or write an article, and even if your story is unsuccessful this time that call can help build a relationship – so do not give up trying!

ALICE HADLEY'S TIPS ON WRITING FOR MAGAZINES

Alice Hadley is the editor of** Love Patchwork & Quilting **magazine (lovepatchworkandquilting.com) and has worked in the magazine industry for over eight years.

First things first: do your research. There are so many craft magazines out there, and it is important to check that the publication you are submitting to is the right fit for your work. Be honest with yourself, and if the brand is not a match for your designs, move on to another!

Introduce yourself. When contacting an editor, it is important that you give them a brief overview of your place in the industry. Have you worked for other publications? Do you self-publish quilt patterns? Let us know so that we can gauge your experience. And, if the content is relevant to your pitch, give them links to your social media pages and blog, so that we can get a good feel for your style.

Be clear and concise when describing your project proposal. Start with the basics: what technique does it use? What skill level is it aimed at? What finished size will it be? Then flesh out with your thoughts on colour schemes, use of print and pattern, quilting designs. Many editors will be commissioning to set issue themes and need a clear idea of what you are putting forward.

Editors are busy people with many and varied demands on their time. Wait a couple of weeks after sending off your submission, and if you have not heard anything, send a polite reminder. If you decide that you would prefer to submit your pattern elsewhere, it is courteous to let an editor know, so that they can take if off the to-do list.

MY FREELANCING

In my experience of freelance writing for craft magazines, the biggest problem I faced was submissions not having images of a high enough quality, or simply not having the correct images available. Do make sure you keep high quality images of all of your products, even if you only need web quality ones to go onto your website.

Another common problem I encountered was people replying after the deadline. Even if it is going to take you a few days to get together everything the journalist is asking for, do reply and let them know that you do want to be included and will send them what they need by the deadline. Journalists have to submit an article on time or risk it not being printed. If we do not hear anything at all, we will look for someone else as we need to ensure we can finish our article.

Activity: Create a contact database

Create a contacts database of the people to whom you could send press releases, both online and offline. Create a spreadsheet with the person's name, their job, the publication for which they work, their website, their e-mail and then have a notes column at the end to make notes about the kind of thing they feature in their publication. This will save you a lot of time when you have something ready to share.

Television and radio features

As with print media, having contacts in the industry will help with television and radio features. If media journalists know you and have your contact details, they may think of you when they need someone. Visiblity and good SEO will also increase your chances of being approached. I have had a few television offers from researchers who found me via Google – it seems some television researchers will simply use a search engine to find experts in the subject they want to talk about, so it really does pay to get your SEO right.

If you are looking to be on television, identify the productions companies that make television programmes that cover your area of business, along with any local television companies. Keep an eye on their websites and follow them on social media. You will then see any announcements when they are looking for people to get involved in what they are filming. You will normally see the production company in the credits, or you can use a search engine to find their details.

MARKETING TIPS

Freelance PR consultant Francesca Weeks (franfreelance.co.uk) provided these useful tips on marketing.

Network Put yourself out there to get work; and attend as many local or national events and meet-ups as you can. As the old saying goes, 'people buy from people' so attending events can be a great way to bring your brand to life.

Target your PR Be targeted with your PR efforts. If you are sending out a press release, for example, spend time researching the journalists and publications you want to send it to and ask yourself why it might be of interest to them or their readers. Try to address each journalist personally and avoid being too generic and blind copying everyone into one blanket e-mail.

Keep your eye on the media Always be aware of the national news agenda and trends. If something is getting a lot of media attention or gaining momentum on social media, have a think about whether it is relevant to your business in any way. If it is, act quickly and make the most of the media hype and buzz!

Watch awareness campaigns Similarly, tapping into national awareness days and weeks is a great way to generate extra publicity. There are a great many awareness campaigns out there, from National Knitting Week to National Cupcake Week, so do some research into the awareness campaigns that might fit with your business and plan your marketing activities ahead of time.

Combining offline and online marketing Combine marketing offline with your online efforts. Make the most of social media! It is such a fantastic free tool and can really help grow your fan base. Make sure you use it to listen and have real conversations with people, not just for broadcasting your own news. Getting social media right is time-consuming but in the end it is worth it. If you are not sure where to start or which platforms are right for you try taking a course.

Follow journalists Make sure you follow key journalists to stay up to date with what they are writing about. You can also search the #JournoRequest hashtag on Twitter. You never know when a journalist might be looking to write about something you make!

Other ways of getting featured offline

Sending out press releases when you have something newsworthy is one way to get featured offline. However, you may not always have something big to publicise but still want to have a presence in the media. How can you do this?

Editorial content Magazines and newspapers are often looking for content to fill the editorial side of their publication. If you can offer them something that fits their usual style, the chances are that they will be very happy to use it. If you can write a project or technique guide for a publication, it creates exposure for your brand. Ensure that the publication credits it to you and includes your business name and a link to your website. This ensures the feature will also be promoting your business.

Writing for publications helps to establish you as an expert in your niche, and raises your profile. Some publications will also pay you for the content, offer you an advert in exchange or give you a feature elsewhere in the magazine for helping them. It also helps with building relevant contacts which could come in useful when you have something you want promoted.

Competitions Competitions are always popular, and if you are willing to give away prizes, most publications will be happy to work with you. Competitions are also a good way of making people aware of your products, which helps to build brand recognition. Remember that your products have a cost to your business, so weigh up the cost of what you provide against the exposure and potential business you will get in return. Ensure your competitions are targeted at people who might potentially buy from you in the future.

Shopping features Many publications do seasonal shopping features such as gifts for St. Valentine's day, Easter-themed products, Christmas decorations and so forth. If you have products that would fit, you could contact them with details, explaining why they would be ideal for their feature. Most publications work a number of months in advance, so contact them in plenty of time, not a few weeks before.

Many magazines run 'new products' features. When you have a new range to promote, try sending details and images to those magazines to see if they will run it.

Awards Winning awards can help to publicise your business. Some awards require you to apply yourself, while others require a third party to nominate you. Local awards often get coverage in local newspapers, trade awards tend to be mentioned in trade publications, and online awards can lead to an increase in traffic, online coverage or support from other winners.

GLITTERING PRIZES

Don't be afraid to put yourself out there. Sometime an award will come with a prize that can be very useful. I won the Theo Pathitis Small Business Sunday (#SBS) award in 2011; and won promotion on the dedicated SBS website. I also gained access to a Facebook group where winners swap advice and help each other, and annual networking events too.

Promoting yourself offline

It may be easier to promote your business online, but not everyone spends their time on the internet. Combining offline and online promotion will help your business reach as many people as possible.

Local promotion

Local advertising can work really well if you sell only in one geographic area. Most of your customers will be local people so advertising nationally is not really going to benefit you as much as promoting yourself in your area. You could look at advertising in the local papers, or local magazines. On a smaller scale, the area or parish magazine and local free ads are good choices.

Look for local publications within your niche in which you could advertise, such as a local quilting group's newsletter if you sell fabric. If your products are for babies or children, will the local toddler group let you put up a poster or display your products?

Well-placed posters or locally delivered flyers could also lead to more business. Many local shops and post offices let you put up an advert for a nominal cost, or some even do it for free. If you do not want to deliver flyers yourself, is there someone you could pay to do it for you?

INDIRECT PROMOTION

If your customers are happy with the products or services you deliver the chances are they will tell others about it. Word of mouth is a great method of promotion for your business, but you can only influence it indirectly. Focus on delivering great customer service alongside quality products.

You can try to encourage word of mouth referrals by offering 'refer a friend' incentives, or even by simply prompting people to spread the word: when you package an order, include a business card or flyer with the note 'if you have a friend who may be interested in what we offer, please pass this onto them.' Sometimes people just need a gentle nudge.

Activity: Publicity research

Set a day aside to research ways in which you can promote your business offline. Draw up a plan of action for the next six months.

- Which publications are you going to contact and how do you want to be featured in them?
- Are there any awards you can apply for?
- What are the deadlines for entering the awards?

Schedule in at least one thing per month to try to generate some offline publicity for your business.

Product demonstrations

Product demonstrations at industry shows or local events can be a good way of getting people to discover your products. It shows people what you sell and gives them ideas of how to use the products. Your aim when demonstrating is to make them think that what you sell is something they cannot live without. Contact local shopping centres, event organizers and your product stockists to see if they would like you to do any product demonstrations.

Measuring the effects of advertising

Advertising can be expensive, especially on a national scale. It is therefore important to avoid wasting money by making sure your adverts target the correct audience. You also need to measure the effectiveness of your adverts to make sure that your money is being well spent.

As with online advertising, one way of tracking an advert's reach and effectiveness is to use a unique discount code. This allows you to track any orders that come from the advert. Similarly, you could put a voucher in the publication which people can cut out and bring with them. This will help to attract people into your premises, looking at whatever it is you have to offer.

Tracking the effectiveness of your offline advertising can be easier if you have an online presence. Look at your website's analytics to see if you can see a spike or other change in traffic and/or sales around the time your advert comes out. If it is a regional advert or local you can go further into your visitor demographics for your website and see if there is an increase of visitors in that particular geographical area.

If you have sales premises, keep a notebook to hand by the till and ask new customers how they found you, while serving them. Make a note of their answer and you can see whether advertising is driving new customers to the store. If they say they saw an advert for your business, ask if they remember where they saw the advert.

Another way to track leads generated from certain advertising is to use a different phone number. You could put your land line number in one advert, and your mobile in another.

> ### RING THE CHANGES
> Changing the artwork for your advert regularly can help attract more people.

Activity: Monitoring advertising

Make a list of your current adverts, how much they cost and whether you see any noticeable increase in business as a result.

If the results are inconclusive, stop all but one advert for a couple of months, and then change it to a different advert for the next two months. This will allow you to measure the effectiveness of each advert in isolation, rather than paying for lots of adverts when only one or two may actually be working for you.

Networking at events

Events like trade shows, craft shows, networking events and even local craft fairs can be great places for networking. Ideal for meeting like-minded crafters with whom you can share business tips for finding new suppliers, finding new buyers or meeting people who can help promote your business.

Time is limited at these events as there are a lot of people to talk to so it is best that you go prepared with a plan of action, ready to make as many useful contacts as you can.

Before you go

Make sure you have plenty of business cards ready to take with you, take a lot more than you think you will need. It is amazing how fast they go!

Notes Take a notebook and pen so you can take down details of people you meet or write down notes.

Know your way around Print a floor plan if possible. They are often available to download on the organizer's website. Organizers sometimes send floorplans by e-mail, so it could be worth signing up to their newsletter.

For big shows you can also normally find an exhibitors list on the organizer's website. Work through the list or floor plan and write down the people you want to see in order of importance and their stall number. It can also help to make notes as to what you want to see them about to remind you on the day.

Research Read up about the exhibitors you want to target before you go. Have a look at their websites and check out their social media, so that you can approach them with knowledge about their businesses and have some concrete ideas about how you can work with them.

Dress appropriately First impressions count, so dress smartly to give the best impression of your business.

NETWORK WITH OTHER ATTENDEES

Look on social media and see if anyone you would like to speak to is attending rather than exhibiting. If so, you could contact them in advance and arrange to meet them at the show.

At the show

Once at the show, work your way through the list of people you wanted to visit, in order of importance. At big shows it can be best to contact people in advance and ask for a meeting so they can schedule you in. If you can see someone is busy, come back later: you will not get chance for a proper conversation if you try to speak to them while there are other people vying for their attention. If you go back to them a few times and they are still busy, ask when the best time to come back would be, or offer to take them for a coffee when they get a break.

Be sociable and strike up conversation where you can – you never know who you will end up meeting. Hand your business cards out and take cards whenever you get the chance. When taking cards, add a note to the back about what that person does, what you talked about or what you would like to speak to them about after the show. If you have space note down where you met them, this will help serve as a little reminder when you get in touch. It is useful to carry an envelope to put all the cards in so you do not lose them.

If they do not have a business card, write their name and business name down in your notebook along with the reason you want to get in touch. You can go online when you get home and find their contact details. If they are exhibiting at an event usually their details will be on the organizer's website.

If you have time left after seeing everyone you wanted to see, take a wander around the show and look at the stalls you have not yet visited. You may find someone you missed off your list, or someone who booked at the last minute, and so was not on the floor plan or exhibitor's list.

PICKING THE RIGHT TIME

Shows are often quieter towards the end of the day, so you may find people are more able to talk then.

NETWORKING AT SHOWS

Many of the tips for selling at craft fairs (see pages 225–229) also apply to attending shows in order to network. In particular, take refreshments; and while you should look smart, comfortable shoes are a godsend for tired feet. In addition, you may want to take some cash. Some shows have no cash machines once you are inside, and there may be exhibitors who are not able to process card payments on their stand.

Paying attention to all of these details can help you stay alert, approachable and making the most of your networking opportunities.

Following up

You will often meet a large number of people at an event or show that you would like to speak to or work with in the future. Attending the show itself is only the first stage of networking; you need to follow up after the event. This ensures people have your contact details, reminds them of anything you discussed and makes it easier for them to get back to you.

Make the subject of your e-mail the name of the event at which you met. Start off with a polite 'nice to meet you at…' sentence, where you can insert a reminder as to where exactly you met them. If it was a big show over multiple days, they probably met many people in different parts of the show. If you remind them that you met them in the queue for the coffee shop on Saturday afternoon, or at a particular social media seminar, it will help them recall exactly which person you are.

Next, explain why you are getting in touch, how you think you can help that person, and how you could work together. Give specific examples and include links to the relevant parts of your site. Anything that saves them time and effort is worthwhile. Make sure you include a telephone number as well as an e-mail address that they can use to contact you.

While contacting people within a few days of meeting them is a good idea because it ensures your meeting is fresh in their mind, the day immediately after a big event may not be the best. They will likely be coming back to an e-mail backlog and you do not want yours to get lost in the midst.

If you do not receive a reply to your initial e-mail after a couple of weeks, follow it up by calling by telephone, or by sending a polite follow-up e-mail asking if they received your previous one – be sure to attach the original e-mail for them.

If you sell products and the contact is a potential stockist, it could be worth posting them a sample and including a letter with your post-show follow-up rather than an e-mail. It will make you stand out from all the other people they met at the show and will remind them of the products you create. This also works for magazine editors too, who are often swamped with hundreds of e-mails after big events.

If you do not have a specific reason for getting in touch with someone, you can still follow them on social media and send a quick message or tweet to say 'nice to meet you at the show'. There may be a way for you to work with them in the future so it is worth establishing an online relationship.

USEFUL LINKS AND FURTHER READING

Craft fairs

How to find craft fairs: ukcraftfairs.com;
stallfinder.com; craftsforum.co.uk;
stallandcraftcollective.co.uk/events

Craft fair display ideas: pinterest.com/
lifethriftylane/craft-show-display-ideas

Craft fair tips:
pinterest.com/kirameku412/for-craft-shows

Lots of useful posts on selling at craft fairs:
blog.folksy.com

Lots of links to craft fair tip posts: ukcraftblog.
com/2011/08/craft-fair-display-tips-and-ideas.
html

How to apply for a craft show:
thedesigntrust.co.uk/how-to-apply-for-a-craft-fair

Useful series of posts on craft fairs:
handmadelives.wordpress.com

Getting your craft products into stores

General information: missmalaprop.com/how-
to-sell-your-product-in-stores; makersrow.
com/blog/2015/02/selling-to-department-stores-
vs-small-boutiques; launchgrowjoy.com/how-to-
sell-to-retail-stores

**Ten reasons gift stores reject
handmade products:**
hubpages.com/business/gift-stores-reject-
handmade-items

Useful information about selling to retailers:
hubpages.com/business/selling-to-retailers

Offline promotion and advertising

How to get featured in magazines:
handmadeharbour.blogspot.co.uk/2012/07/how-
to-get-your-products-in-magazine.html

Ideas for getting magazine features:
info.thatsgreatnews.com/2015/05/20/18-ways-to-
get-featured-in-a-magazine/

How to get press features: blog.folksy.
com/2010/11/09/get-featured-in-the-press

Tips for creating an advert that sells:
business.com/articles/how-to-make-a-magazine-
ad-that-sells

Tips for magazine advertising: ephealy.
com/2012/01/24/7-magazine-advertising-tips

Networking tips from The Design Trust:
thedesigntrust.co.uk/networking-if-you-dont-like-
or-cant-network-the-usual-way

Useful networking tips:
entrepreneur.com/article/223468

How to run a successful competition:
success.com/article/how-to-run-a-promo-contest

Word of mouth promotion strategies:
businessknowhow.com/marketing/
wordofmouth.htm

How to encourage word of mouth promotion:
bit.ly/1ime2bc

YOUR LINKS AND NOTES

You can use this space to keep a list of links to websites and services you find helpful.

ENDNOTES

Your business

Now that your business is up and running, you can look at ways of streamlining your processes so you can do things more quickly, and be more efficient. Over the years I have learnt ways to save time, cut costs and generally make running a business easier. On the following pages I have listed fifteen free tools which I use to make my life easier. Hopefully you will find them useful too.

The biggest thing I have learnt is not to give in to what other people think. There is no 'one size fits all' for your business. We all have different needs and what matters is what you want from your business, not what someone else tells you that you should want from it.

Remember that the business is yours. Keep striving towards making it the perfect business for you; whether this is working as much in order to earn as much as possible, or something that fits around the rest of your life and earns you enough to cover the bills or for some extra pocket money. There is a lot of pressure to keep your business growing and building all the time, to start employing people and managing staff, but this may not be for you.

Personally, I just want to pursue the craft I love without any extra pressure. For me, my focus is streamlining my business so that I keep the same level of income but gradually reduce the hours I put in; by improving my productivity and gradually cutting out the work that earns me less.

Your goals may be different to mine, but it is crucial that you make sure you know what your goals are and that you do not let other people distract you from them. It is your business, so make it work for you.

THE TEMPTATIONS OF OVERWORK

When you run your own business it is easy to put all your time and energy into it, and hard to take time away from your business to recuperate. You can easily find yourself working seven days a week, and before you know it, you burn out. This leads to you being too exhausted and ill to work for weeks or even months, which sets you back a lot more than if you had just taken a day or two off when you first started to feel tired or ill.

Understandably, you want everything to be perfect with your business, and this can lead to setting yourself impossibly high standards. Even after many years of running my business, I must confess I still struggle with the temptation to overwork, but I have finally come to realize that close to perfect is just as acceptable and much less stressful!

My top tips

These are my favourite free services that I use in my own business. They will all help you save time, money and effort when running yours.

1 Dropbox (dropbox.com)

A free online cloud storage for your documents, photos and other files. You can earn free space by inviting friends to also use Dropbox, or you can upgrade to a paid account if you need more space. It is very useful for backing up your computer as well as sending large files that will not fit into an e-mail.

2 Google calendar (google.com/calendar)

Most of us have Google accounts nowadays. One is essential if you want to use Google Analytics on your site, or Google Plus, so why not take advantage of its other free programs? Google have a free calendar app which you can use to synchronize appointments and reminders between your computer, tablet and mobile phone. It works with Apple devices as well as Android.

3 Image resizer (imageresizer.codeplex.com)

Image resizer is a free download which allows you to select single or multiple images on your computer and resize them. This is ideal for when you need images for your website and social media, or if your camera takes very high quality, large sized images.

You can either use one of their standard sizes or specify your own, and you can set it to keep both the original file and a smaller version. This allows you to keep a high-resolution image for print and have a smaller web-sized version too. Using this service only takes a few seconds to resize big batches of images – so much easier than opening each image individually and re-sizing it!

4 and 5 Google Analytics and Google Webmaster Tools (google. co.uk/analytics and google.com/webmasters)

As you will see in the SEO section of this book, Google gives you huge amounts of useful information about your website, and all for free! You would be a fool not to make the most of them. Information on how to use these programs is on pages 200–207.

6 Hootsuite (hootsuite.com)

Ideal for prescheduling your social media updates, and for streaming your Twitter lists, Hootsuite allows you to view several of your social media platforms at once and manage multiple accounts. Note that it does not work so well for Facebook, as your posts will have less reach.

7 Evernote (evernote.com)

A popular multiple device app that allows you to store to-do lists, research and similar notes. It allows you to snip things from the internet and separate your notes into different projects.

8 Google Keep (drive.google.com/keep)

I use this in a similar way to Evernote, but find it easier to use. It is essentially a collection of digital post-it notes into which you can add images and schedule alarms in order to remind you when to do the things on the note. It works well for to-do lists and storing ideas for future use. I also use it for saving links that I want to look at properly when I have more time.

9 PicMonkey (picmonkey.com)

Free image-editing software that will allow you to create adverts; images to use on social media or your website (such as banners and shareable images) and also to enhance images. If for any reason you do not get on with PicMonkey try Pixlr (pixlr.com) which offers a similar service.

10 Bitly (bitly.com)

Bitly shortens unsightly long web address (URL) links so they look neat and tidy. It also stores statistics for those links so that you can see how many people clicked on them, when they clicked and where those people are geographically.

11 Survey Monkey (surveymonkey.com)

This site lets you run free surveys which are great for market research. Just be aware that only the first one hundred responses to your survey are free to view. After that you need to pay. Google forms is an alternative that is free regardless of the number of responses.

12 Mailchimp (mailchimp.com)

A newsletter creator. It is free for up to two thousand subscribers, though once you pass that limit, you are required to pay. Design software for your newsletter, manages your list and allows you to create bespoke sign-up forms and autoresponders too.

13 Rafflecopter (rafflecopter.com)

Allows you to run giveaways for free. Their software randomly picks winners for you, allows you to export entrant data and to create your own entry forms. You can also integrate it with your social media accounts.

14 Trello (trello.com)

Project management software that is ideal for teams of people working collaboratively. It also integrates with many of the other programs on this list to help boost your productivity.

15 Open Office (openoffice.org)

If your start-up budget does not stretch to Microsoft Office, Open Office is a great free alternative. Be careful to save your files in an extension that can be opened by Microsoft Office if you are sending documents to others.

A few tips for going forward with your business

- Set aside some time each week to read business sites, SEO sites and marketing sites to keep up to date with changes that could affect your business, and to learn new things. If you keep learning, you can keep ahead of new trends and continue to work efficiently, without wasting time on things that no longer work, or are not very effective any more.

- Thinking of a second business? If you have another business idea make sure it will not adversely affect the first (or your health from doing too much) and plan carefully. It will be easier the second time around in many ways because you will have learnt a lot of lessons from the first business. However, a second business will add new pressures. Do not stretch yourself too far and end up doing neither business properly. The problem with being an entrepreneur is that we have too many ideas and not enough time!

- Take the time to build relationships with other entrepreneurs, with magazines, with blogs and enjoy the social side of business. Working for yourself can be very isolating, especially when working alone, or from home. Make plans to go to events regularly, or meet with other people in a similar situation to you so you do not feel lonely or depressed. Social media is great, but it does not compare to leaving the house and meeting up with people in real life.

- Have a clear goal. Knowing what you are working for will help you through hard times, while having a clear goal in mind keeps you focused. Make sure the goal is of your choosing, and that you do not let other people distract you from it or allow them to dictate your aims.

- Repeat custom is the easiest way to grow your business. It is easier – and cheaper – than attracting new customers, so do your best to make sure your customers are very happy with the service and products they receive.

- Have fun! Most of all, have fun and enjoy what you are doing. There is so much freedom that comes with self-employment so make the most of it. If it is a lovely sunny afternoon and you want to go to the beach, then go. If you are having an 'off day' and do not feel like working, take some time off. So long as you are sensible and still get your work done, it is up to you when you do it.

  As a self-employed businessman or woman, you no longer have a boss dictating that you must work on set tasks at set times. Instead, you get to spend your time doing something that you love. Make sure you enjoy it.

Good luck on your new creative adventure.

Growing your business

If all goes well with your business, you will inevitably find that it will start to grow. Before long, you may find it grows beyond the point that it can be run by just one person, and you will have to start thinking about how to manage that growth.

Learning to share

One way is to try and control the expansion and not let it go beyond a certain size, by turning down orders, reducing promotion, streamlining your tasks, or creating a waiting list. Another alternative is to get help from someone else.

It can be hard to make this decision; your business is your baby and it is hard to share it with someone else – not to mention the fact that you have put in so much hard work to get to this point, it can be hard to imagine that anyone else will ever care as much about it as you do. It is tough to let go and trust other people to get involved. You need to take a good look at all the individual roles you perform to keep your business running and decide where you need help, or what you are prepared to let someone else do.

In my case with The Sewing Directory I was finding that the content side of the site was taking a lot of time and, although it was also my favourite part, it would be the easiest area to bring someone else in. Once I identified where I needed help, I could then start thinking about the kind of person I needed to help me and what skills they needed to have.

I needed someone who knew the core topic of sewing well. They also needed to be good at coming up with content ideas and writing them up, or finding the right people to commission to write them. Fortunately, I knew the editor of *Sewing World* Magazine, Julie Briggs, from writing for the magazine. When I approached her about joining me, she said yes.

The next thing to figure out was in what way we would work together. Would she be freelance and just help me when I needed? Would she work part time on whatever jobs I allocated her or would I bring her fully into the business and make her an equal partner? Julie would be giving up a full-time job to work with me. She wanted job security, not just freelance or part time work. I did not want to commit to paying a fixed monthly wage as the business income varies from month to month, so in the end we decided the best solution for both of us was that she would buy a share of the business and become my partner.

The working relationship

Once you have identified where you need help, you need to think about what kind of working relationship works best for you. If you need someone to pack orders then paying someone part-time would probably work well for that. If you want help with the accounts or marketing, you could consider outsourcing it or employing a freelancer rather than directly employing anyone. If you want someone as invested in the business with you to ride the highs and lows together you may want to consider partnership. If you need someone in your shop you will need to employ them.

It is a very big change when you are no longer running your business alone, and it has both pros and cons. The biggest downside is having to be more structured and not just working when you feel like it, or as much as you feel like doing. Another is having to consult someone else about the plans for the business when you are used to making all the decisions. There are also many perks too: being able to delegate tasks to someone else, having someone to bounce ideas off, or cover for you when you are unable to work for any reason.

The most important thing is finding the right person. I had several discussions with Julie in advance to ensure we had similar goals, working practices and plans for the business before committing to anything. There were several people who had offered to join the business in the past but I did not feel it would lead to a successful partnership. Go with your gut, especially when considering partnership, as it is a very big step. If you have misgivings, then do not do it – it can be both very complicated and expensive to break a partnership agreement. With staff or freelancers it is easier, but it still wastes your time and money if you pick the wrong person.

GROWING AND CHANGING

There were several things that changed for me when I bought someone else into my business:

- All of my business processes had to be formalized and written up, so that Julie could refer to those guides when working, especially in the beginning.

- I had to learn to let go. This was very hard! I still struggle with it now. I had to trust someone else to do the things that I had been doing for years.

- We had to find a way of keeping track of how much time we were each spending working, in order to keep it equal. In the end, we decided to do this by agreeing a set number of weekly hours and logging the time we worked on a shared calendar.

- We had to find a way of logging who was doing what and making sure we were not duplicating tasks. We do this via Excel spreadsheets that we share through Dropbox.

- We had to make time for regular catchups and planning, especially as we live hundreds of miles apart. We have weekly telephone calls, quarterly meet-ups and daily conversations through Google chat.

- We had to agree a formal working structure with things like annual leave allowances, sick leave, a set number of hours to work per week and fixed pay dates – none of had which needed consideration when working alone.

- We had to agree how to split the workload: as Julie learned more about the business, she was able to take on more responsibilities.

My top tips

If you decide you want freelance help with your business some sites that might come in handy are:

1 People by the Hour (peopleperhour.com)

This site has skilled freelancers who will work for a set hourly rate making it easy for you to budget.

2 Fiverr (fiverr.com)

A site of freelancers offering to complete jobs for you starting from $5, which is where the site got its name. You can search for the job you need doing and will see people's starting prices to complete that job.

3 Etsy (etsy.com)

There are plenty of sellers on Etsy who offer custom logo design, website templates and custom packaging and labels for your business.

4 Creative Market (creativemarket.com)

Although you do not technically hire freelancers through this site, it has a big selection of logos, graphics, website templates, business card designs, social media icons and so forth, which saves you having to create your own.

There is also useful advice on hiring freelancers, plus some other handy sites you could use in this guide from Ramsay Taplin, aka Blog Tyrant: (blogtyrant.com/hire-a-freelancer)

THE LONG AND SHORT OF IT

Be aware that bringing someone new into your business will initially create more work for you, not less. Not only do you have to spend time finding the right person and dealing with any contracts necessary, you then have to train them, and allow time for them to get up to speed. However, in the long run it will give you more free time and freedom.

GROWING YOUR HANDMADE BUSINESS ... OR COPING WHEN IT GROWS!

__Poppy Treffry (poppytreffry.co.uk) shares her advice on expanding your handmade business:__

I started my eponymous textile design company thirteen years ago. Within a year it had grown and become too much for me to cope with alone. Today, I have ten employees, two shops, a busy studio and a group of local outworkers who make all of our products. The most important things I learned when my business became too much for just me were:

- *__Ensure you continue to enjoy your work__* Think long and hard about what you want to do in your business – what are your favourite tasks? Why are you doing it? Make sure your plan for the future means doing more of what you love – not less of it! It can be hard to find time for this if you are expanding due to demand, but it is essential.

- *__Processes__* Look at all the processes involved in your product and identify the tasks which someone else can do. In my case, I was able to delegate the cutting-out first, then some of the administration. That gave me the time to begin to train other people to do the embroidery.

- *__Pay__* Decide how you will pay someone to do these things – will they work in your studio and be employed? Will they work freelance from home and be paid a piece-work rate? How much training will they need?

- *__Pricing__* You will need to change your pricing model and check that your prices still make sense when you are paying someone else to do things. It is critical that you have a proper understanding of your costs and the margin you need to make your business sustainable.

- *__Trust__* You will need to trust other people to do things well. You will need to be very clear about what you expect from them; you should have a trial so you can be sure they are up to the job; and you should pay them a decent amount – if you are going to invest lots of time into someone, you want them to stick around.

- *__Enjoy the benefits__* Once you have done all that you can enjoy the benefits of delegating as well as finally having someone else to talk to!

INDEX